IMPOSSIBLE NATURE

☞ Books in the RENAISSANCE LIVES series explore and illustrate the life histories and achievements of significant artists, rulers, intellectuals and scientists in the early modern world. They delve into literature, philosophy, the history of art, science and natural history and cover narratives of exploration, statecraft and technology.

Series Editor: François Quiviger

Already published

Albrecht Dürer: Art and Autobiography *David Ekserdjian*
Aldus Manutius: The Invention of the Publisher *Oren Margolis*
Andreas Vesalius: Anatomy and the World of Books *Sashiko Kusukawa*
Annibale Carracci: Art, Wit and Authority *F. M. Gage*
Artemisia Gentileschi and Feminism in Early Modern Europe *Mary D. Garrard*
Benvenuto Cellini and the Embodiment of the Modern Artist *Andreas Beyer*
Bernard Palissy and the Arts of the Earth *François Quiviger*
Blaise Pascal: Miracles and Reason *Mary Ann Caws*
Botticelli: Artist and Designer *Ana Debenedetti*
Caravaggio and the Creation of Modernity *Troy Thomas*
Descartes: The Renewal of Philosophy *Steven Nadler*
Domenico Ghirlandaio: An Elite Artisan and His World *Jean K. Cadogan*
Donatello and the Dawn of Renaissance Art *A. Victor Coonin*
Erasmus of Rotterdam: The Spirit of a Scholar *William Barker*
Filippino Lippi: An Abundance of Invention *Jonathan K. Nelson*
Francis I: The Knight-King *Glenn Richardson*
Francisco de Zurbarán and the Fabric of the World *Jeremy Robbins*
Giorgione's Ambiguity *Tom Nichols*
Hans Holbein: The Artist in a Changing World *Jeanne Nuechterlein*
Hans Memling and the Merchants *Mitzi Kirkland-Ives*
Hieronymus Bosch: Visions and Nightmares *Nils Büttner*
Impossible Nature: The World of Giuseppe Arcimboldo *Jessica Keating*
Isaac Newton and Natural Philosophy *Niccolò Guicciardini*
Jan van Eyck within His Art *Alfred Acres*
John Donne: In the Shadow of Religion *Andrew Hadfield*
John Evelyn: A Life of Domesticity *John Dixon Hunt*
Leon Battista Alberti: The Chameleon's Eye *Caspar Pearson*
Leonardo da Vinci: Self, Art and Nature *François Quiviger*
Lorenzo Ghiberti: Designer *Scott Nethersole*
Lucas Cranach: From German Myth to Reformation *Jennifer Nelson*
Machiavelli: From Radical to Reactionary *Robert Black*
Michelangelo and the Viewer in His Time *Bernadine Barnes*
Paolo Veronese and the Nobility of Painting *Tom Nichols*
Paracelsus: An Alchemical Life *Bruce T. Moran*
Petrarch: Everywhere a Wanderer *Christopher S. Celenza*
Piero della Francesca and the Invention of the Artist *Machtelt Brüggen Israëls*
Piero di Cosimo: Eccentricity and Delight *Sarah Blake McHam*
Pieter Bruegel and the Idea of Human Nature *Elizabeth Alice Honig*
Raphael and the Antique *Claudia La Malfa*
Rembrandt's Holland *Larry Silver*
Robert Hooke's Experimental Philosophy *Felicity Henderson*
Rubens's Spirit: From Ingenuity to Genius *Alexander Marr*
Rudolf II: The Life and Legend of the Mad Emperor *Thomas DaCosta Kaufmann*
Salvator Rosa: Paint and Performance *Helen Langdon*
Thomas More: Humanism and Heresy *Andrew Hadfield and Joanne Paul*
Thomas Nashe and Late Elizabethan Writing *Andrew Hadfield*
Titian's Touch: Art, Magic and Philosophy *Maria H. Loh*
Tycho Brahe and the Measure of the Heavens *John Robert Christianson*
Ulisse Aldrovandi: Naturalist and Collector *Peter Mason*

IMPOSSIBLE NATURE

The World of Giuseppe Arcimboldo

JESSICA KEATING

REAKTION BOOKS

To Larry

Published by Reaktion Books Ltd
2–4 Sebastian Street
London EC1V 0HE, UK
www.reaktionbooks.co.uk

First published 2026

EU GPSR Authorised Representative
Logos Europe, 9 rue Nicolas Poussin, 17000, La Rochelle, France
email: contact@logoseurope.eu

Printed and bound in India by Replika Press Pvt. Ltd

A catalogue record for this book is available from the British Library

ISBN 978 1 83639 260 6

COVER: Arcimboldo, *Vertumnus*, 1590, oil on panel. Skoklosters slott, photo Erik Lernestål/SHM.

CONTENTS

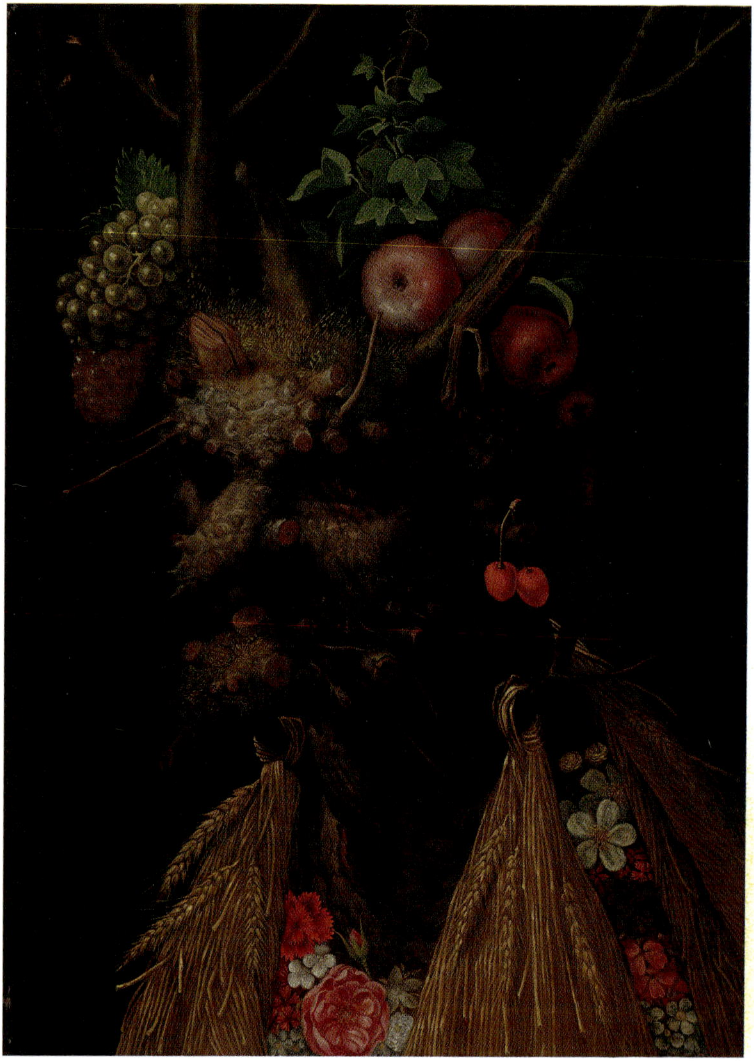

Introduction

A painting by Giuseppe Arcimboldo (1526–1593) depicts a lone bust-length figure in three-quarter view against a dark ground (illus. 1). Though the painting is in the format of a Renaissance portrait, the conventions of the genre stop there. Instead of flesh and blood, the figure is made up of branch and bark. Instead of garments cut from cloth, the figure is dressed in sheaves of autumnal wheat and a tunic of spring flowers. Instead of a ruby earring, the figure sports summer cherries. Instead of a diadem of gold, the figure dons a crown of leafless branches and freshly harvested fruit. Instead of a vigorous face, cuts where tree limbs were removed make the figure appear diseased, and twigs sprouting like errant whiskers mark it as decayed.

Four Seasons in One Head, as the painting is now titled, is not a large work.[1] Measuring 60 cm tall and 44 cm across (24 × 17 in.), it was probably intended to be hung on the wall of a palace, among other works of art, in the collection of a learned European ruler who appreciated artistic virtuosity and ingenuity. The work would have been valued, in large part, because it is a contradiction. Though Arcimboldo used the customs of portraiture to portray the arboreal man, he replaced a particular human subject with an allegorical one he invented; and even though the painting is not a record of a specific person at a precise moment in time, the pictorial description of the external and internal particularities of the subject

1 Arcimboldo, *Four Seasons in One Head*, c. 1590, oil on panel.

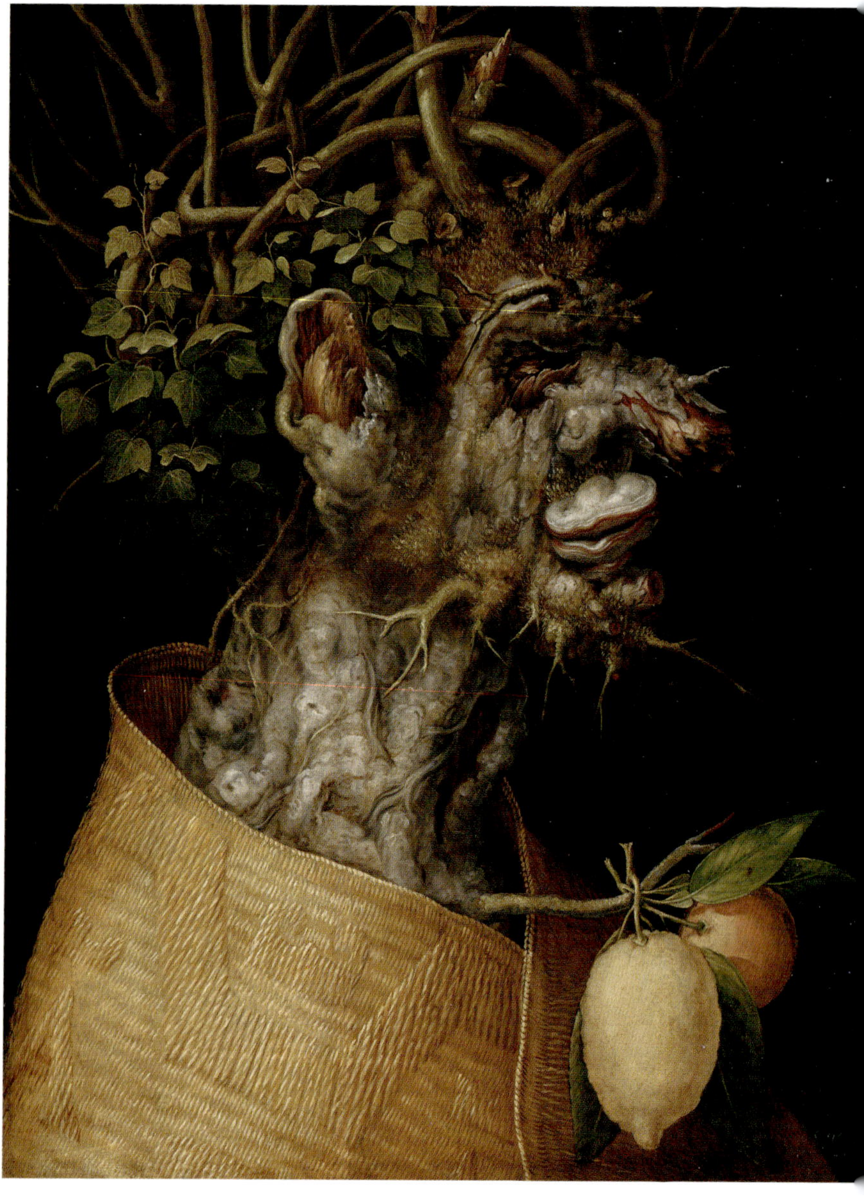

2 Arcimboldo, *Winter*, 1563, oil on panel.

prevails. The pronounced and irregularly shaped 'nose', the deep-set 'eyes' and the jutting 'underbite' give the figure an individualized physiognomy. Additionally the figure has an inward 'gaze' and rounded posture which convey a contemplative character.

Four Seasons in One Head also evidences Arcimboldo's remarkable ability to allow the qualities of nature's products at once to liberate and to determine the image he created. To compose it, he leaned on formal analogies to govern which natural feature would come to stand in for a human one. To make it appear plausible, he seamlessly joined these natural elements together, as if the fantastic figure was posed, observed and documented in the artist's own spatial milieu. At the same time, the impossibility of this arboreal man makes clear that we are not witnessing a product of nature, but a product of the artist's fecund imagination and distinctive wit.[2]

Almost all Arcimboldo's extant easel paintings were, like *Four Seasons in One Head*, made for European nobility and were composite in nature.[3] In fact, his paintings are often referred to as 'composite heads', or *teste composte* in Italian. But the works are not only composites of disparate elements, they are often composites of different artistic genres. For instance, as we will see, in the composite heads he made for his patron, Holy Roman Emperor Maximilian II (1527–1576) – like his famed series of the Seasons (1563) (illus. 2, 3, 4 and 5) and the Elements (1566) (illus. 6, 7, 8 and 9) – the artist wedded natural history illustration and portraiture to develop novel imperial allegories that elaborated on longstanding cosmological systems for political ends. In others, such as the invertible *Vegetable Gardener* (1590) (illus. 10), Arcimboldo coupled the nascent genre of still life with portraiture to raise questions about his own pictorial intentions.

The works addressed in this book span Arcimboldo's career and include not just his composite heads, but his designs for stained glass and tapestries; his painted frescoes, plant and animal studies; and his choreographed courtly spectacles, such as tournament processions. Some were created between 1549 and 1562, in Arcimboldo's native city of Milan. Others were painted or devised between 1562 and 1587, while Arcimboldo was the imperial painter at the court of Maximilian II in Vienna and then at the court of his successor as Holy Roman Emperor, Rudolf II (1552–1612), in Prague. Still more works considered in these pages were painted at the end of Arcimboldo's life, between 1587 and 1590, after he retired from the imperial court and returned to Milan.

Though we are fairly certain where and when Arcimboldo was active as an artist, the rest of his life is shrouded in mystery. He was born to a family of Milanese painters in 1526, but we know nothing about his childhood and can only surmise how he was trained. Presumably, he was taught by his father, Biagio Arcimboldo (d. 1555), and his paternal uncles, Ambrogio and Gian Giacomo. If this was the case, he was trained by painters whose livelihood was maintained by ecclesiastical commissions. Initially, Arcimboldo followed in their footsteps and cobbled together commissions from churches in and around Milan. Somehow, somewhere, he caught the eye of the imperial court and crossed the Alps to work for two consecutive Holy Roman Emperors. After 25 years in Vienna and Prague, he returned to Milan in old age to live out his life as a famous and admired artist. If, amid all this, he married and had children, we do not know their names.

Arcimboldo lived during a tumultuous time in early modern European history. In 1527, the year after the artist was born, Holy Roman Emperor Charles V (1500–1558) sacked Rome. Eight years later, in 1535, Charles V took control of the Duchy of Milan after the Duke of Milan, Francesco Sforza II (1495–1535), failed to produce an heir. That same year, King Henry VIII (1491–1547) of England deemed himself head of the Church of England after being excommunicated from the Catholic Church. Nicolaus

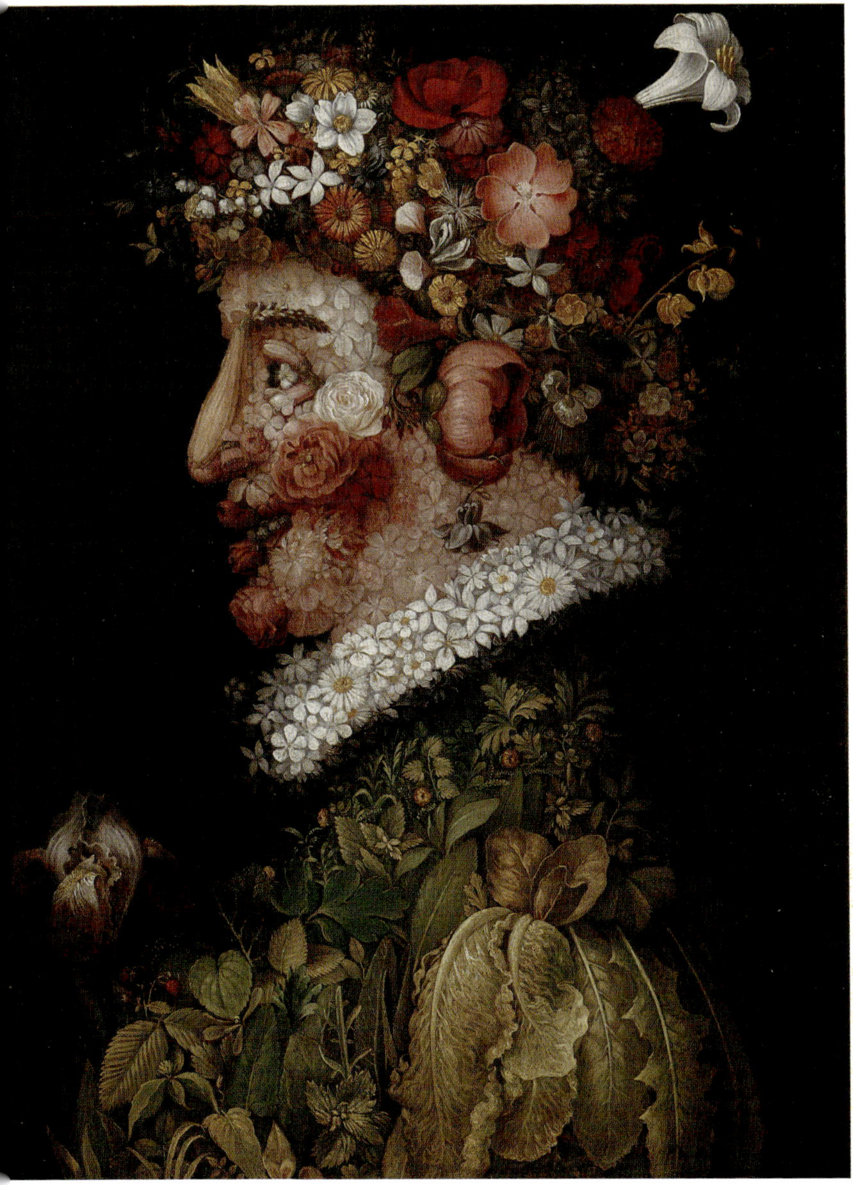

3 Arcimboldo, *Spring*, 1563, oil on panel.

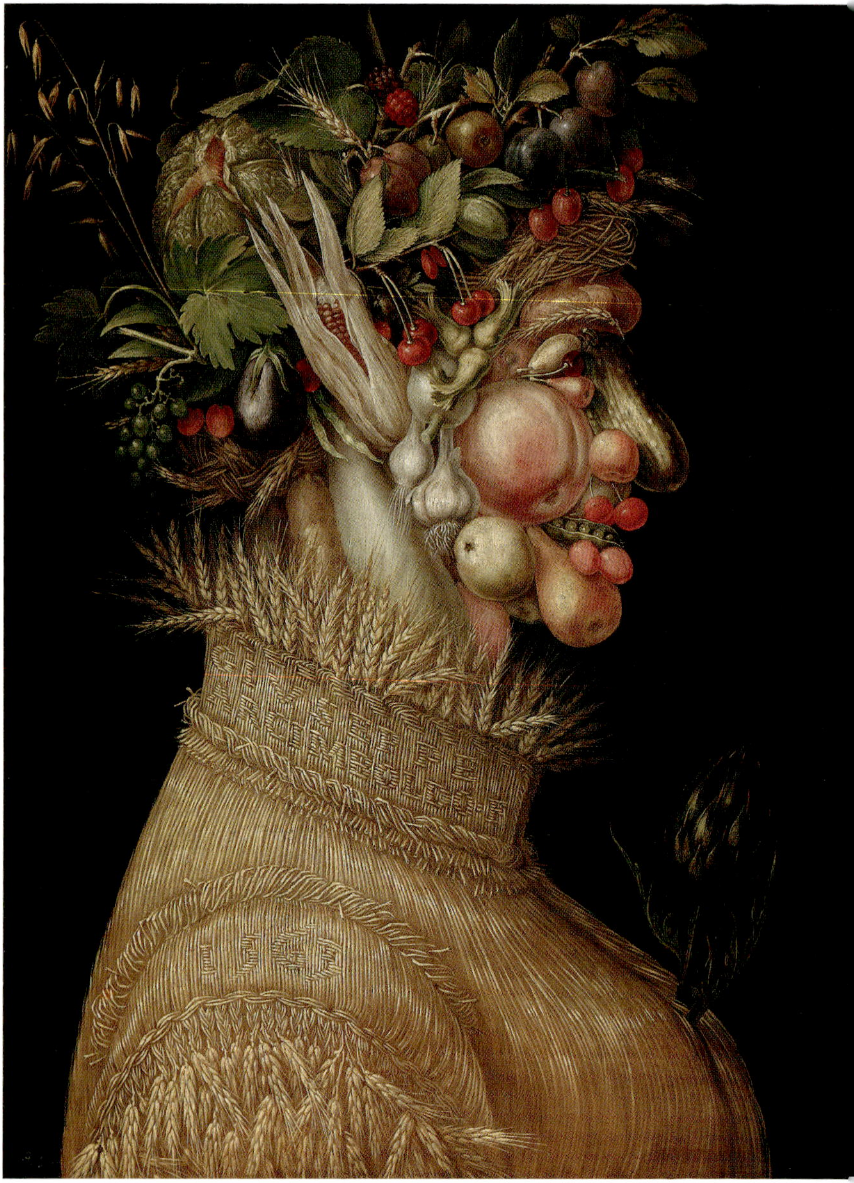

4 Arcimboldo, *Summer*, 1563, oil on panel.

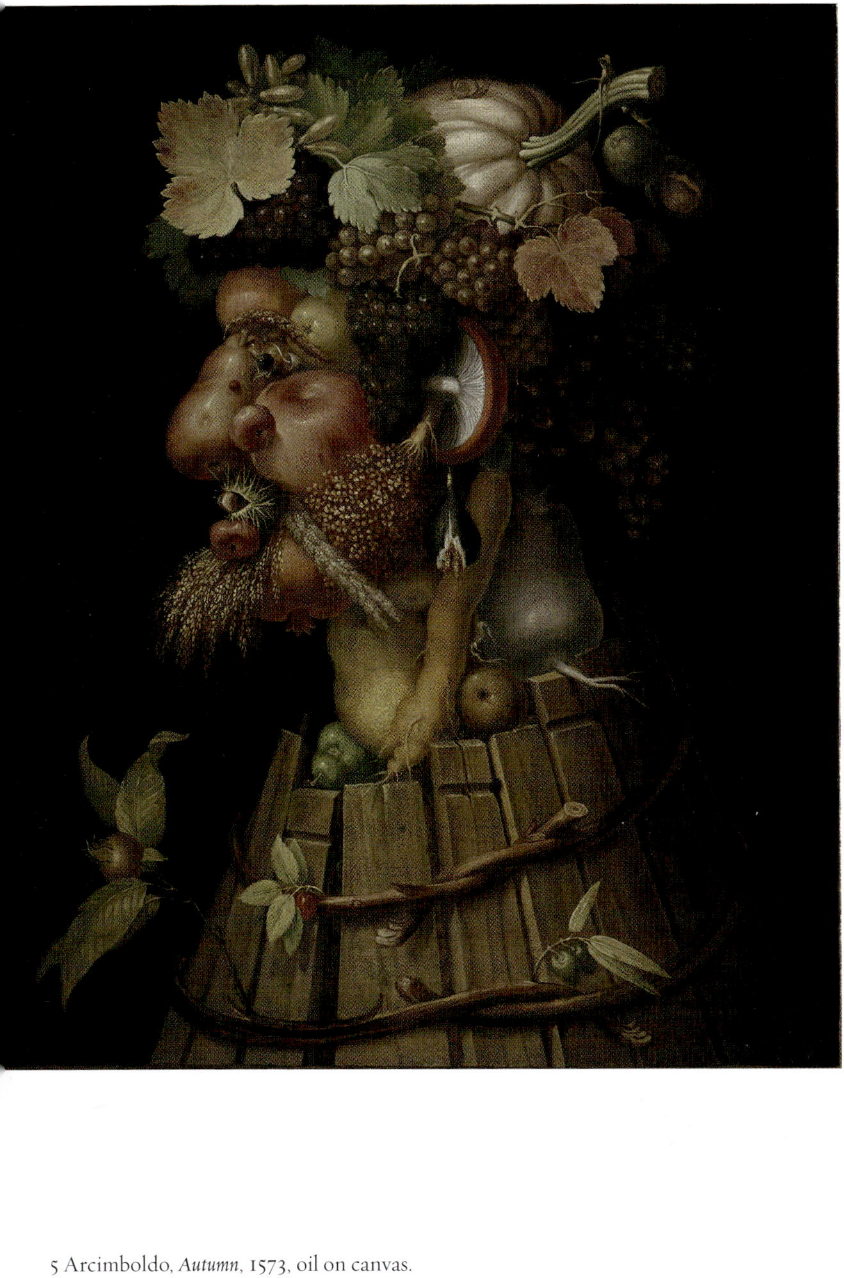

5 Arcimboldo, *Autumn*, 1573, oil on canvas.

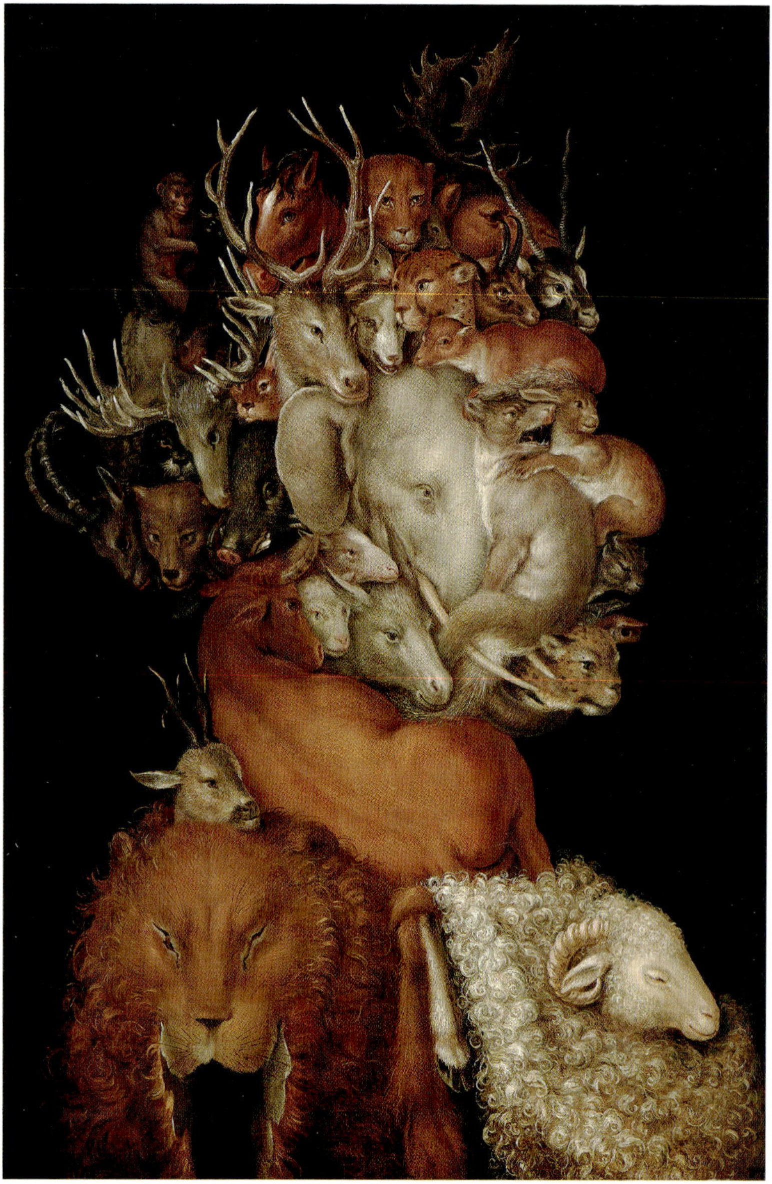

6 Arcimboldo, *Earth*, 1566, oil on panel.

Copernicus (1473–1543) published his *On the Revolution of Heavenly Bodies* in 1543, just two years before the Catholic Church began convening the Council of Trent to stem the tide of Martin Luther's (1483–1546) Protestant Reformation.

Arcimboldo made his paintings amid a fraught moment in imperial politics. Not only were Maximilian II's and Rudolf II's reigns dogged with fear of an Ottoman invasion, but both Maximilian's and Rudolf's sovereign legitimacy was doubted by many of their own subjects. This was due to questions surrounding the imperial line of succession after Charles V abdicated the imperial throne in 1558, as well as to the Protestant Reformation. Since Protestant reformers refused to recognize the spiritual and political authority of the Pope (who since the reign of Charlemagne (d. 814) anointed and crowned the Holy Roman Emperor), the political legitimacy of the Holy Roman Emperor was called into question. It did not matter that the emperor was technically elected by the seven princes or 'Electors' of the Holy Roman Empire; the fact that the emperor was crowned by and had an allegiance to the Catholic Church made his position as leader of the Holy Roman Empire suspect to many Protestants. Thus, during the period taken up here there was no clear consensus in the Holy Roman Empire as to where the sovereign's power originated, who authorized his rule or the extent of his reach.

Though he was recognized by the Pope, Maximilian II was ambivalent about his own religious sentiment. Indeed, in a conversation between himself and the Polish bishop Stanislaus Hosius (1504–1579) in 1560 he is reported to have said that he considered himself neither a Catholic nor a Protestant, but a Christian.[4] It is therefore not surprising that Maximilian did not mandate confessional uniformity in the empire. Rather, Maximilian sought to reconcile the many theological disputes among his subjects. Rooted in the Christian humanism of Erasmus of Rotterdam (d. 1536), this desire for religious moderation is now referred to as 'Irenicism'.

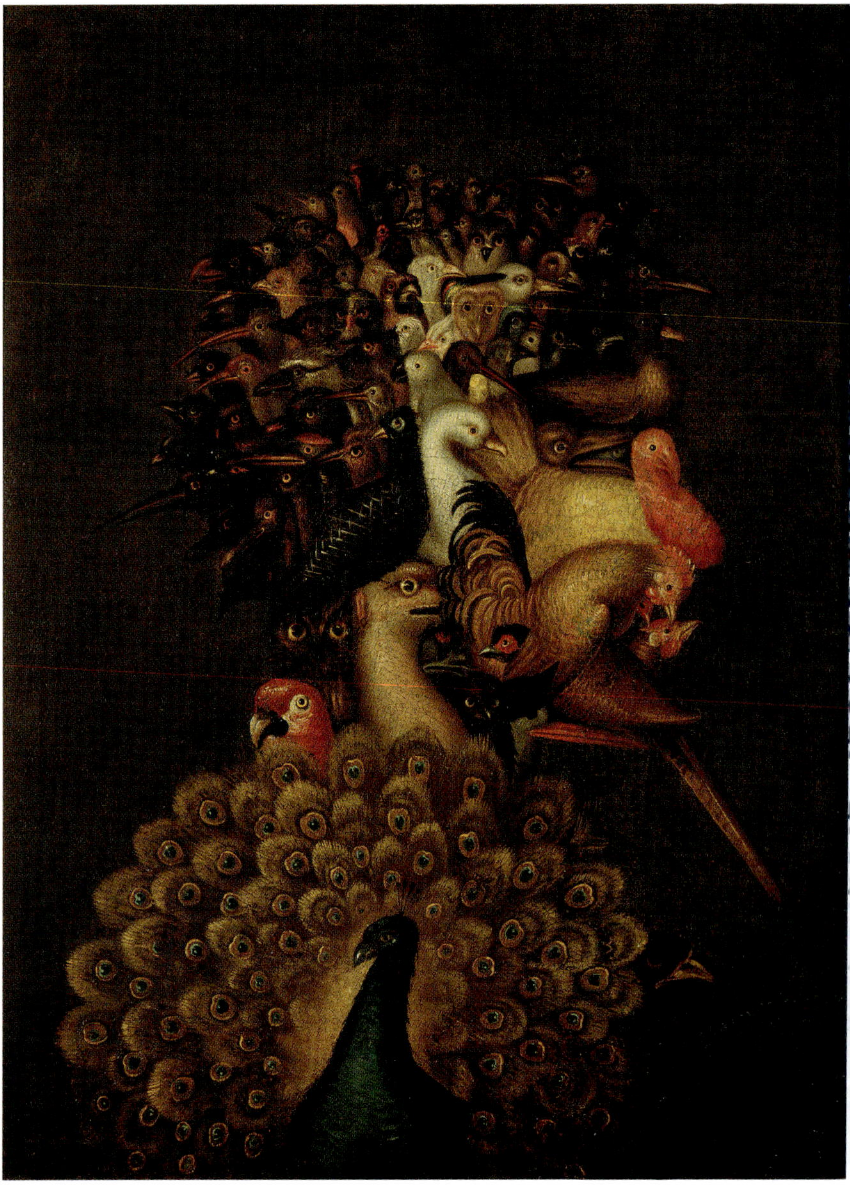

7 Copy after Arcimboldo, *Air*, after 1566, oil on panel.

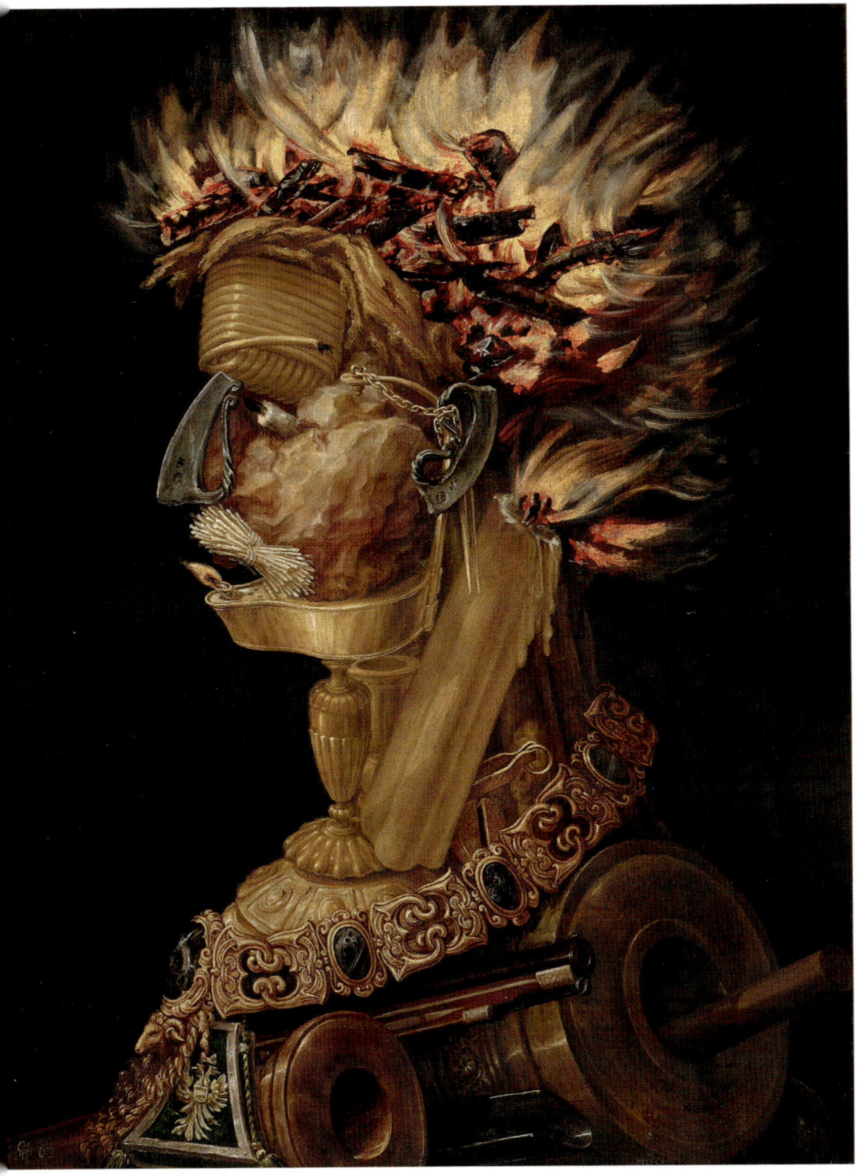

8 Arcimboldo, *Fire*, 1566, oil on panel.

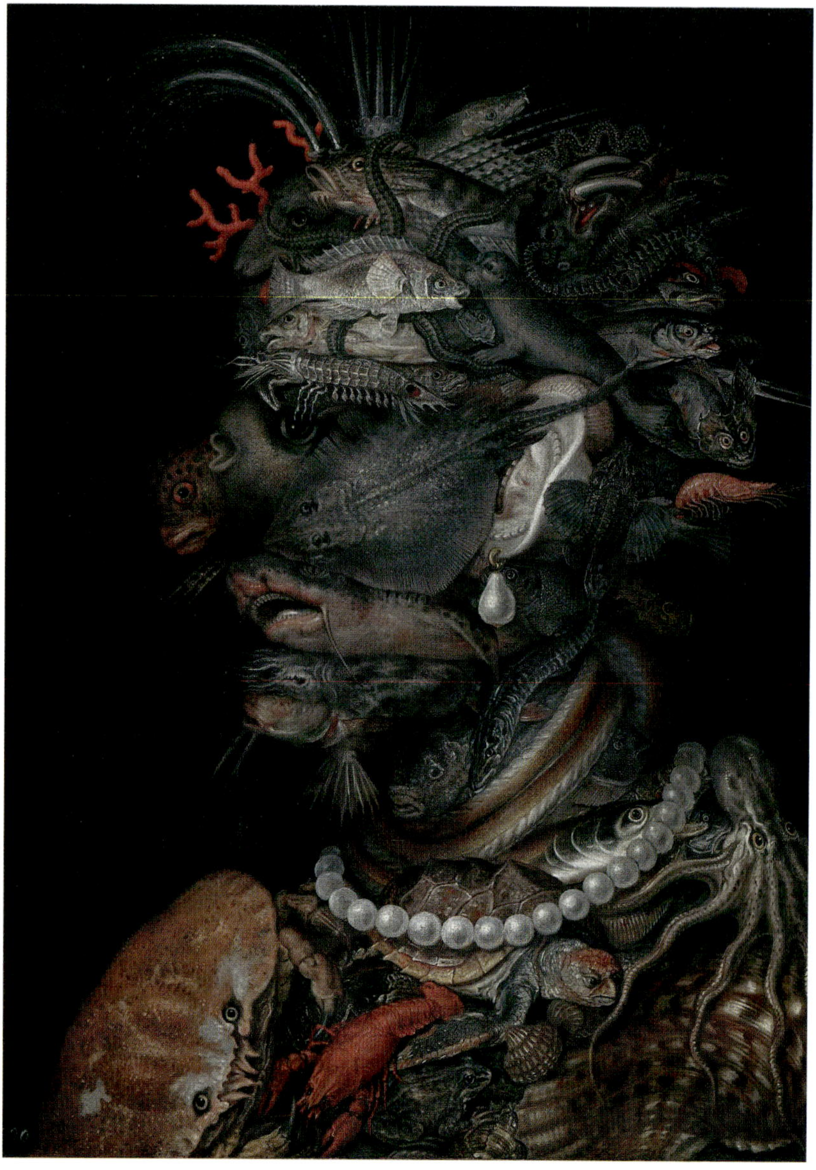

9 Arcimboldo, *Water*, 1566, oil on panel.

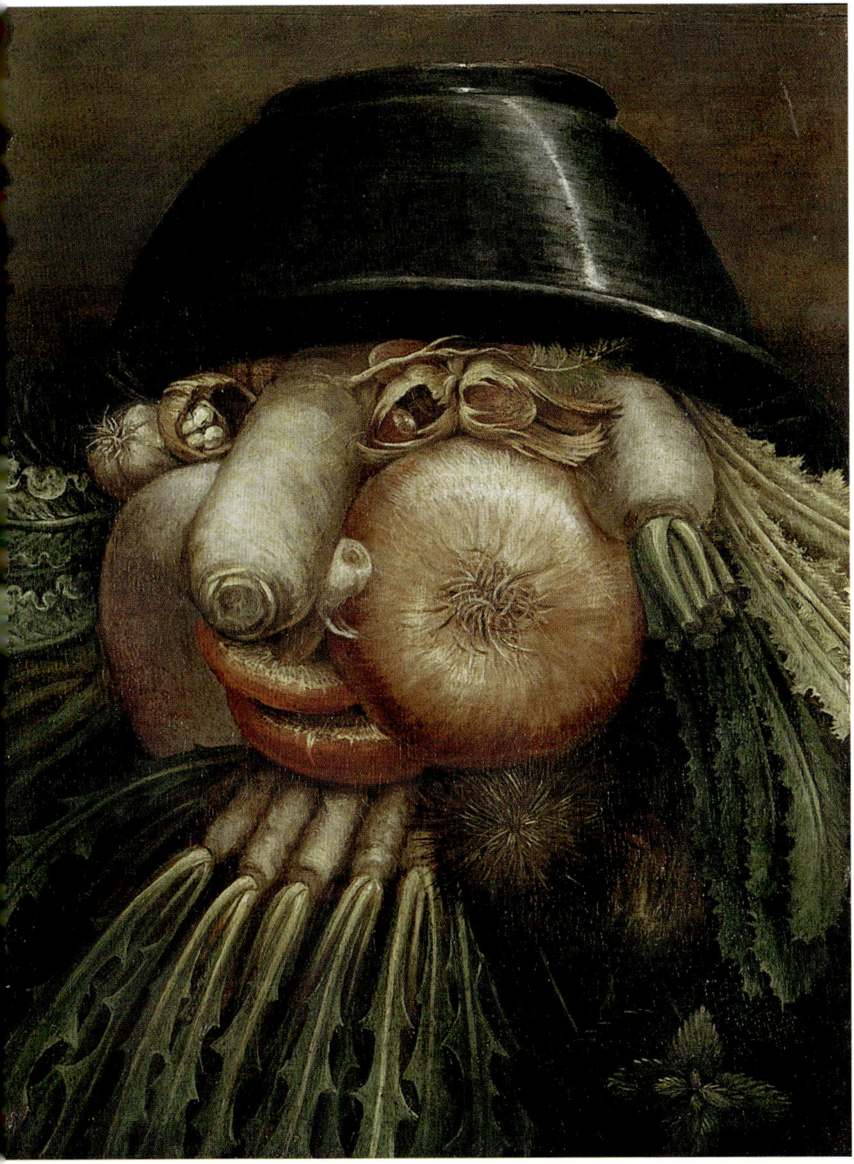

10 Arcimboldo, *The Vegetable Gardener*, *c.* 1590, oil on panel.

One way Maximilian tried to promote confessional compromise was by inviting numerous Protestants to take up positions at his court, and he promoted an image of the House of Habsburg that was not mired in confessional strife. Not until after 1576, during Rudolf II's reign, did the perception of the imperial court shift. Raised at the Spanish court, Rudolf II fashioned himself as both more Catholic and more religious than his father. For instance, in May 1578 he took part in a procession through the streets of Vienna during the feast of Corpus Christi. At that time, Habsburg rulers had not participated in the Corpus Christi festivities for over fifteen years.

As the issue of sovereign legitimacy loomed, and the divide within the empire between Protestants and Catholics remained, images of the emperor diversified. Not only was the emperor portrayed as a courtier, an intellectual, a military leader or a representative of Christ during the reign of Maximilian and Rudolf, but the Holy Roman Emperor began to be represented as nature itself. The portrayal of the emperor and other Habsburgs as nature was a means to avoid the question of sovereign legitimacy and to claim that the Habsburg ruler was a 'natural' ruler who controlled the powers of nature. The animal and plant studies, painted allegories and courtly spectacles that Arcimboldo produced and that helped propel this new imperial persona stand at the heart of this book. I frame discussions of the projects Arcimboldo completed while he was at the imperial court with examinations of works of art he produced in Milan before and after his time at the imperial court. In the end, *Impossible Nature* shows that Arcimboldo instantiated and cultivated a new imperial persona and message, and at the same time undermined them by unintentionally revealing that the very idea of a natural ruler is not only unnatural but impossible. It is rifts like this that this book seeks to highlight.

Impossible Nature tracks Arcimboldo's career. However, it is not a catalogue or a survey of all Arcimboldo's works and accomplishments, but an argument about the relationship between art, nature and politics in the Holy Roman Empire in the second half of the sixteenth century. The works are read as evidence of Arcimboldo's self-conscious role as a mediator of nature, as an index of doubt surrounding imperial authority and as instances in which works of art fall short of expressing their own political arguments.

To be sure, there are other significant examples of Arcimboldo's work, but in the interest of telling a focused and coherent story I have not addressed them here. A famous example is Arcimboldo's drawings of sericulture, which he devised to adorn rooms in Baron Ferdinand von Hoffman's (1540–1607) palace in Prague (illus. 11 and 12). There are also composite portraits like *The Jurist* (1566) (illus. 13), which, on account of this book's short length, are also not given their fair due. The imperial focus of this book is not arbitrary, nor a mere consequence of the magisterial scholarship on Arcimboldo's career in the Holy Roman Empire. It is justified by the radicalism of the pictures and the political arguments they attempt to articulate. The topic of Arcimboldo's work for the imperial court has hardly been neglected by recent scholarship. Arcimboldo's importance to the development of the genre of still life, his ancient textual sources, his invention of new imperial allegories as well as how the empirical study of nature was indispensable to the creation of his most fantastic works have been the focus of some of the most innovative research in the study of sixteenth-century art history over the last 45 years. The present book relies and builds on this scholarship.[5]

Chapter One, 'Lost Origins', presents what little we know about Arcimboldo's training and career before he moved from Milan to Vienna to take up a position as a portrait painter at Maximilian II's court. It focuses on the work Arcimboldo produced for various ecclesiastical and civic patrons between the years 1549 and 1562 in Milan and throughout the Duchy of Milan.

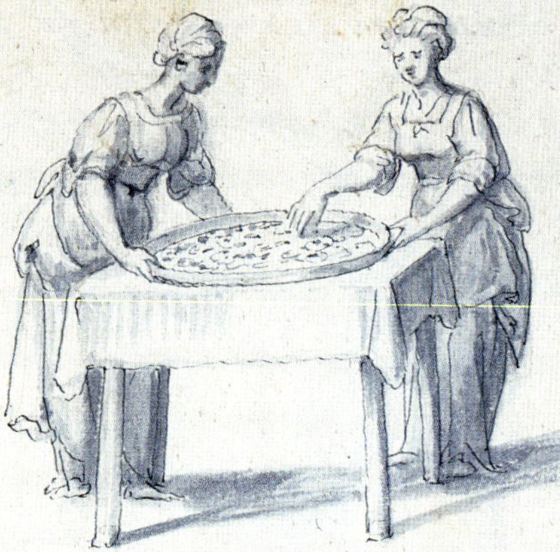

Questo p° capitulo dimostra la semenza del bigatto
la uerso la pª vera quando il tempo e caldo le
femine pigliano il seme et lo mettano nel seno e con
quel calore la si comenza a mouere tenendola a
lochi piu caldi e temperati che a lochi fredi il
semo e di questa grossezza ° e quando quel bigat
to uermino e nato et che per far la galla e di
questa grossezza et faciono

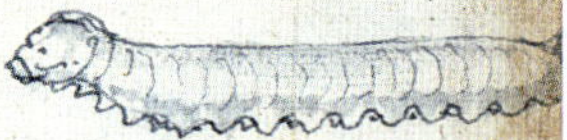

la galla e di tal grossezza

come qui si uede

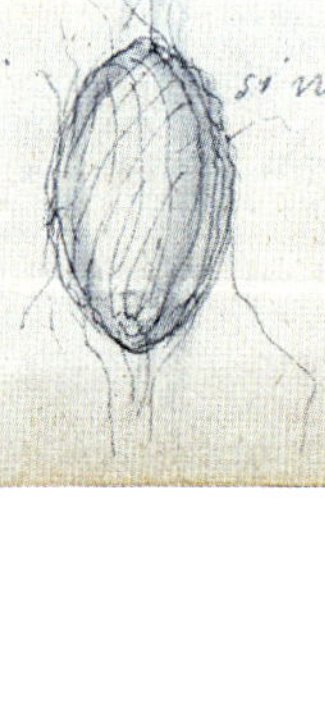

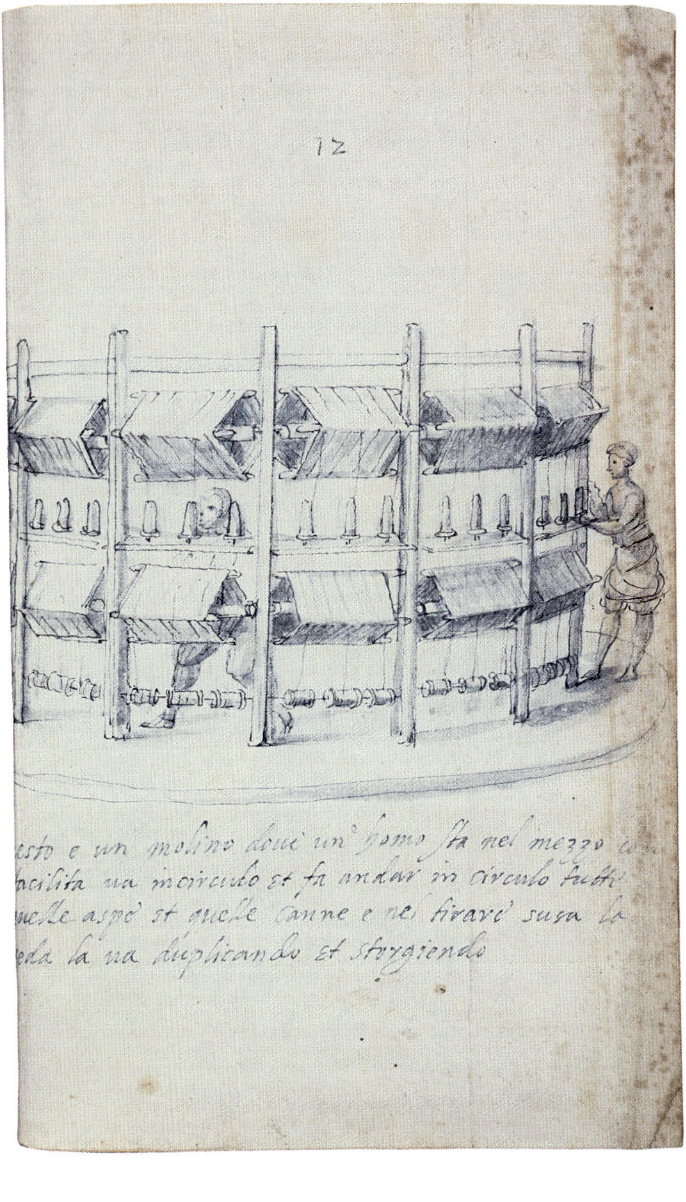

11, 12 Folios from Arcimboldo, 'Treatise on Silk Culture and Manufacture', *c.* 1586, pen and blue ink and brush with blue wash.

The first chapter also examines Arcimboldo's social network in Lombardy and explores how these contacts may have been instrumental to the artist's development of his famed composite heads. Finally, the chapter sheds light on how effectively Arcimboldo went from an artist whose works were religious and collaborative in nature, in Milan, to one whose secular works are still considered products of a singular creator at court.

Chapter Two, 'Nature Studies', takes up the plant and animal studies Arcimboldo completed while he was at the imperial courts in Vienna and Prague throughout the 1560s, 1570s and 1580s. Not only did these diverse studies of plants and animals form some of the components of Arcimboldo's famed series of the Seasons and the Elements, but they make evident the burgeoning confluence of early modern collecting, the study of nature and the representation of imperial power. At the same time, the chapter shows that Arcimboldo's plant and animal studies were collected and displayed in such a way as to promote the notion that nature was made up of distinct entities that could be ordered into a unified whole, even though many of Arcimboldo's studies exist uneasily between the modern art-historical categories of preparatory study and natural history illustration.

Chapter Three, 'Nature and Empire', centres on two series of paintings, the Seasons and the Elements, that Arcimboldo completed between 1562 and 1566 at Maximilian II's court in Vienna. Given to Maximilian on New Year's Day in 1569, along with an explanatory poem by the Milanese humanist Giovanni Battista Fonteo (1546–1580), the works portray composite representations of the four seasons and the four elements. Intended by the artist to be hung together, the eight paintings make the bold claim that Maximilian II was the supreme ruler not just of the Holy Roman Empire, but of nature itself. To do so, however, the paintings had to reduce the emperor to mere matter. Thus, this chapter shows that to understand the works' artistic conceit and

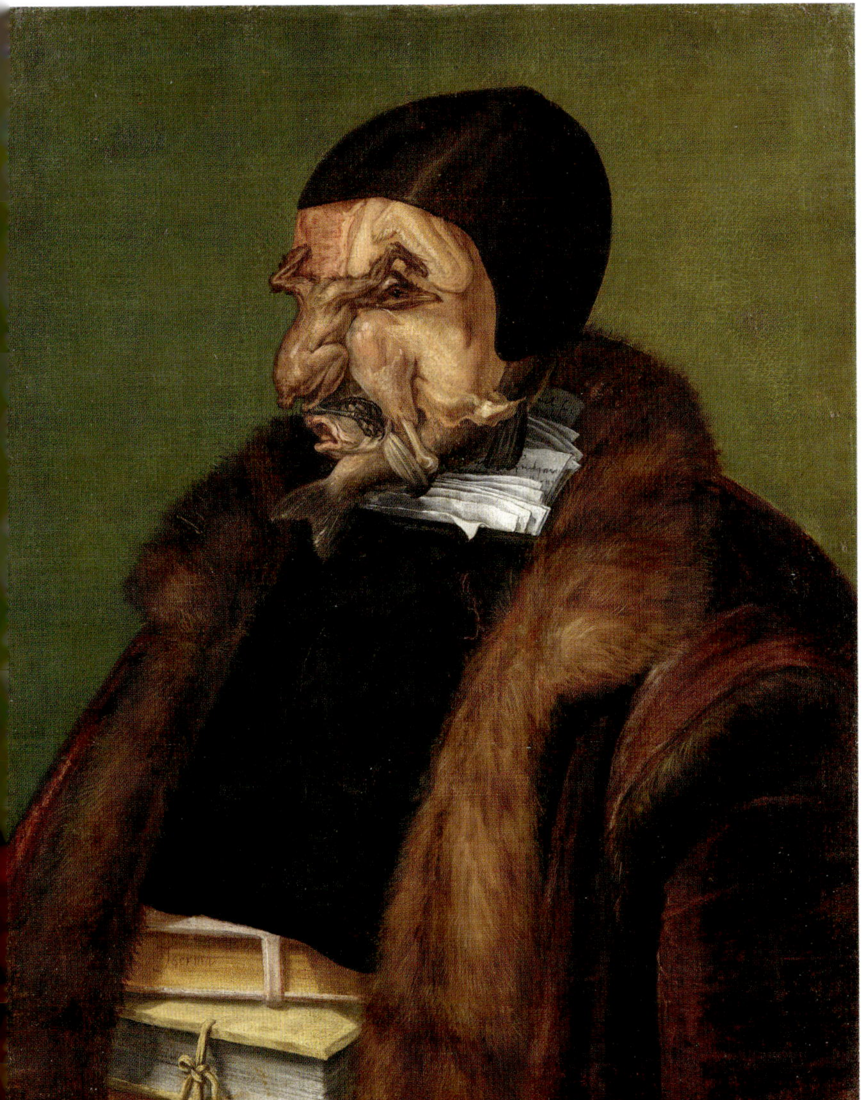

13 Arcimboldo, *The Jurist*, 1566, oil on canvas.

political meaning fully, one had to divorce the component parts of the work from one another, which in turn dismembered not only the pictures but Arcimboldo's political allegory as well.

Chapter Four, 'Harmonious Bodies', looks at a tournament procession Arcimboldo designed in 1571 for the festivities celebrating the nuptials of Maximilian II's brother, Archduke Charles of Steiermark (1540–1590), and the staunchly Catholic Maria Anna von Wittelsbach (1551–1608) of the Bavarian court. According to cartels, or programmes, of the procession, Arcimboldo elaborated on his novel imperial allegory, which portrayed Maximilian as a natural sovereign and sovereign of nature, so that it could be legible to a large international audience and so that the allegory could explicitly address contemporary geopolitics. Doing so afforded Arcimboldo the opportunity to articulate a vision of power that was secular, thereby avoiding confessional tensions inside and outside the empire. This secular argument also allowed Arcimboldo the opportunity to add an explicitly dynastic component to his allegory as well as laying the groundwork to claim Asia, Africa and the Americas into the Habsburg domain.

Chapter Five, 'Impossible Desires', investigates Arcimboldo's final imperial allegory – his portrait of Holy Roman Emperor Rudolf II in the guise of Vertumnus, the Roman god of the seasons (illus. 14). Based on verses by the Roman poet Propertius, the painting claims that Rudolf II's reign ended history by ushering in a new golden age; an age defined by peace and natural abundance. Like other composite paintings, *Vertumnus* accomplishes this by reducing the human subject of the painting to disparate inanimate objects. In doing so, it creates a fiction of a sovereign that is suffused throughout the world, and thus lays bare an impossible political ambition.

Chapter Six, 'To Make a Face', works to understand three composite paintings Arcimboldo made towards the end of his life in Milan, after he retired from Rudolf's imperial court. These

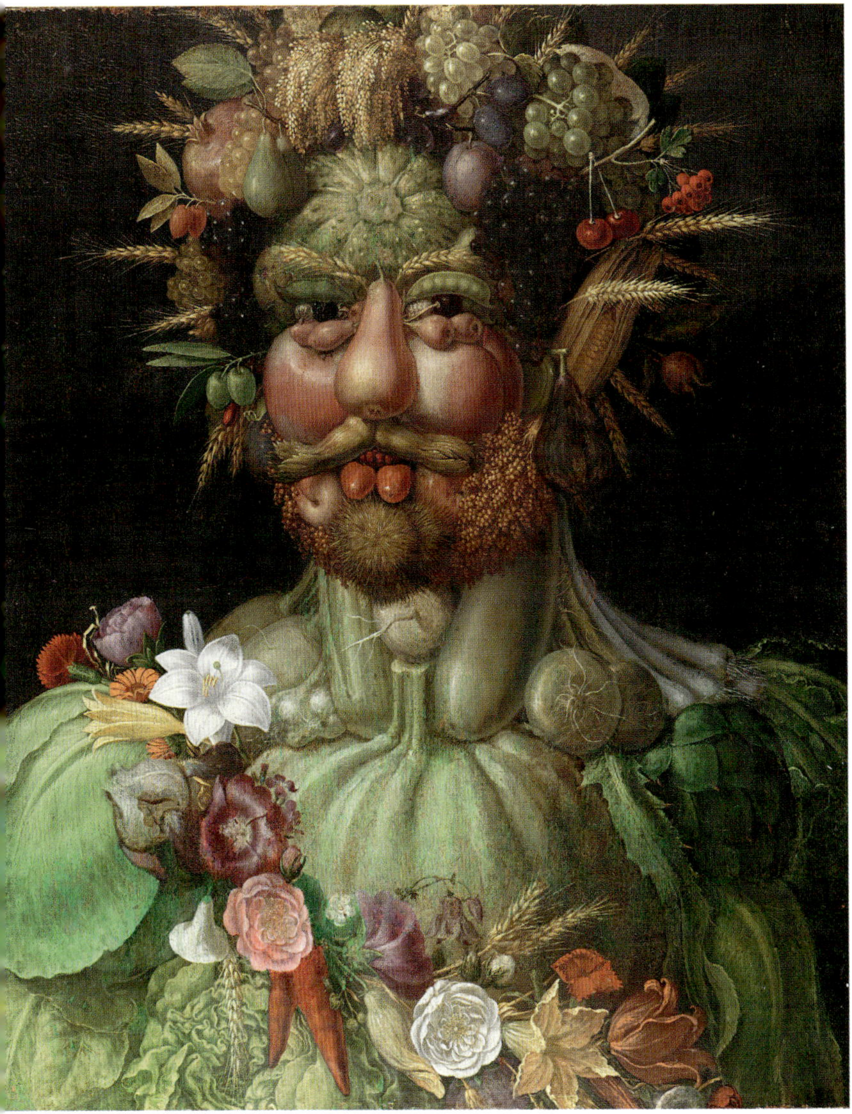

14 Arcimboldo, *Vertumnus*, 1590, oil on panel.

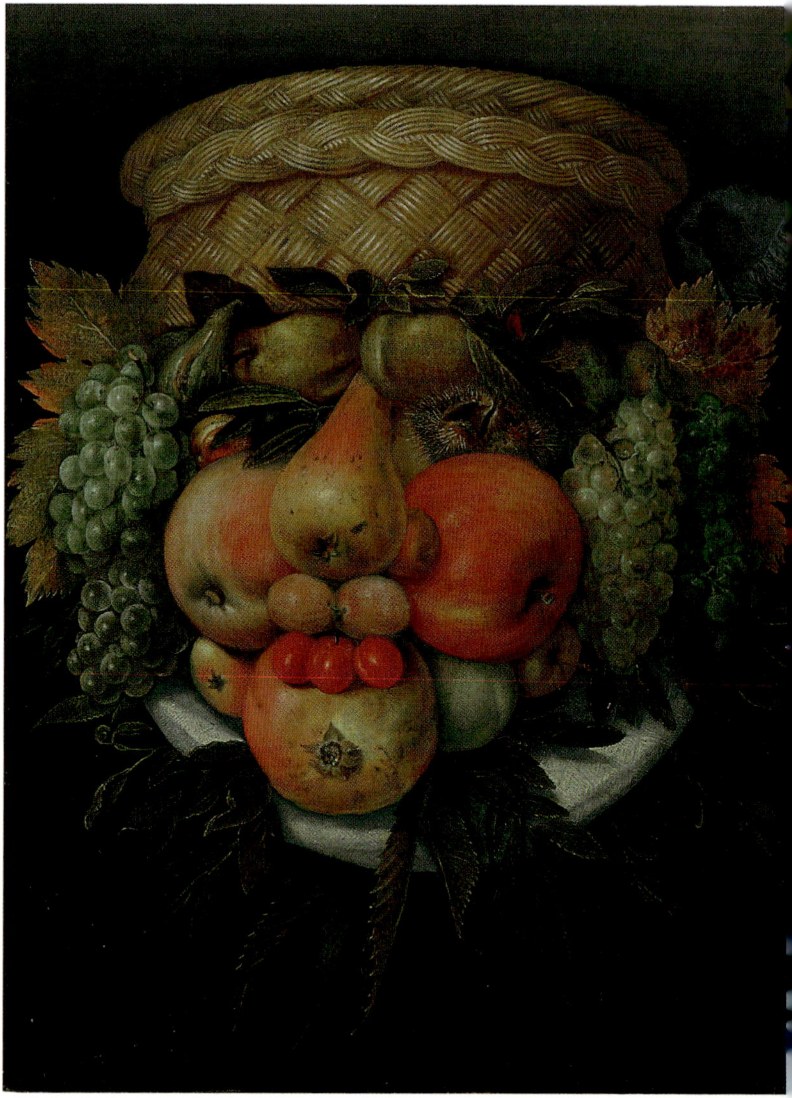

15 Arcimboldo, *Invertible Head with Basket of Fruit*, *c.* 1590, oil on panel.

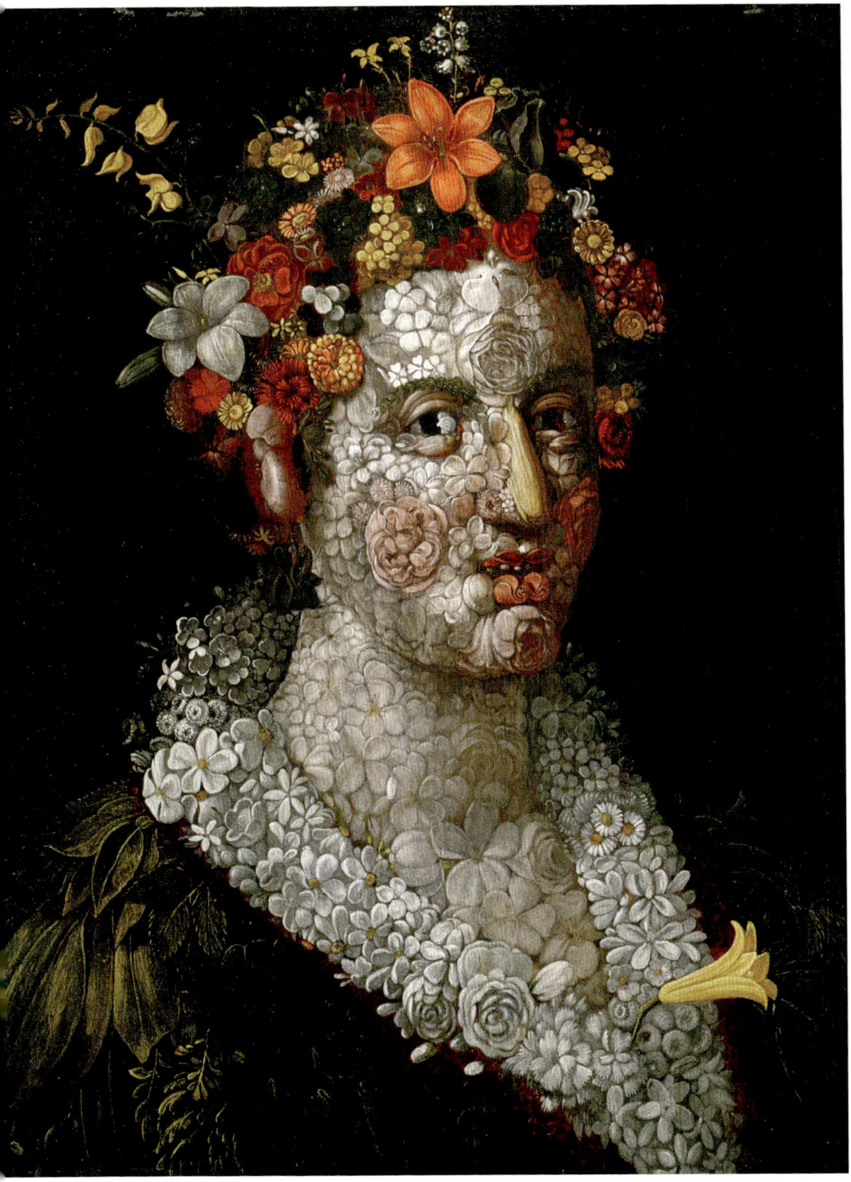

16 Arcimboldo, *Flora*, 1591, oil on panel.

are works that portray two subjects at once. In two, *The Vegetable Gardener* (illus. 10) and *The Basket of Fruit* (1590) (illus. 15), when oriented in one direction the painting is a conventional still life, and when turned upside down the still life morphs into a humanoid face. *Flora* (1590) (illus. 16), the third painting examined in the chapter, also has a double subject. However, rather than inverting the painting to induce a second subject to appear, one must alter one's proximity to the work. This chapter makes clear that these works not only blur the distinction between art and nature's ingenuity but, like his imperial allegories, attempt to generate uncertainty in the viewer's experience of nature.

Arcimboldo's works are filled with moments like this: the ambiguous divide between nature and art, suggestive similarities of human, animal and vegetable, objects curiously isolated through their proximity to other objects. Meaningful in their politics and their design and execution, such works trouble art historians who want to explain how they came to be. This makes Arcimboldo's works a singular phenomenon of the Renaissance. Their birth remains as difficult to understand as our own.

ONE

Lost Origins

The date of the first known document to record Giuseppe Arcimboldo's existence is 24 December 1549. The document in question was issued by Milan's Fabbrica, the organization responsible for the construction, decoration and maintenance of Milan Cathedral. It authorized a payment of 6 lire to Arcimboldo for four stained-glass window designs.[1] Such designs (there would have been hundreds) were drawn up by local artists for a glazier who would transfer the designs to the windows and colour them. By the time Arcimboldo was paid for his contribution, the Fabbrica had been sporadically compensating his father, Biagio Arcimboldo, for over 31 years. Biagio's projects for the cathedral included painting the houses of the cathedral vestry board, panels of the Virgin in majesty and banners for the altar of the cathedral. In 1549 Biagio was remunerated for thirty designs for the cathedral's stained-glass windows.[2] From the start, then, Giuseppe seems not to be following in his father's footsteps but standing by his side.

While Arcimboldo's designs for the windows do not survive, the windows do. They depict scenes from the Hebrew Bible and scenes from the life of St Catherine (illus. 17 and 18). The former are now on the south side of the cathedral's nave, and the latter rise over what is now the south entrance of the cathedral. There is consensus among the scholarly community that father and son worked on these designs together.[3] Arcimboldo's earliest

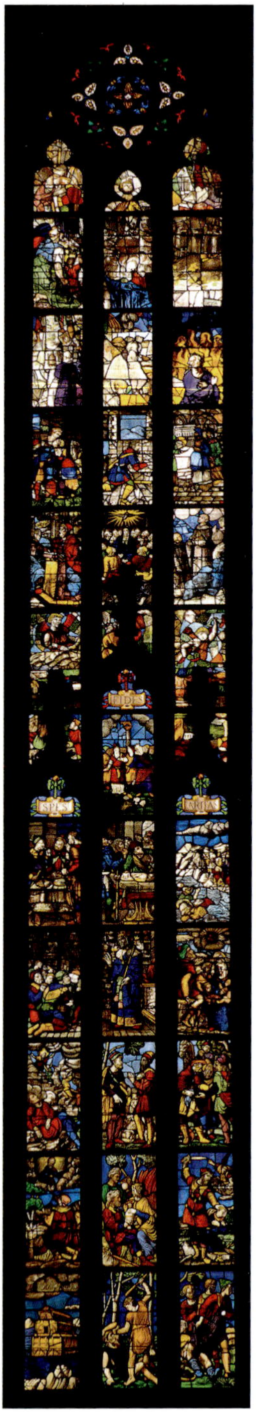
FIDES
SPES
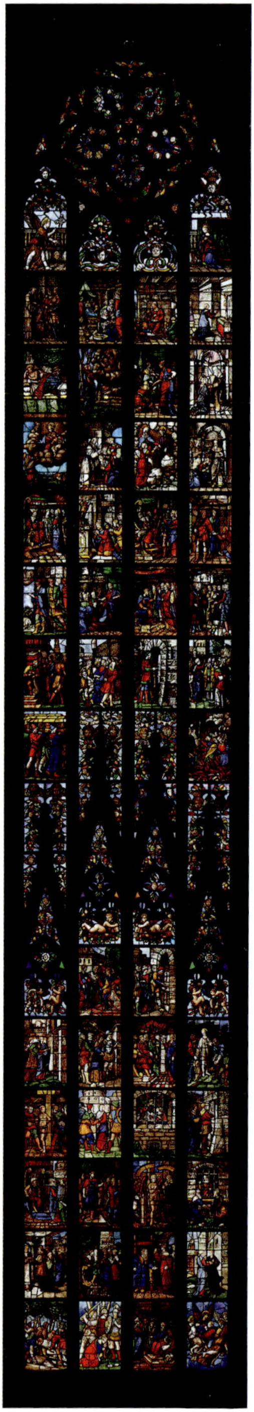

work, then, adheres to the style of his father. This stylistic conformity is but one of several distinguishing features between his earliest projects and the paintings he would later create and that were collected by courts north of the Alps.

Besides the fact that they were a collaborative endeavour and intended for a pre-existing, architectural programme, the designs for Milan Cathedral's windows differ structurally from the artist's later composite paintings in other ways. Perhaps the most striking contrasts are the windows' biblical and hagiographical subject matter. After leaving Milan in the early 1560s, Arcimboldo, to our knowledge, never portrayed another explicitly religious subject in a painting, a drawing or any of the courtly performances and tournaments he orchestrated. Nor did Arcimboldo openly rely on prose for his subjects. In his later work he dispensed with any reliance on established iconographic traditions. Multifigured works are also few and far between in his oeuvre. Indeed, as we will come to see, Arcimboldo's work, his aims and his professional persona changed considerably over the course of his career. Like Proteus, whom he was likened to towards the end of his life, Arcimboldo transformed himself several times over.[4] To appreciate his remarkable mutability, it is vital to familiarize ourselves with his early career in Milan, as it not only makes clear how clever and inventive Arcimboldo was but provides a fleeting glimpse of his desires and ambitions.

SOURCES FOR ARCIMBOLDO'S LIFE

We come to the beginning by way of the end. Arcimboldo died in Milan in 1593 at the age of 67. Scholars have derived his age from a self-portrait (illus. 19).[5] Dated 1587, the red chalk drawing bears the face of the artist in three-quarter view. Standard in its format, the drawing is unusual in its portrayal. The artist has converted his own materiality from bone, skin and hair into crumbled,

17, 18 Stained-glass windows with scenes from the Old Testament and scenes from the life of St Catherine of Alexandria, Milan Cathedral, *c.* 1546, after cartoons by Biagio Arcimboldo and Giuseppe Arcimboldo.

creased, curled and torn scraps of paper. Upon his brow Arcimboldo penned '61'.[6] The artfully placed numeral functions as a sign of age, twice over. Standing for both a bodily sign of age – a wizened brow – and a numerical one, this self-conscious sign has allowed scholars to determine his birth year as 1526.

Born two years after a plague that took over 50,000 souls in Milan and one year before Holy Roman Emperor Charles V plundered Rome, Arcimboldo's early life is a mystery.[7] Though he was born into a family of painters, little is known about the young artist's training. Some scholars contend that Arcimboldo studied under his father, Biagio. Others maintain that he was taught by one of his uncles, Ambrogio or Gian Giacomo Arcimboldo, who were also local painters. Beyond Arcimboldo's surviving works, the complicated trajectory of his early activity in Milan has been reconstructed on textual traces of the artist discovered in both civic and ecclesiastical archives. Much of what we know with confidence about this period in Arcimboldo's life comes from documented payments to the artist for various works. Silvio Leydi, R. S. Miller and Thomas Kaufmann have attributed an array of work produced in the city and Duchy of Milan to Arcimboldo by means of these payments along with stylistic features evinced in the St Catherine windows of Milan Cathedral.[8] Many of the payment records provide dates for the works Arcimboldo completed for various ecclesiastical institutions. These documents also contain evidence of Arcimboldo's collaboration with artists such as Giuseppe Meda (1534–1599) as well as pointing to his connections with notable Lombard painters, like Bernardino Luini (d. 1532) and his son Aurelio Luini (1530–1593) and Leonardo's protégé Francesco Melzi (1493–1570). Besides the works, dates, payments and social networks, nothing else is known about this period in Arcimboldo's life.

It is only after Arcimboldo retired from Rudolf II's imperial court in Prague in 1587 and returned to Milan that the picture

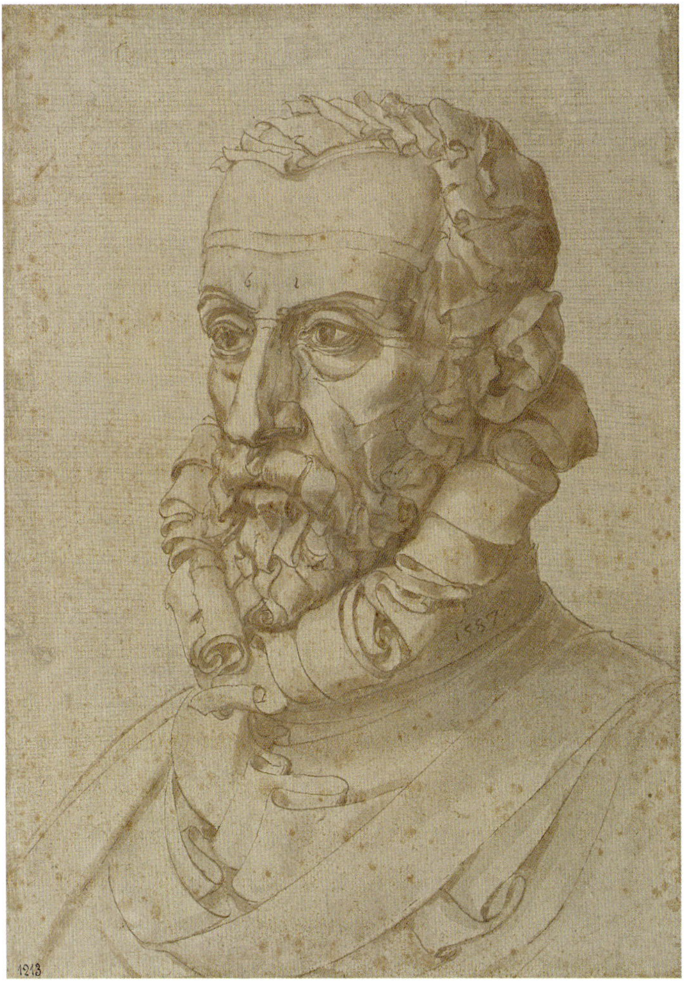

of his life begins to take shape, albeit not always reliably. For instance, in his *La nobiltà di Milano* (1595) the famed chronicler of the city, Paolo Morigia (1525–1604), laid out an entirely invented genealogy of the Arcimboldo family.[9] The family name 'Arcimboldo', which according to Morigia meant 'mine in a wood', was

19 Arcimboldo, *Self-Portrait (Man of Letters)*, 1587, pen and ink on paper.

a consequence of the family's supposed origin in the dense and rich forests of ancient Germany. Morigia reported that Arcimboldo learned of his family's ancestry from a German doctor at the imperial court. The doctor in question could have been Maximilian II's court antiquarian, Wolfgang Lazius (1514–1565), who was practised in determining, etymologically, the roots of noble families.[10] Morigia must have learned of the family's pedigree from the artist himself. Whether Arcimboldo was aware that this learned reconstruction of his familial lineage was a fiction, we may never know. We can infer that Arcimboldo was keen to relay the nobility and antiquity of his family to his acquaintance for publication and posterity.

As far as we can surmise, Arcimboldo was neither a member of an ancient clan nor a descendant of the Arcimboldis – a politically powerful Milanese family who counted several Archbishops of Milan among its members. Rather, Arcimboldo was born into a modest family of painters who worked in Milan and in nearby Monza and Como – all locations where he would eventually work. His father, Biagio, was son to Pasio Arcimboldo. Pasio was a master but we know not of what, as his guild affiliation was not documented. However, since Biagio's two brothers, Ambrogio and Gian Giacomo, also took up the trade of painting, it is highly probable that Pasio too belonged to the profession.[11]

MILAN

The Milan that the Arcimboldo family lived and worked in was a vast and flourishing city (illus. 20). Situated in the Po valley and linking trade routes between the Italian peninsula and the lands north of the Alps, Milan was an effervescent urban centre where commerce, craftsmanship, politics and religion were deeply entangled. Giovanni Botero (1544–1617), author of *The Reason of the State* (1589), wondered: 'Is there a duchy more abundant in

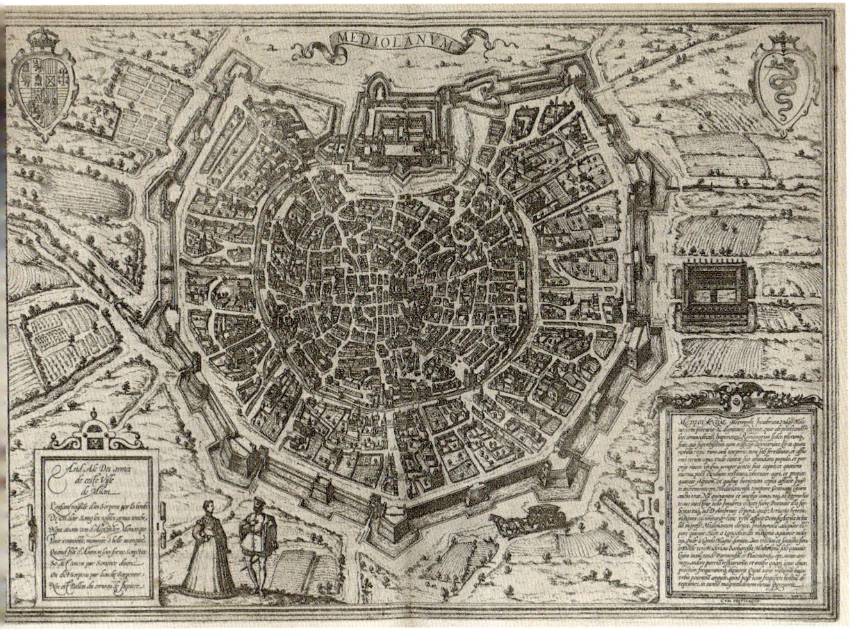

victuals, grains, rice, livestock, cheeses, wines, and flax; more replete with artificers and traffic, more densely populated or more conveniently located?'[12] All this abundance was governed by the ruler of the Duchy of Milan, a region that included most of modern-day Lombardy as well as parts of Liguria, Emilia and Venetia. Holy Roman Emperor Charles V took control away from the Sforza family in 1535 (when Arcimboldo was but nine years old) and the duchy became an imperial fief. In 1546 Charles invested his son, Prince Philip II (1527–1598) of Spain, with control of the duchy. Milan's location, between the Iberian peninsula, the lands of the Austrian Habsburgs and Flanders, fostered its importance for the movement of both goods and soldiers throughout the Habsburg imperial lands.[13]

Beyond the city's value to the Spanish Habsburgs, it was also a jewel in the crown of the church. Located in the largest diocese

20 Georg Braun and Franz Hogenberg, *Mediolanum* (Milan), from *Civitates orbis terrarum*, vol. I (1575).

in all of Italy, the city was home to 238 churches, 30 monasteries and 34 convents by the time Arcimboldo could pick up a brush.[14] The sheer number of ecclesiastical institutions afforded local artists and artisans opportunities to work, interact and collaborate. The prevalence of artisans and tradesmen in Milan was frequently commented on by locals and foreigners alike. Morigia wrote: 'It is worth seeing the union of all trades in this city. One can see all goldsmiths and jewelers gathered in two streets, all those making armors and coats of mail in another; those who make swords, and daggers and arquebuses in another, the same can be said about the union of all other trades.'[15]

The remarkable cooperation of the trades is made apparent in Arcimboldo's early forays into art making. Almost all the works attributed to Arcimboldo in the 1540s and 1550s in Milan and its environs were the result of a collaboration of artists and artisans from different trades. In addition to the glaziers and weavers who brought the artist's designs to fruition, we know that Arcimboldo worked closely with at least one other painter, Giuseppe Meda, on frescoes for the cathedral in Monza and on organ shutters for Milan Cathedral. Thus, it is fair to say that when we examine many of Arcimboldo's works from the 1540s and 1550s in Lombardy, it is difficult to assess confidently where Giuseppe Arcimboldo begins and ends.[16] To make matters more tricky, recent archival discoveries have thrown some long-held attributions into doubt. In other cases (particularly with regard to tapestry designs attributed to Arcimboldo), new workshop practices have come to light that have thrown into question the presence of the artist's hand in certain elements of the tapestry design, such as the borders.[17] It follows, then, that we must approach works from this period of the artist's career with some caution and resist the urge to read too much of the artist into them. Instead, we should consider these works as examples of the types of object the young artist was acquainted with. Only by familiarizing ourselves with them will we be able to apprehend the dramatic turn his career took after he crossed the Alps.

EARLY WORK

The payment on 24 December 1549 was the first of several Arcimboldo received from the Fabbrica. A payment on 20 May 1551 for another set of designs for stained glass lists him as a 'master'. The change in rank may have created opportunities for new commissions. On 17 June 1551 the freshly minted master was paid 8½ lire for painting the crest of the Fabbrica on the facades of the cathedral's vestry.[18] This commission is notable: it makes clear that the young artist was adept at working at diverse scales, and it also demonstrates that he was making pictures that shaped the public image of an institution and his patron. That Arcimboldo was accomplished at reproducing heraldic imagery is attested to by his next commission – painting banners that featured the coat of arms of the King of Bohemia (illus. 21), who at that time was Ferdinand I (1503–1564) of the House of Habsburg, the father of Arcimboldo's future patron, Holy Roman Emperor Maximilian II.[19] It is tempting to speculate that the 25-year-old artist dazzled Maximilian II's father with his portrayal of two crowned, rearing and roaring lions against a red ground; it is also inviting to wonder if the complex superimposition of six other Habsburg family crests, masking the bodies of the lions, impressed Ferdinand upon his visit to Milan in 1551. Whether or not this was the case we will never know. What we can say about the banners is this: to our knowledge this was the first time Arcimboldo represented the House of Habsburg by way of a composite and emblematic image, although one he did not design.

Despite these commissions, and others he received from the Fabbrica between 1549 and 1557 (roughly 150 designs for

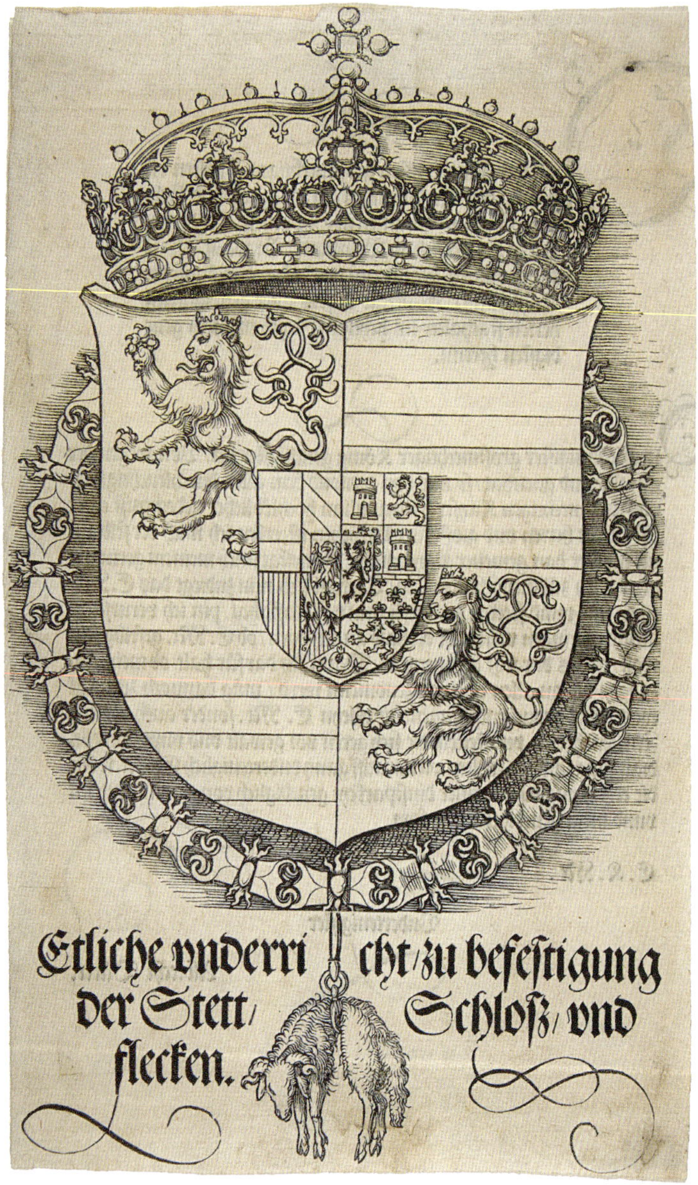

21 Albrecht Dürer, *The Arms of Ferdinand I, King of Bohemia and Hungary*, 1527, woodcut.

stained-glass windows), Arcimboldo still had to seek work elsewhere to make ends meet. In 1556 he was awarded a major commission. He and Giuseppe Meda were contracted to paint the ceiling and wall of the south transept of Monza Cathedral – roughly 19 kilometres north of Milan. According to the commission, Arcimboldo and Meda were to paint the four evangelists along with eight angels on the ceiling above the Virgin and John the Evangelist flanking Christ nailed to the Tree of Jesse.[20] The tree was to cradle fifteen of Christ's male ancestors in its branches. Still in the cathedral today, this fresco is markedly different from Arcimboldo's composite heads (illus. 22). Massive in their scale and against a gold ground, the frescoes in Monza Cathedral evoke an older tradition of sacred painting. Christ's monumental ancestors (all listed in the Gospel of Matthew and Luke) twist and turn atop frothy clouds among the tree's branches. Each male ancestor holds aloft and presents an identifying scroll or tablet. The Virgin and John the Evangelist adore the body of Christ at the base of the tree, while Jesse, out of whom Christ's family tree grows, lays beneath their feet. This entire schematic genealogy is set against a screen of the tree's lush foliage and colossal citrus fruit – the abundance of life and nature's fecundity at odds with Christ's dead body.

Because of the naturalistic portrayal of the tree and its fruit, the frescoes in Monza have been considered a harbinger of Arcimboldo's composite paintings' descriptive tendencies.[21] However, the contract drawn up for the Monza frescoes specified that Arcimboldo and Meda were to be equal contributors.[22] Therefore, we must be prudent when attributing a particular hand to specific passages of the fresco, especially because all of Arcimboldo's previous works – such as the St Catherine windows – were designed by him, but not executed by him. Even so, the frescoes in Monza are significant because they further demonstrate that prior to his arrival at the imperial court Arcimboldo

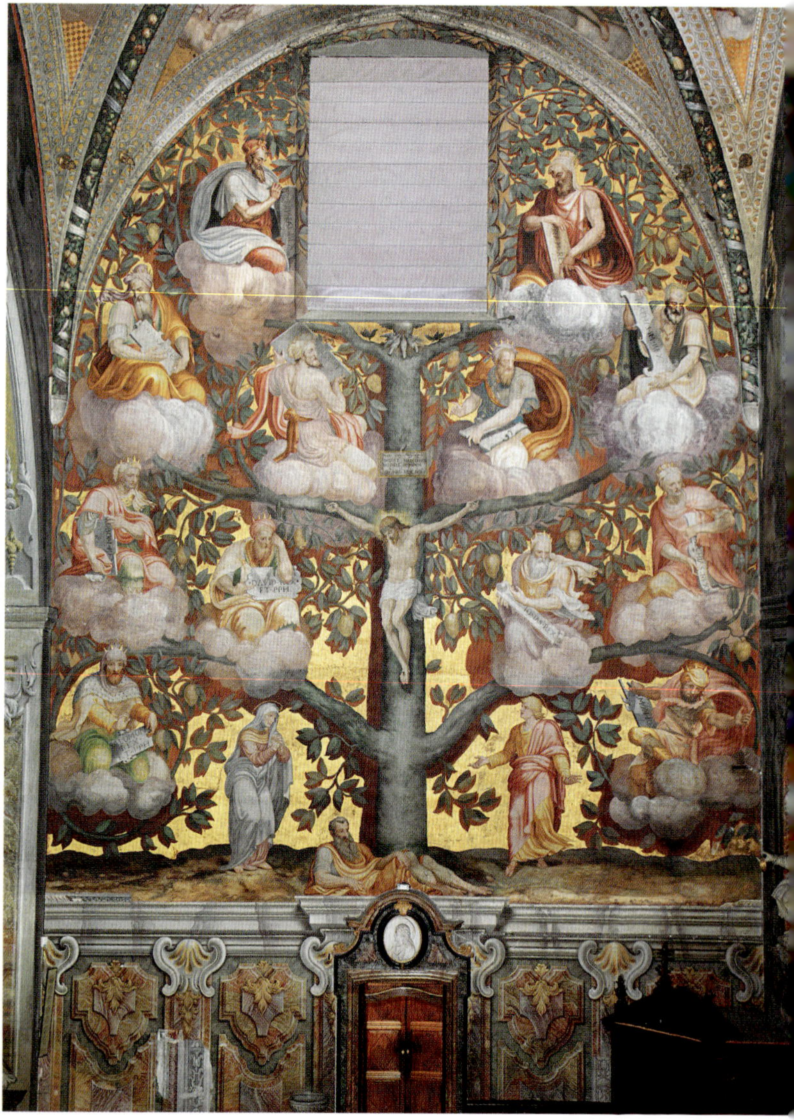

22 Arcimboldo and Giuseppe Meda, *Tree of Jesse*, 1556–62, fresco, Monza Cathedral.

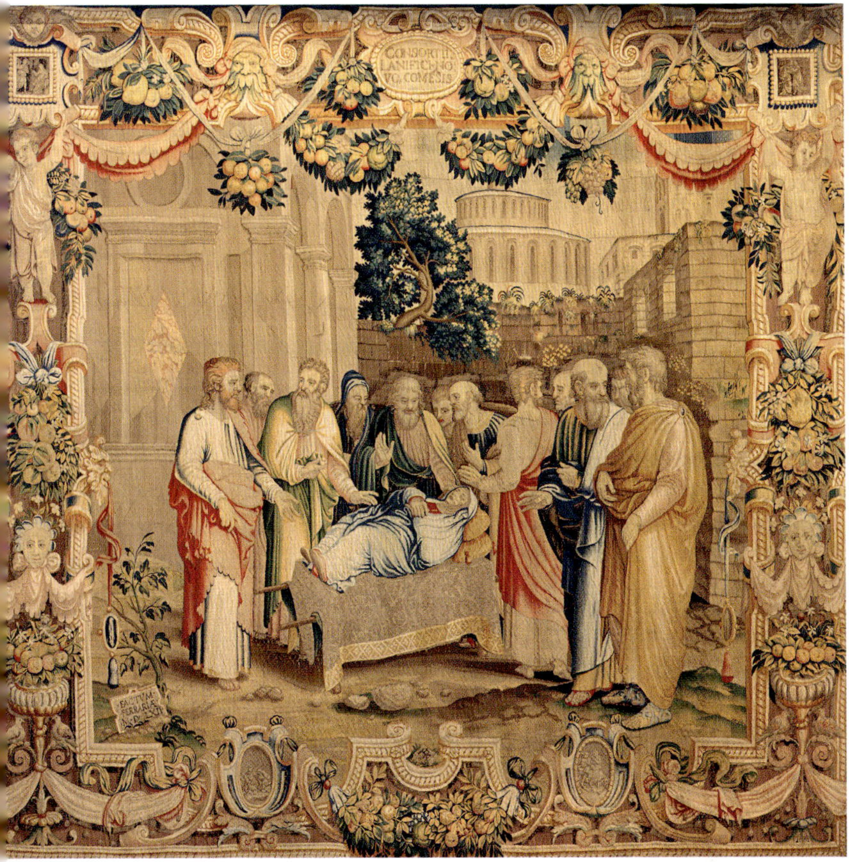

was spending most of his time focusing his attention on large-scale, multifigured religious subjects for an ecclesiastical setting. As far as we can tell, he adhered to his contract as well as convention and was able to coalesce his style with another artist. These are elements of his painting that he would come to shake off in less than eight years.

Before leaving Lombardy, however, Arcimboldo completed two more commissions – one is documented while the other

23 Arcimboldo, *Dormition of the Virgin*, 1558, tapestry.

has been attributed to him on stylistic grounds. The documented work is a now-lost cartoon for a tapestry of the *Dormition of the Virgin* (illus. 23).[23] Destined for Como Cathedral, the tapestry was one of seven in a series of the Life of the Virgin. Situated between two structures, one pristine and adorned with classical ornamentation and the other a ruinous stone wall, the twelve apostles congregate around the Virgin, who lies, arms crossed, on her deathbed. The festooned border of the tapestry contains five cartouches portraying scenes from the life of the Virgin that centre on the immaculate conception and Christ's infancy. Made of foliage, bunches of hanging fruit, swaths of drapery, grotesque masks and two childlike Atlas figures, the festooning exceeds the limits of the frame and spills into the funerary scene.[24] Like the fresco in Monza of the Tree of Jesse, the *Dormition of the Virgin* tapestry evidences Arcimboldo's familiarity with representations of an extra-biblical tale. The second tapestry, which has been attributed to Arcimboldo, is the *Preaching of John the Baptist*, currently housed in the treasury of Monza Cathedral (illus. 24).[25] However,

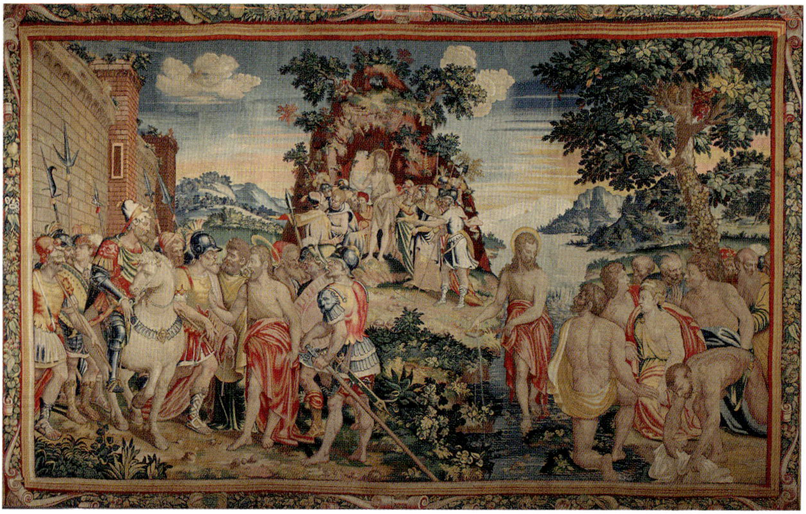

24 Arcimboldo, *Preaching of John the Baptist*, *c.* 1550–59, tapestry, Treasury of Monza Cathedral.

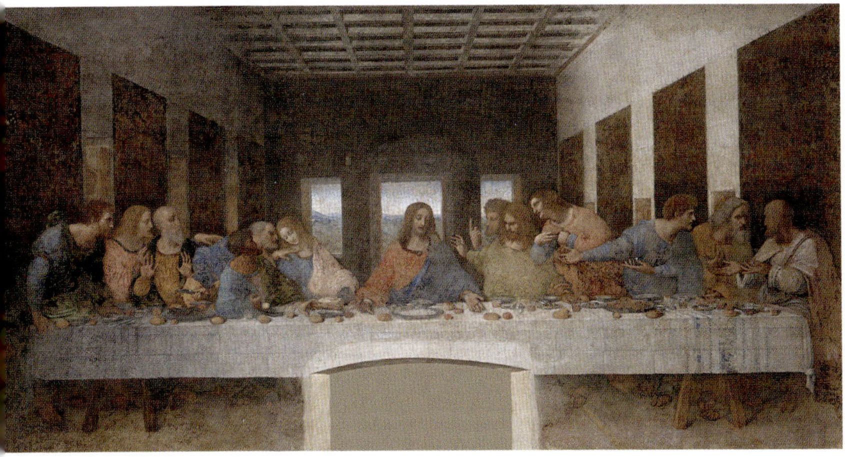

new documents have come to light that suggest the tapestry attributed to Arcimboldo may have been designed and woven not long after Arcimboldo's birth in 1526, and if anything may have been the design of Biagio.[26]

In 1554 Arcimboldo took on a small commission that may have had major consequences for the artist's later work at the imperial court. In November of that year Arcimboldo was paid 49 lire to paint and gild the frame of Titian's *The Crowning with Thorns* (1542–3) (illus. 26).[27] The painting was commissioned by and in the possession of the Confraternity delle Grazie in Milan. It was hung in the Chapel of the Holy Crown in the church of Santa Maria delle Grazie – the same complex which housed Leonardo's *Last Supper* (1495–8) (illus. 25). Besides housing Leonardo's fresco (which included a table laid with an assortment of hyper-naturalistically rendered plates, vessels and food), the church was also home to two works by Gaudenzio Ferrari (1480 or 1484–1546): *The Flagellation* (1513) (illus. 27) and *The Crucifixion* (1513) (illus. 28).[28]

As far as we know, Arcimboldo's early Milanese activity concluded with a competition to design the banner of St Ambrose,

25 Leonardo da Vinci, *The Last Supper*, 1494–8, tempera on gesso, pitch and mastic.

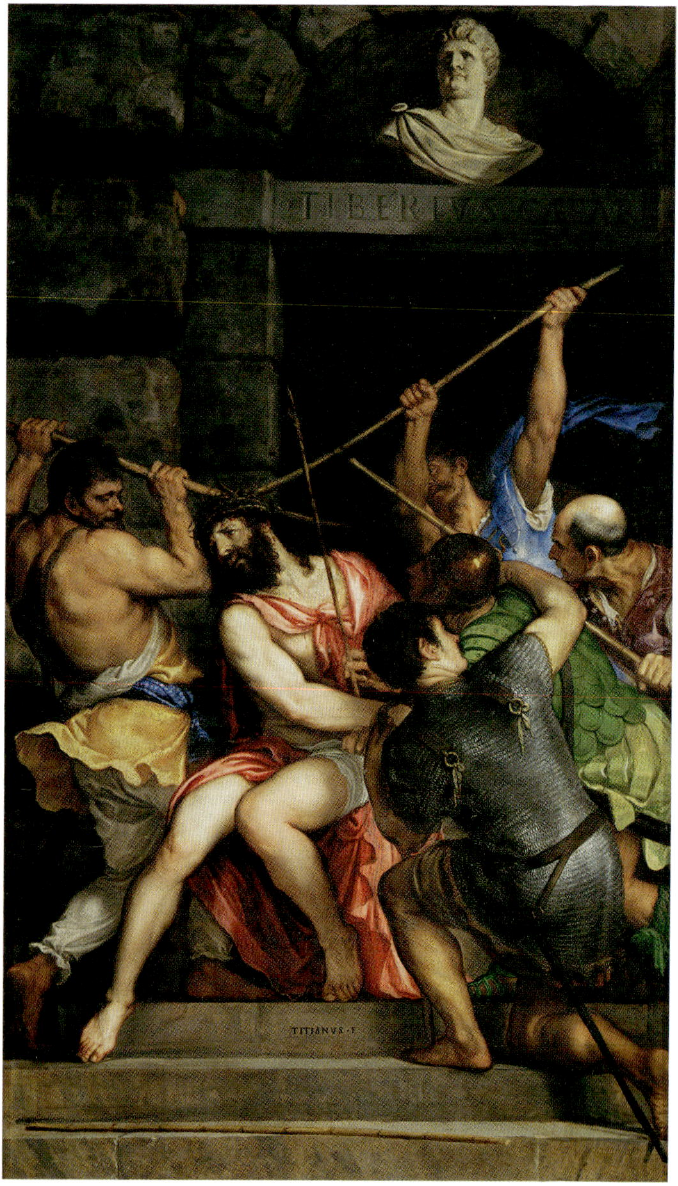

26 Titian, *The Crowning with Thorns*, 1525–50, oil on canvas.

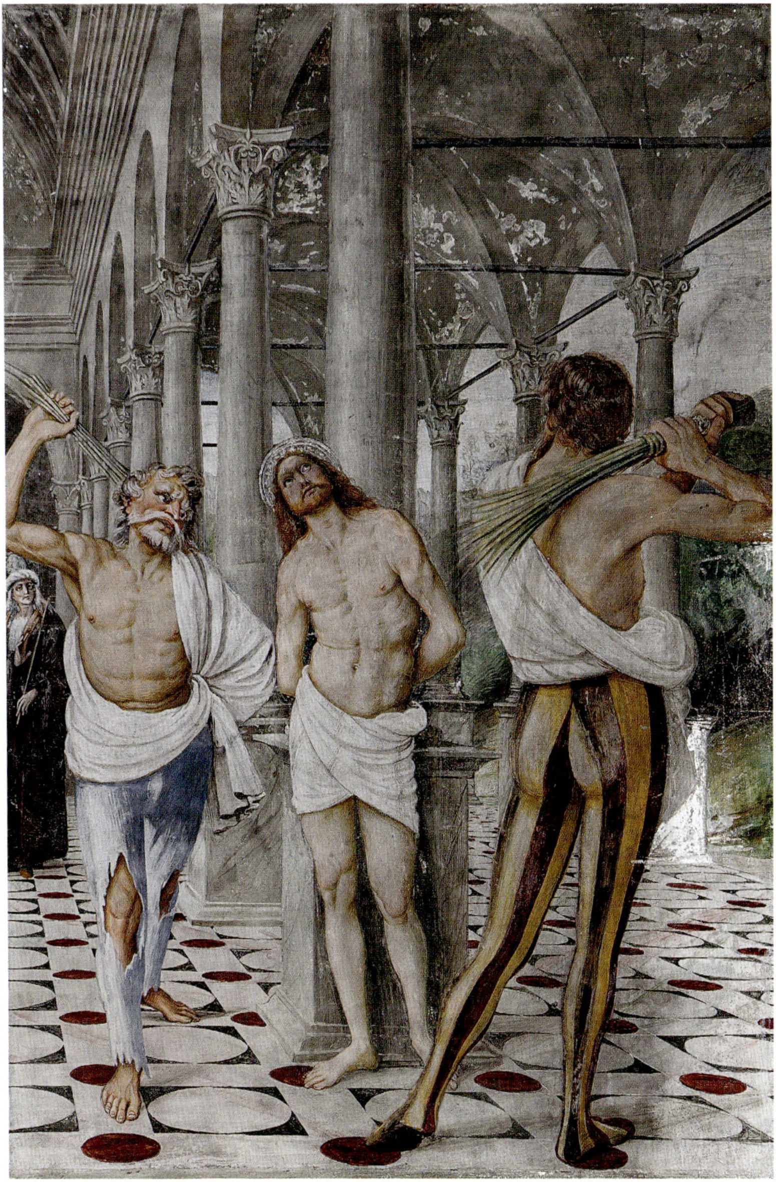

27 Gaudenzio Ferrari, *The Flagellation*, 1513, fresco, Santa Maria delle Grazie, Varallo Sesia.

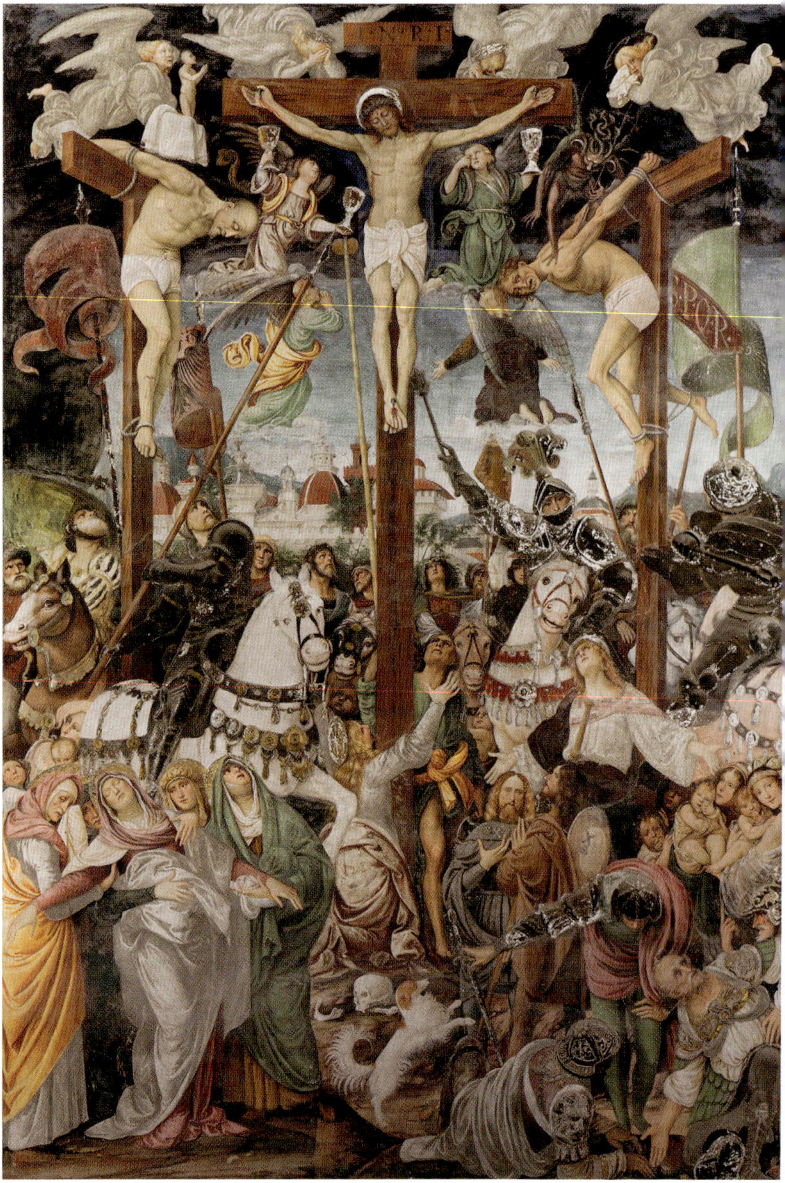

28 Gaudenzio Ferrari, *The Crucifixion,* 1513, fresco, Santa Maria delle Grazie, Varallo Sesia.

the patron saint of Milan. A drawing in the Metropolitan Museum of Art in New York is believed to be an early design for the banner by Arcimboldo (illus. 29, 30).[29] In it a nude male figure stands in an elaborately decorated classical niche, which bears blank cartouches awaiting heraldic imagery. Remarkable in its architectural detail, the drawing formed the basis of the design which was eventually completed by Meda, Arcimboldo's collaborator in Monza. Though the banner was an enviable commission, and perhaps would have cemented Arcimboldo's fame in Milan, documents suggest that the artist may have ceded the commission to Meda when he departed Milan around 1562.

Even though the information we have about Arcimboldo's life, training and work in Milan during his first 36 years is thin at best, we can draw some tentative conclusions about this early work that casts light on the innovative qualities of his artistic production north of the Alps. First, apart from one work, the design for the banner of St Ambrose (which remained incomplete), Arcimboldo's early years in Milan were dominated by collaborative ecclesiastical commissions. He designed objects that were produced in an array of media – stained glass, tapestry, fresco. As far as we know, upon his arrival at the imperial court, he abandoned these forms of media for watercolour, oil painting and festival design. The audience for his work also shifted. Whereas in Milan his works were aimed at clergy, Milan's lay population and, of course, other artists, once at court his works were made for the eyes of other artists, learned members of the imperial court, noble visitors to the imperial court and the emperor himself. Unlike his time in Milan, at court Arcimboldo rarely had to accommodate or blend his style with that of other artists or collaborators, as all his paintings were by and large solo projects. Perhaps this new and sustained artistic autonomy contributed to his presentation of a novel pictorial sensibility to the imperial

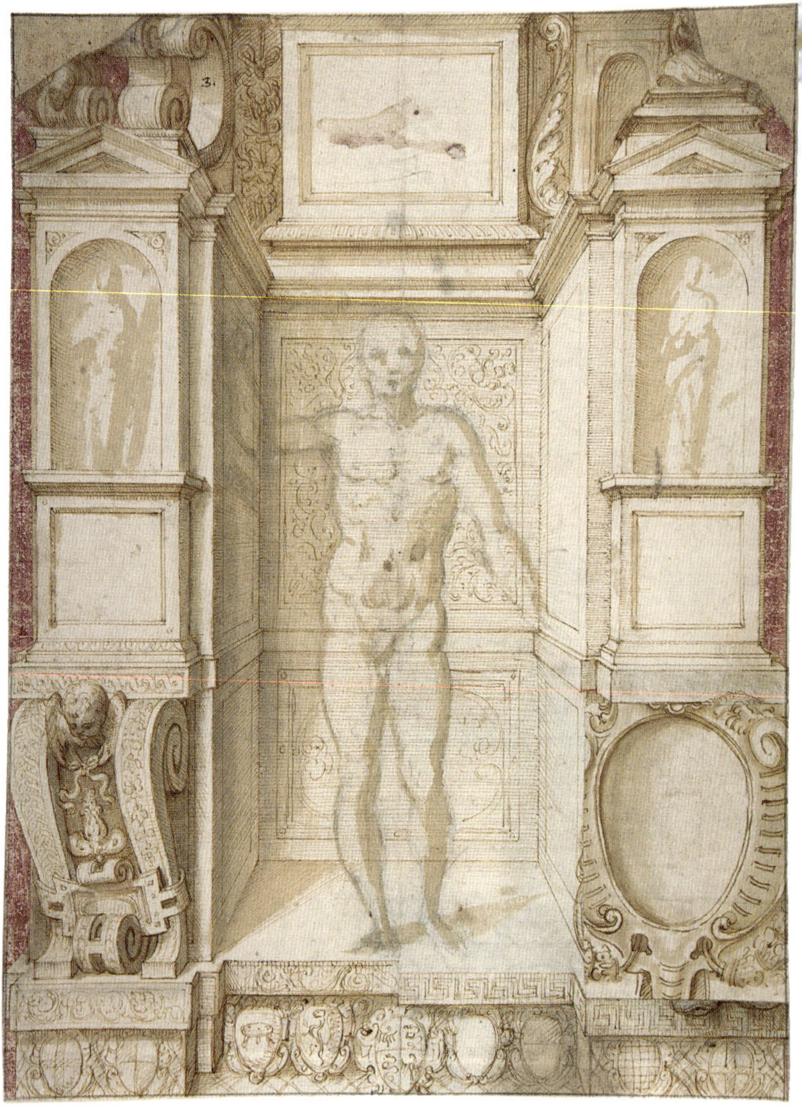
3.

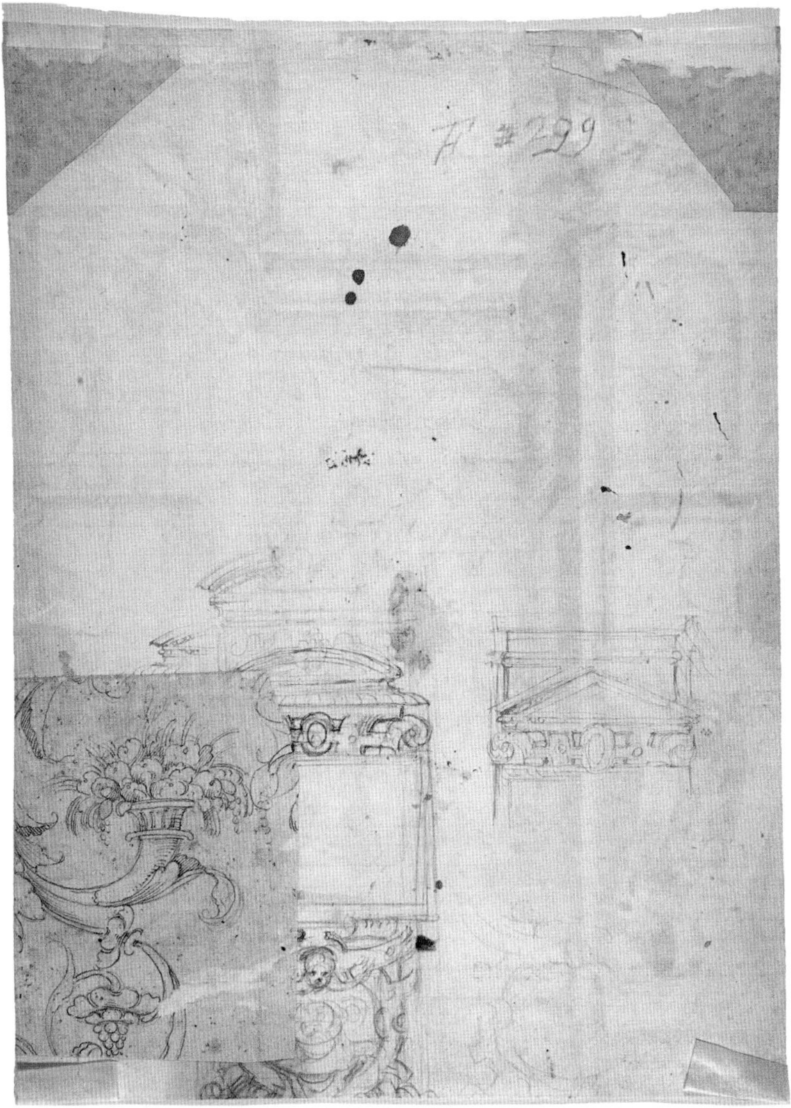

29, 30 Arcimboldo (attrib.), *Study of a Figure in a Niche (Saint Ambrose)* (recto); *Architectural Studies: Four Alternative Designs for Fictive Niches and an Unrelated Design with Garlands* (verso), *c.* 1560–67, pen and ink on paper.

court; a pictorial sensibility grounded in the idioms of portraiture, neo-Platonic cosmology and natural history that distinguished his work from many others at court and beyond.

THE ORIGIN OF THE COMPOSITE PAINTINGS

Despite these important conclusions that we can draw from the early part of his career, the existing scholarship disagrees on the origin of Arcimboldo's composite painting. For some scholars, the conceit of the composite heads can be traced back to long-standing Lombard traditions; for other art historians, the composite paintings point to Leonardo and his followers; and still others claim that the conceit was developed because of Arcimboldo's exposure to the courtly art of the Holy Roman Empire. Assertions of the essential Lombard nature of his work rest on a stylistic convention and on a generic convention of early sixteenth-century Lombard painting – detailed and naturalistic descriptions of nature and the *pitture ridicole* tradition, a regional genre that often portrayed grimacing and grotesque heads in a 'crude' style to induce laugher and amusement, such as Bartolomeo Passerotti's *Head of a Man* (illus. 31).[30] Sylvia Ferino-Pagden and Andrea Bayer, for example, see Arcimboldo's naturalistic but fantastic heads arising from the mimetic veracity of Lombard painting.[31] Resistant to classicism and idealism, Lombard painting has become increasingly associated with the innovative optical effects that artists like Fede Galizia (1578–1630) and Giovanni Girolamo Savoldo (1480–1548) were experimenting with in paintings such as Galizia's *Portrait of Paolo Morigia* (1592–5) (illus. 32) and Savoldo's *Saint Matthew and the Angel* (*c.* 1534) (illus. 33).[32] In these paintings and others, Lombard painters were paying careful attention to light in the atmosphere, the way light is absorbed and reflected off different surfaces, the portrayal of light moving through transparent materials, the variety and texture of the

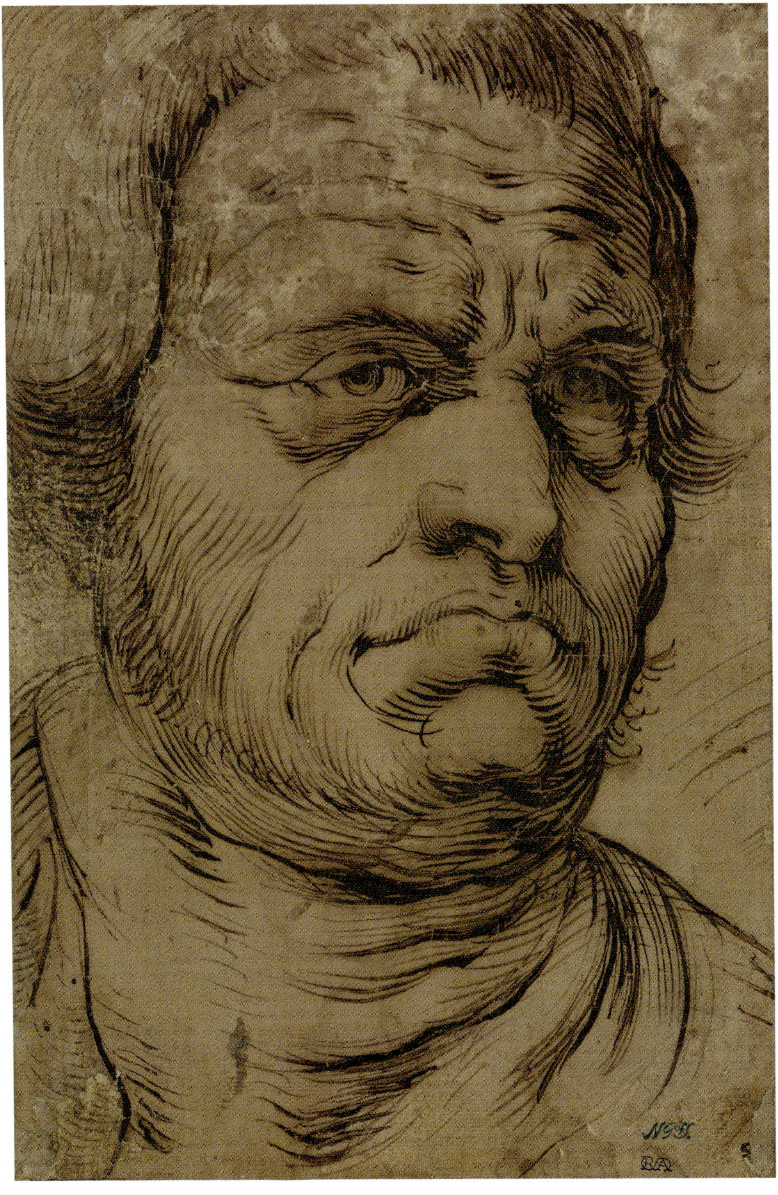

31 Bartolomeo Passerotti, *Head of a Man*, *c.* 1570, pen and ink on paper.

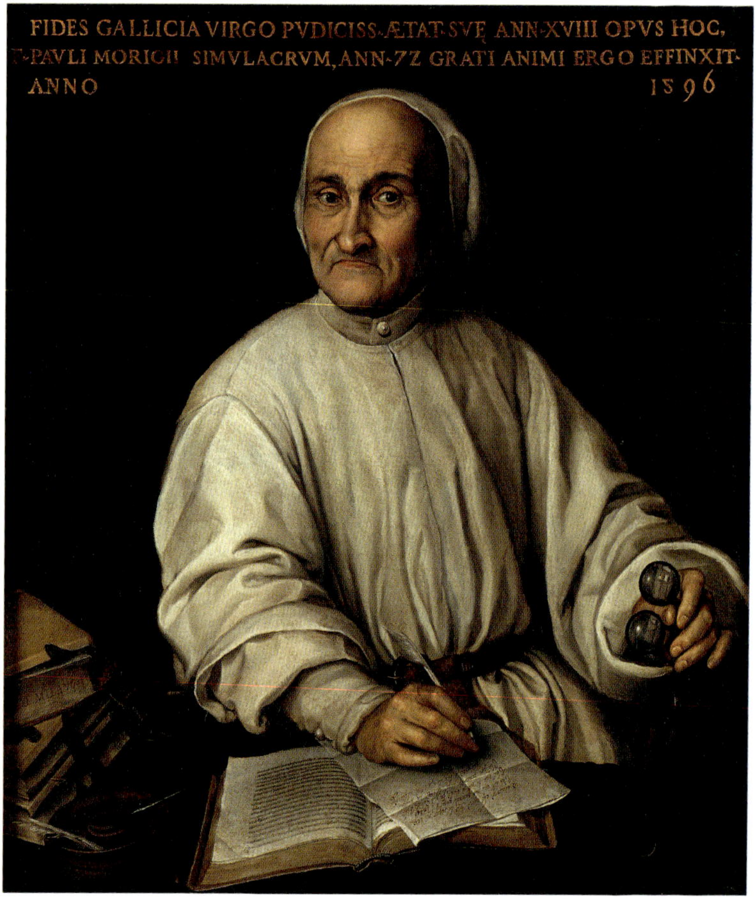

material world and describing minute details. In addition to his careful description of the components of his pictures, Arcimboldo, like other Lombard artists of the *pitture ridicole*, was not bound to traditional subject matter and focused his attention on articulating irregular physiognomies for his audience's delight. Some scholars have worked to connect Arcimboldo's imperial paintings to local carnival traditions in and around Milan. But as

32 Fede Galizia, *Paolo Morigia*, *c*. 1592–5, oil on canvas.

Kaufmann has pointed out, there is little evidence to support that association.[33]

Another fascinating potential prefiguration of Arcimboldo's paintings are heads composed of flaccid penises and fulsome scrota frequently portrayed in profile and found on early sixteenth-century pieces of majolica and not-so-easily identifiable portrait medals (illus. 34, 35 and 36).[34] However prurient it is to compare the profiled phalloi heads to Arcimboldo's composites, one should not lose sight of the differences between the two. Whereas the head on a majolica plate is made up of malleable components that can seemingly be contorted into all sorts of diverse shapes, Arcimboldo's heads were composed of elements that are analogous in form to the body part they have been made to replace. A portrait medal of the poet Aretino, in which the satirist's profiled head is composed of an assortment of animals, is more in line with

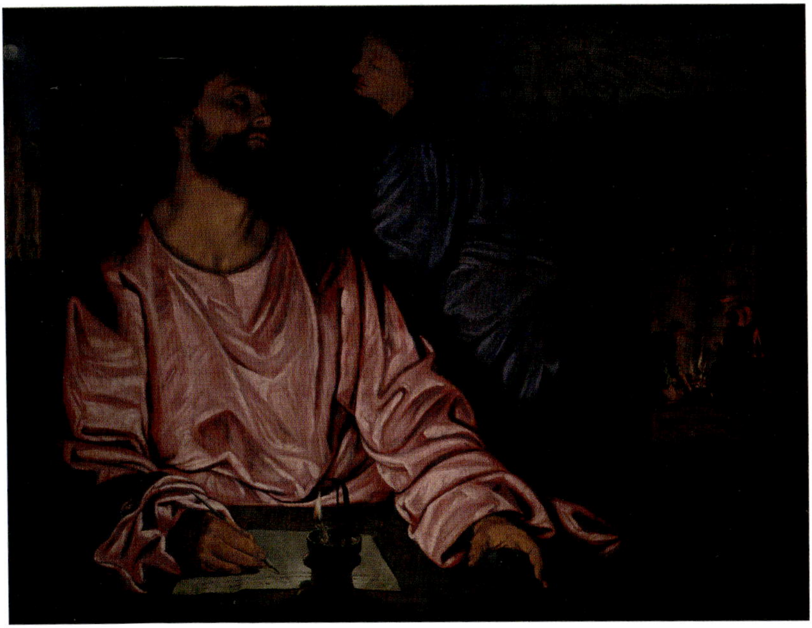

33 Giovanni Gerolamo Savoldo, *St Matthew and the Angel*, c. 1534, oil on canvas.

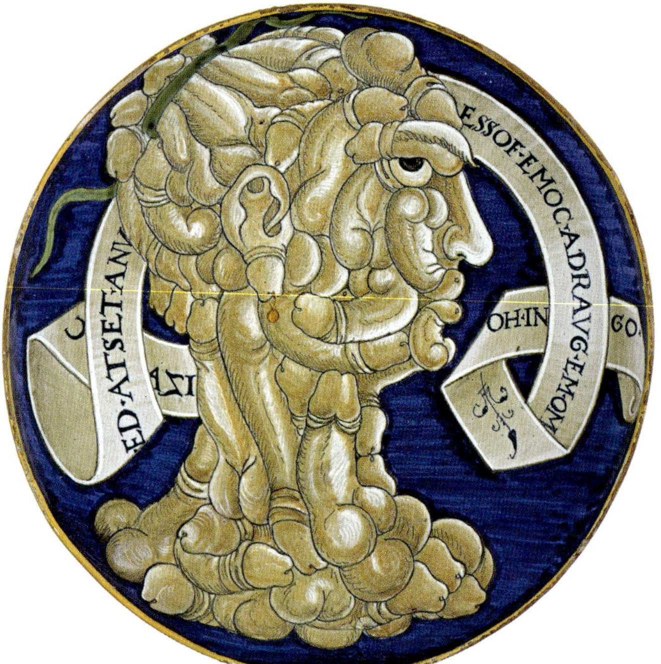

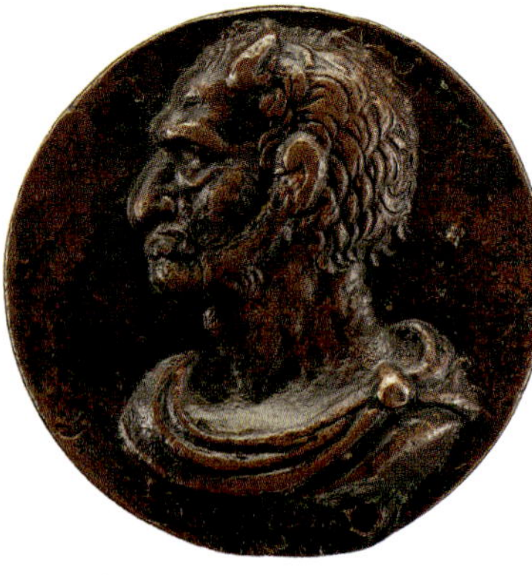

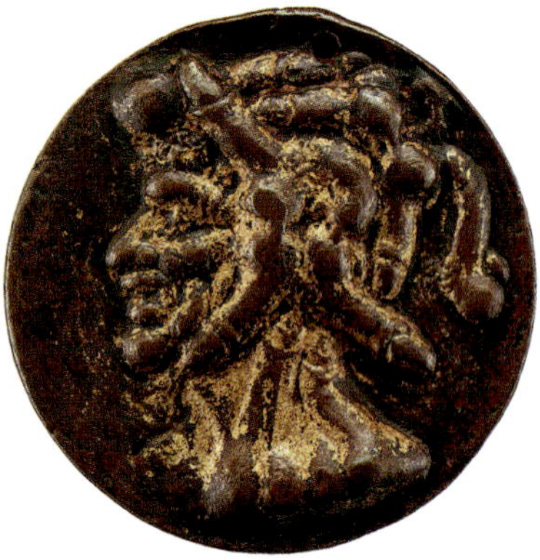

34 Francesco Urbini (attrib.), dish with a composite head of penises ('Testa de cazi'), 1536, tin-glazed earthenware (majolica).
35, 36 Anonymous, *Portrait medal of Paolo Giovio* (?), *c.* 1526–50, bronze.

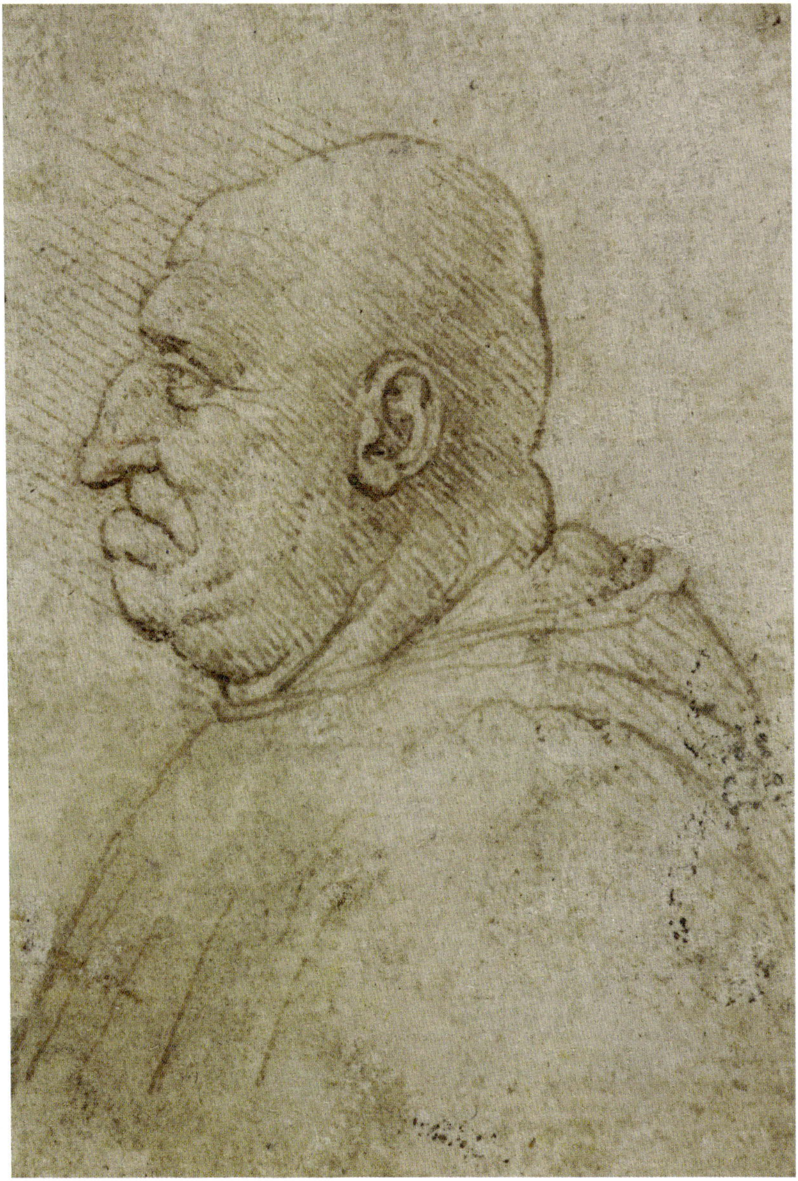

37 Leonardo da Vinci, *Caricature of an Old Man*, *c*. 1485–90, pen and ink on paper.

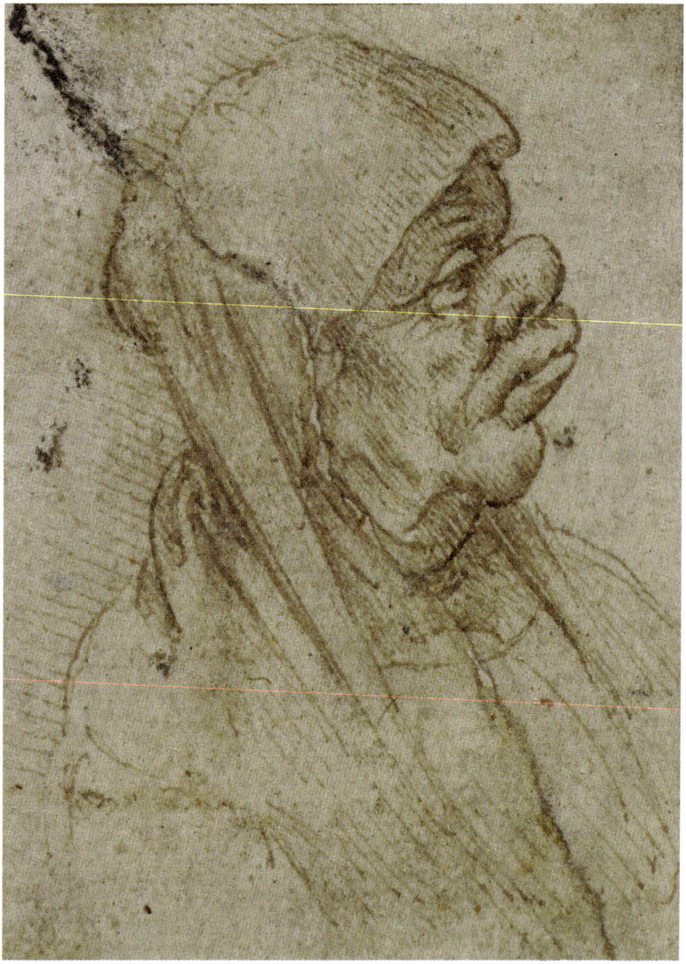

Arcimboldo's heads, but we cannot be certain if the artist ever encountered the medal in Milan or in Vienna.

Kaufmann understands the composite paintings to be, in part, a consequence of Arcimboldo's probable exposure to Leonardo's physiognomic studies, such as his drawings of an *Old Woman*

38 Leonardo da Vinci, *Caricature of an Old Woman*, *c*. 1485–90, pen and ink on paper.

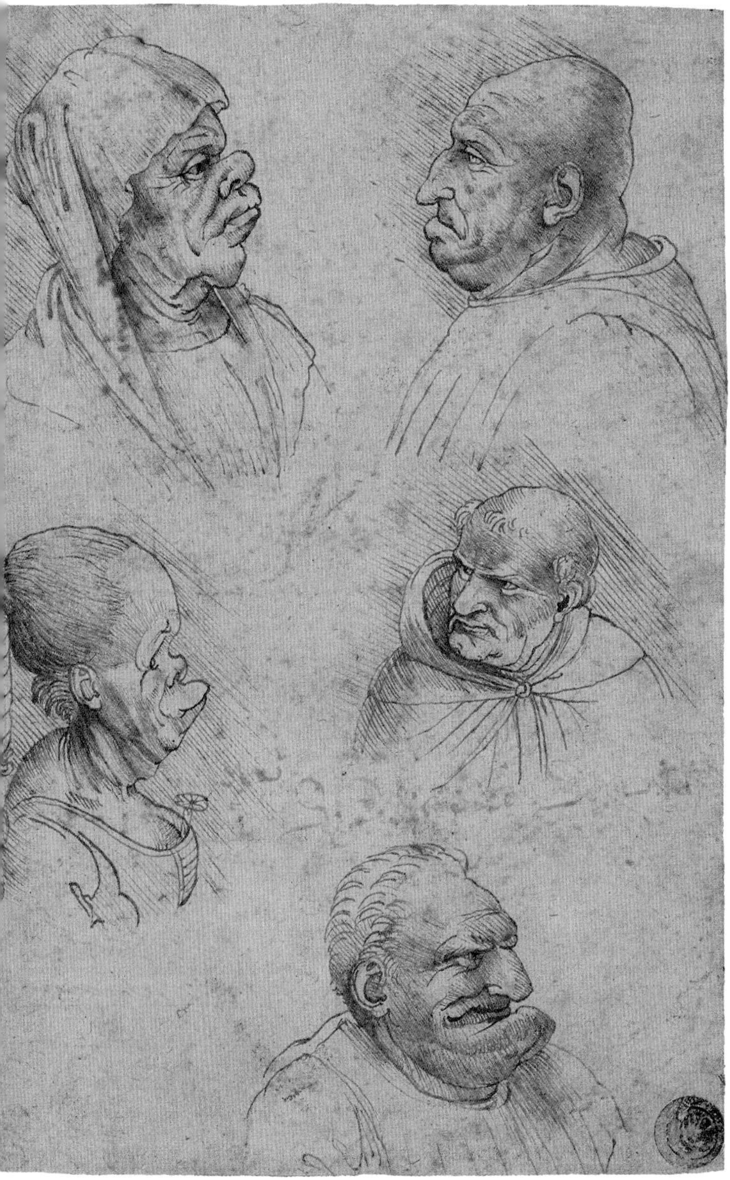

39 Francesco Melzi (attrib.), after Leonardo da Vinci, *Five Studies of Grotesque Faces*, c. 1550, red chalk on paper.

and an *Old Man* (illus. 37 and 38) now in the British Museum. In these works and others, Leonardo has portrayed ageing figures in strict profile. Their features are elongated, inflated, deflated, malformed and out of proportion.[35] Melzi and others in Leonardo's circle made copies of Leonardo's physiognomic studies, and we know that they were circulated among artists in Milan (illus. 39).[36]

LEONARDO

Leonardo was active in Milan from 1483 to 1499/1500 and again from 1508 to 1513. While in Milan, Leonardo took on several students whose duties entailed copying the master's paintings and drawings. It is probable that Arcimboldo encountered at least three of Leonardo's students. Bernardino Luini, one of Leonardo's Milanese 'disciples', was dear friends with Arcimboldo's father, Biagio. The British Museum houses *A Portrait of Biagio* in Bernardino's hand; though informal, it looks to have been done with affection and care – perhaps as a token of friendship (illus. 40). A student of Leonardo, Bernardino began working in Milan in 1483 and not only based several of his paintings, such as *Christ Among the Doctors* (1515–30) (illus. 41) and *The Virgin and Child with St John* (1510) (illus. 42), on Leonardo's compositions, but may have been in possession of a stash of Leonardo's drawings and writings.[37] Bernardino may have entrusted his teacher's drawings and writing to his youngest son, Aurelio. According to the Milanese artist and theorist Gian Paolo Lomazzo (1538–1592), Aurelio Luini owned a sketchbook by Leonardo that contained lifelike drawings of peasants laughing.[38] Remarkably, Aurelio and Arcimboldo worked together at the church of San Maurizio in Milan. Thus, supposing Arcimboldo did not encounter Leonardo's drawings through Biagio or Bernardino, he might have been able to study them with Aurelio.

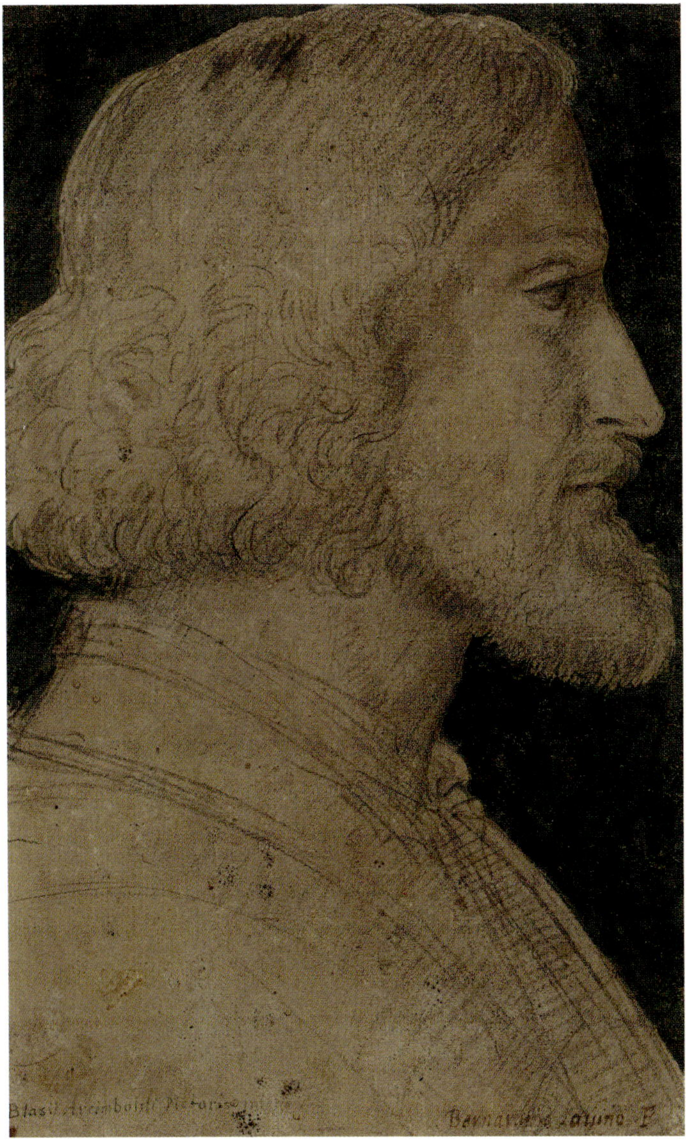

40 Bernardino Luini, *Biagio Arcimboldo*, n.d., black chalk on paper.

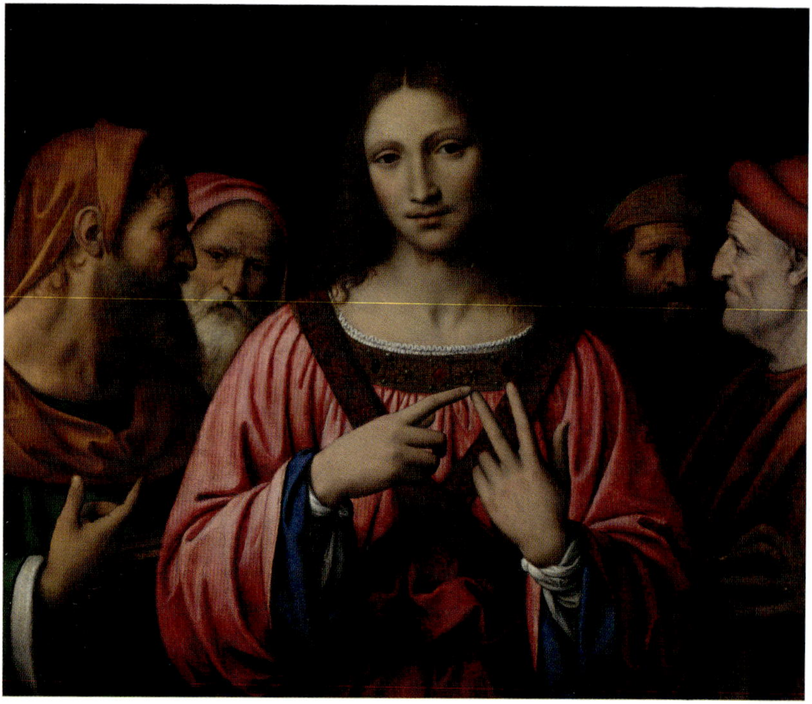

If the Luinis were not the conduits of Leonardo's drawings, Leonardo's other Milanese student and later 'heir', Francesco Melzi, may well have been. After studying with Leonardo for eight years in Milan and Rome, Melzi travelled with his teacher to France in 1513. Melzi remained in France with Leonardo until the latter's death in 1519, upon which Leonardo bequeathed Melzi 'each and every book [Leonardo] ha[d] . . . as well as other instruments and portraits related to the painter's art and industry'.[39] Melzi transported the drawings and manuscripts back to Milan after Leonardo's death and spent the rest of his days organizing and compiling the documents into a treatise, which we now refer to as *The Treatise on Painting*. Though Melzi was born of a noble family, and did not need to paint to support himself, he

41 Bernardino Luini, *Christ Among the Doctors*, *c*. 1515–30, oil on panel.

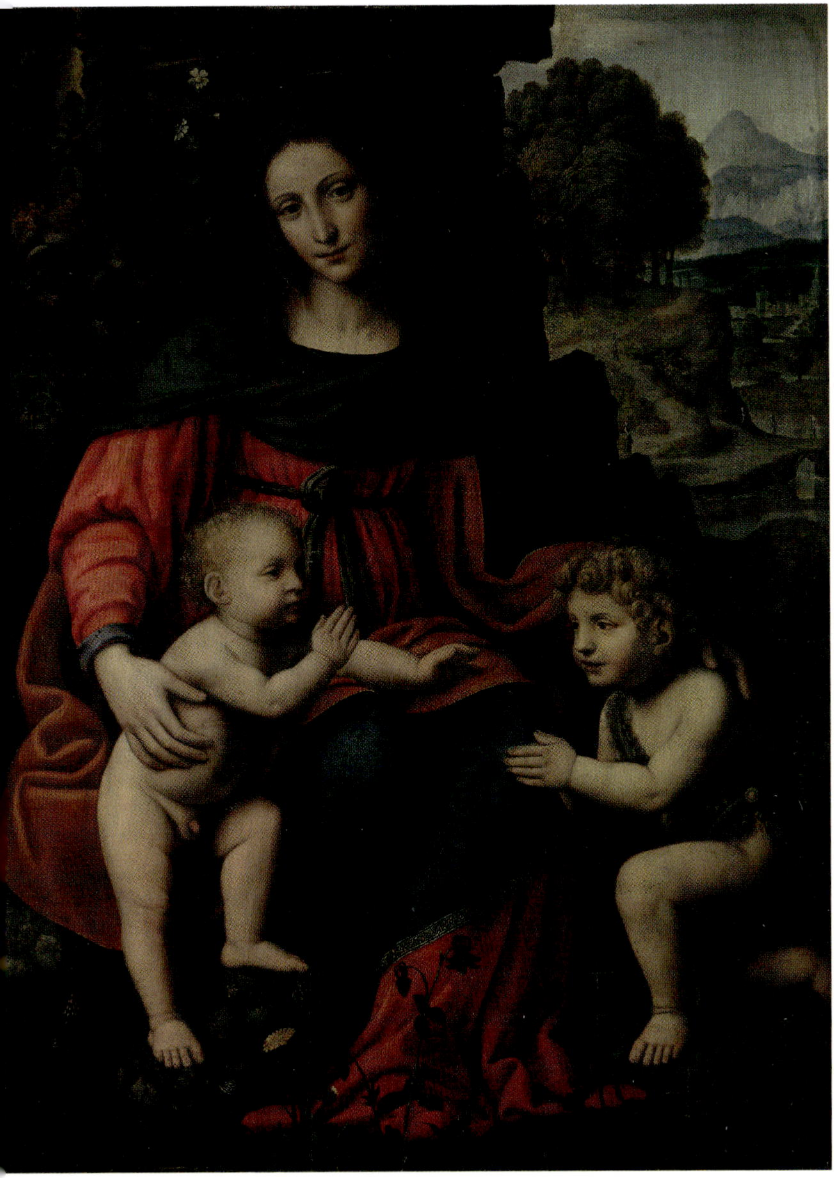

42 Bernardino Luini, *The Virgin and Child with St John*, late 1510, oil on panel.

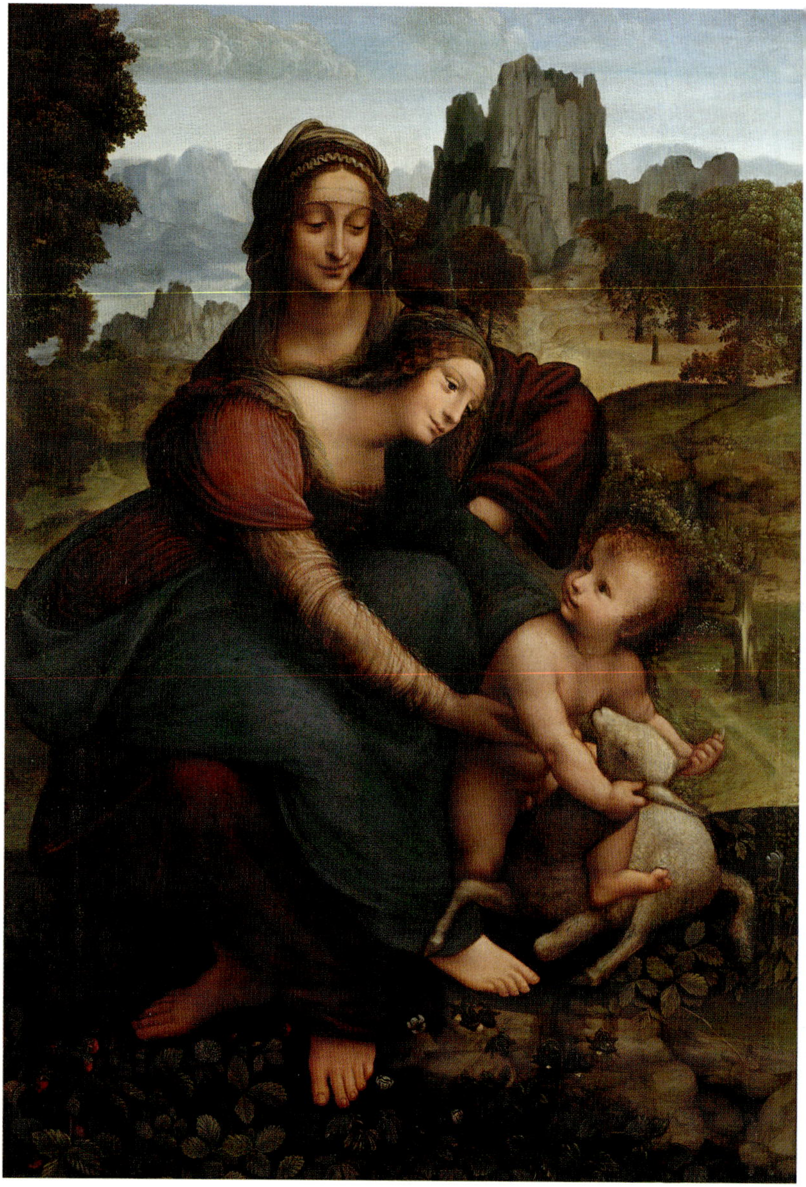

43 Francesco Melzi, *St Anne with the Virgin and Child Embracing a Lamb*, 1520–25, oil on panel.

did not retire to a life of complete contemplation upon his return to Milan. Notably, in 1564 the Fabbrica consulted Melzi over a competition to paint Milan Cathedral's organ shutters that involved Meda, Arcimboldo's collaborator on the Monza frescos. Though Arcimboldo was no longer in Milan, Melzi 'invoked' Arcimboldo during the deliberations, indicating that the two may have known each other. Kaufmann has suggested that Arcimboldo's contact with Leonardo's drawings may have come about through his acquaintance with Melzi.[40]

While it is tantalizing to see Arcimboldo's works as a direct consequence of his exposure to Leonardo's students, drawings and writings, it is important to remain aware of the salient differences between Arcimboldo's composite paintings and Leonardo's work. Even though Arcimboldo clearly had an interest in physiognomy, and playful physiognomy at that, and even though Arcimboldo's work, like Leonardo's, displays a descriptive potency, Arcimboldo largely resisted the principles of monumental narratives that Leonardo helped to codify. Neither did Arcimboldo delicately model his figures in a Leonardesque *sfumato* nor did he regularly give his figures a tawny complexion, as Francesco Melzi did in his *St Anne with the Virgin and Child Embracing a Lamb* (1520–25) (illus. 43).

An important exception to this rule is a set of the Seasons that has been tentatively attributed to Arcimboldo and which now forms part of the Bavarian state's collection of painting (illus. 44, 45, 46 and 47). As Francesco Porzio has pointed out, in three of the four paintings of the series on view in Trausnitz Castle in Landshut (*Autumn* is severely damaged), the details of the components that make up the composite heads are not as isolated from the atmosphere of the painting as other versions of the Seasons in Vienna and later versions in the Louvre. Scholars have long believed that the paintings in Landshut were inferior workshop copies based on the paintings of the Seasons in Vienna

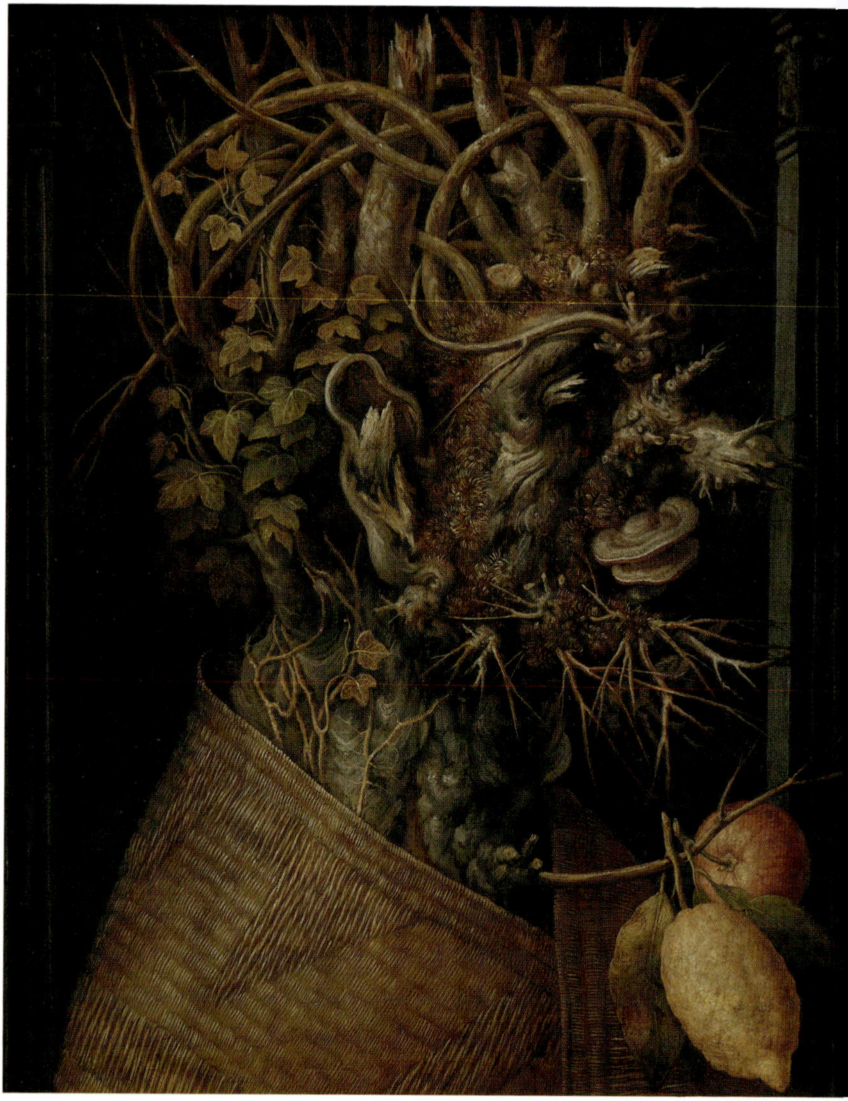

44 Arcimboldo, *Winter*, *c.* 1555–60, oil on panel.

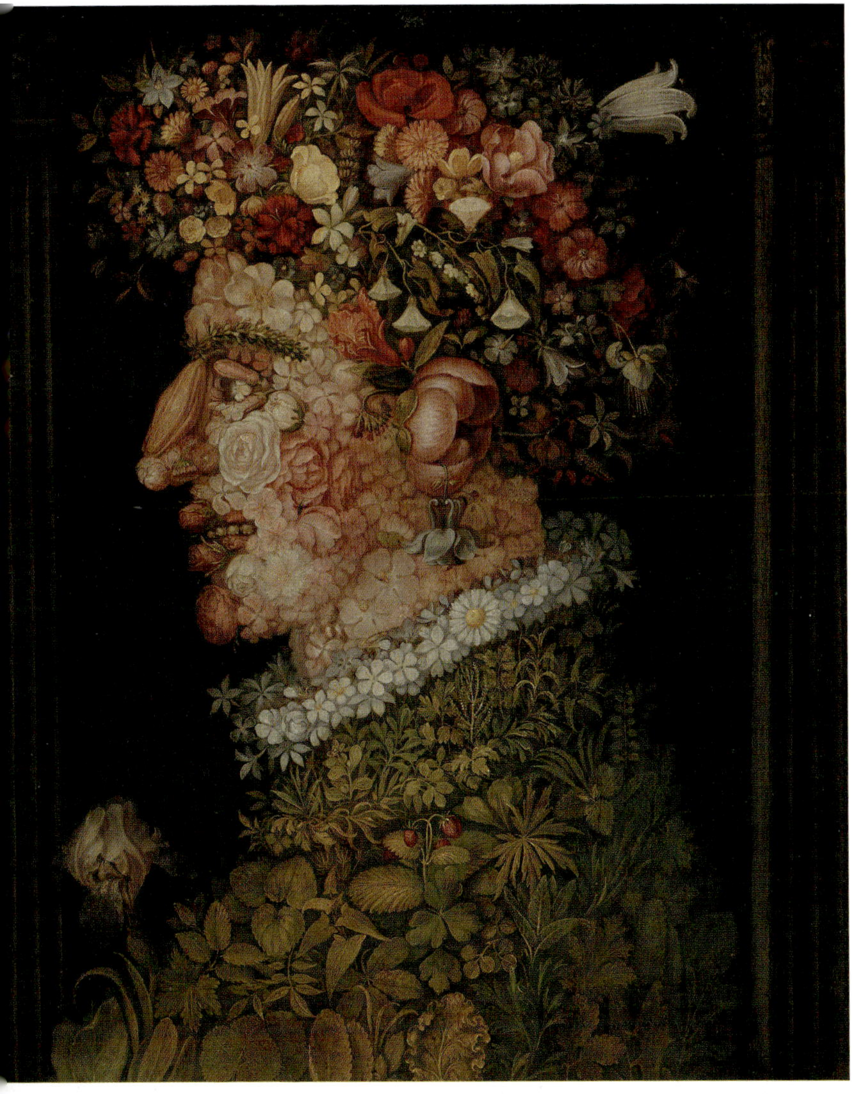

45 Arcimboldo, *Spring*, *c*. 1555–60, oil on panel.

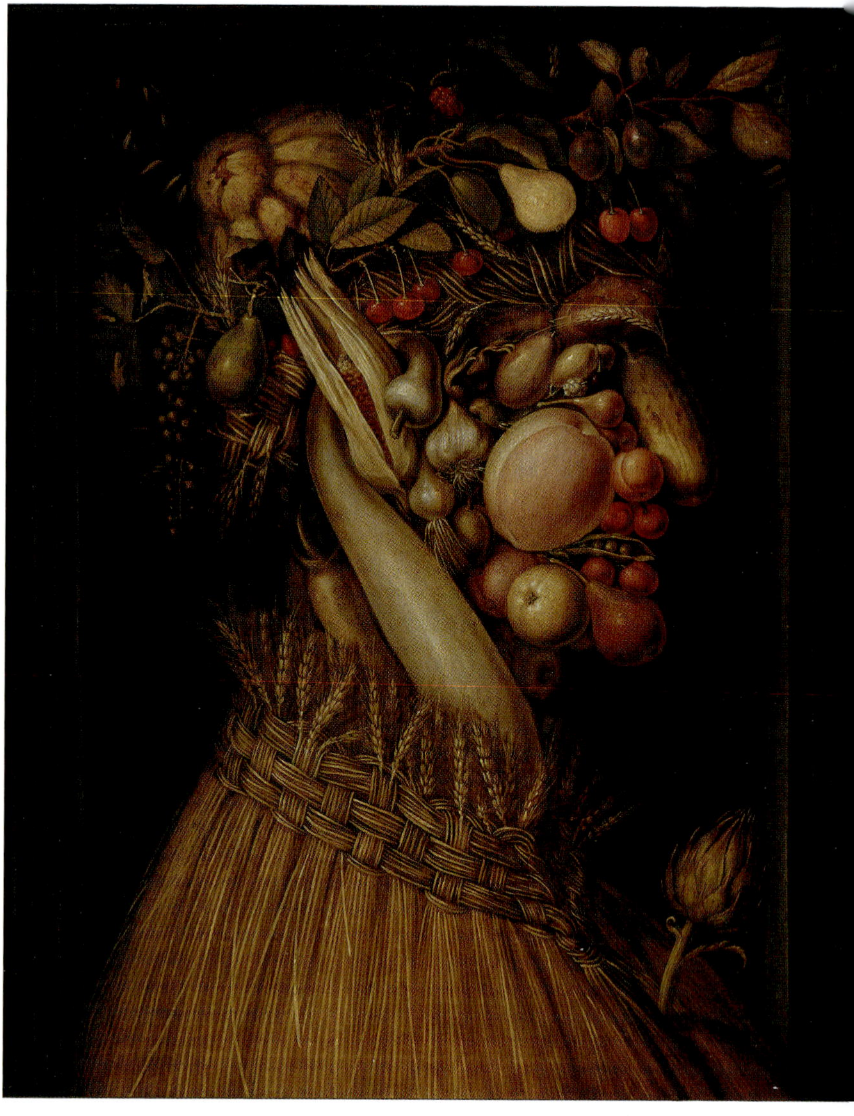

46 Arcimboldo, *Summer*, *c.* 1555–60, oil on panel.

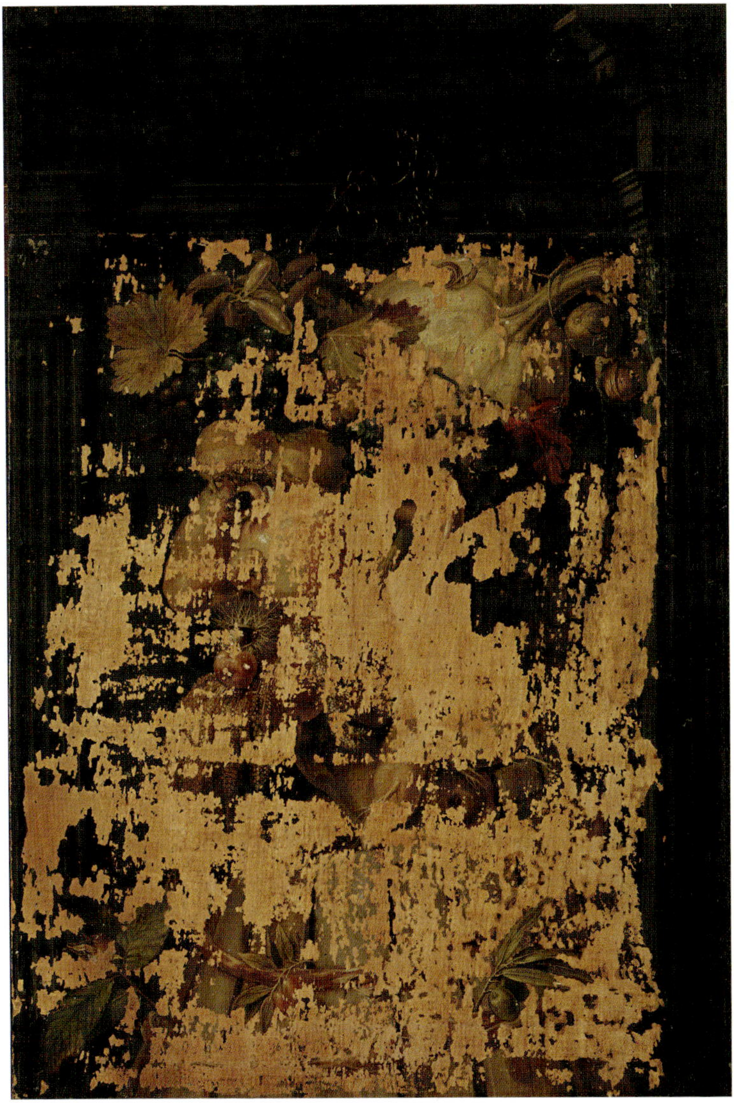

47 Arcimboldo, *Autumn*, *c.* 1555–60, oil on panel.

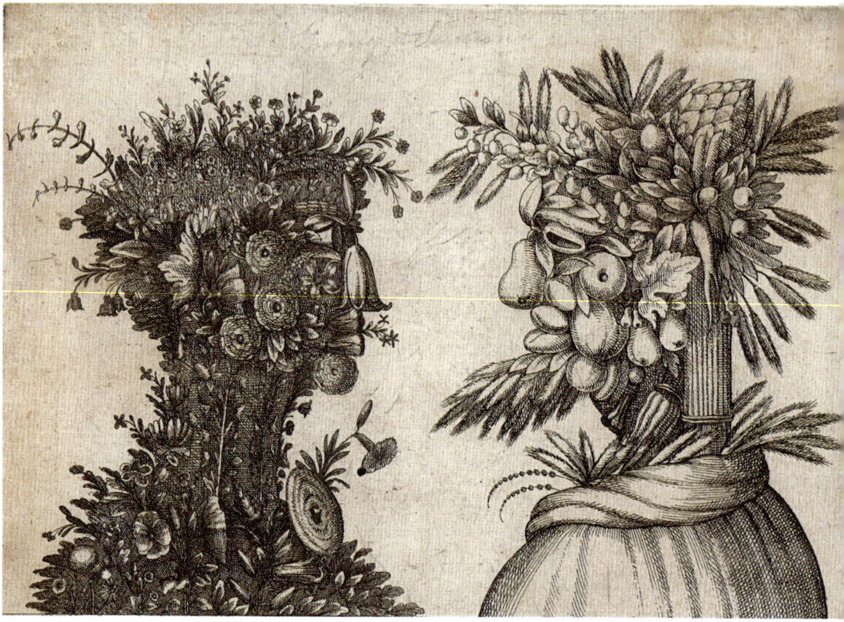

(1563). According to this view, the paintings wound up in Munich because they were gifted by Maximilian II to Duke Albrecht V of Bavaria upon the marriage of the emperor's brother, Charles of Steiermark, to Albrecht's daughter, Maria Anna, in 1571.

In 2011, however, the dating of the paintings in Landshut was thrown into doubt. In a lengthy and detailed essay, Francesco Porzio draws attention to subtle differences between the series in Vienna and the series in Landshut.[41] He highlights that the versions in Landshut lack certain elements that are present in the Viennese versions, such as an 'M' woven into Winter's straw cloak. Porzio also points to several improvements to the 'anatomical effectiveness', a softening of caricatural harshness as well as a greater emphasis on the nobility of the figures in Vienna. Given these stylistic discrepancies, Porzio argues that the paintings in Landshut pre-date those in Vienna. Moreover, he claims that

48 Anonymous (Giovanni Ambrogio Brambilla?), *The Four Seasons: 'Primavera' and 'Estate'*, c. 1565–80, etching on paper.

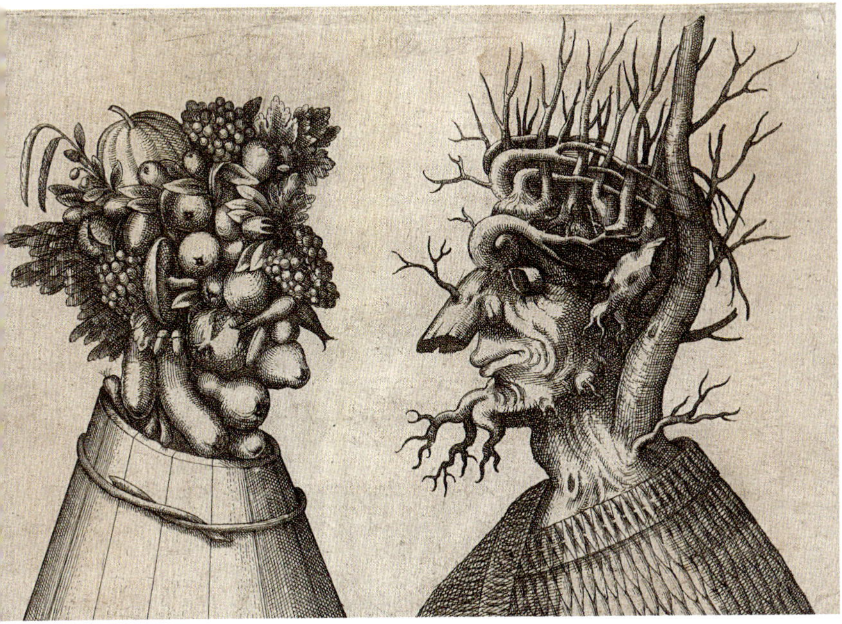

Arcimboldo modelled the paintings in Vienna on those in Landshut. To bolster his stylistic analysis, Porzio points to two engravings which may document versions of the Seasons that, he claims, perhaps even pre-date the panel paintings in Bavaria (illus. 48 and 49). In one engraving Spring and Autumn face off, while in the other Autumn and Winter do. Porzio also maintains that the engravings and Arcimboldo's paintings of the Seasons in Landshut evoke popular comedic imagery that was prevalent in Lombardy during Carnival as well as during agricultural festivals. In the case of the former, the contrasting pairs recall popular Lombard prints of Carnival facing off Lent, and in the case of the latter, the composite heads are reminiscent of puppets made up of actual fruits and vegetables that were paraded through the streets during harvest festivals in Milan. If Porzio is correct, it would mean that Arcimboldo conceived of and executed the

49 Anonymous (Giovanni Ambrogio Brambilla?), *The Four Seasons: 'Autunno' and 'Inverno'*, *c.* 1565–80, etching on paper.

paintings that are currently in Landshut before he left Milan, sometime around 1560. Porzio's claims contrast with Kaufmann's argument that the composite heads were the direct consequence of Arcimboldo's exposure to humanistic cosmological theories and the nascent practices of natural history and natural philosophy at Maximilian's court in Vienna.

Given the lack of any hard evidence that Arcimboldo conceived of and executed the first composite heads in either Milan or Vienna, the origin point of the conceit may remain a mystery. Whatever the case, if Arcimboldo was drawing on local Lombard traditions in his composite heads, he made a serious effort to elevate the conceit, not only in terms of his chosen medium – oil on panel – but in terms of its function, a gallery picture.

The lack of clear origins for Arcimboldo as well as his composite paintings has provoked somewhat polarizing consequences regarding how the artist and his work have been characterized. On one side, there are scholars who see Arcimboldo and his composite paintings as a nexus of regional Lombard painting styles, painting genres and popular Milanese civic and ecclesiastical practices. On the other, there are those who view the artist and his work as having transcended his Lombard roots. In this view Arcimboldo and his composite paintings embody a form of early modern humanistic cosmopolitanism that was flourishing at the imperial court in Vienna on account of Maximilian II's promotion of classical learning, the emperor's moderate position on the confessional divide in the empire and, as we will see in the next chapter, his interest in the natural world and those who studied it. The first is invested in portraying the artist and his work as parochial; the other, as international. At the heart of these different takes on the artist and his work is a concern to locate the origins of Arcimboldo's singular, novel and intense artistic imagination. If in the end we cannot precisely know whenever and wherever Arcimboldo devised his first composite paintings, we can say with confidence that much of the allure of his seemingly impossible composite paintings rests on his ability to observe and describe the natural world, and it is to the traces of Arcimboldo's study of the natural world that we now turn.

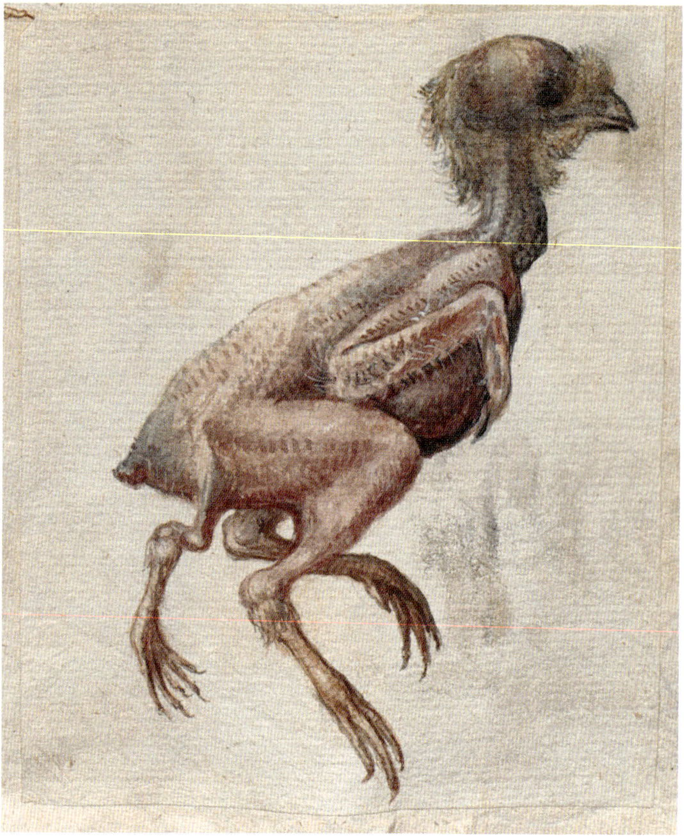

TWO

Nature Studies

Sometime after arriving at Holy Roman Emperor Maximilian II's Viennese court in 1562, Arcimboldo posed a dead and plucked three-legged chick so that he could portray it in profile (illus. 50). Possibly based on an embalmed specimen in the imperial Kunstkammer (Art Collection), Arcimboldo's watercolour invites us to picture the artist cradling the bird's body in his hands and gently placing it on a surface so that he could carefully observe its typical and atypical features. Isolating the specimen and setting it against a neutral ground, the artist provides the viewer with a virtually unmediated view of the denuded chick, its avian frame and its extra appendage. Placed in profile, purged of any context and afforded no suggestion of movement or behaviour, Arcimboldo's carefully executed watercolour exemplifies certain conventions of late sixteenth-century plant and animal studies produced by artists employed by early modern courts, universities and naturalists.[1] Its subject, a monstrous bird, is also representative of an early modern interest in nature's penchant to veer off course.[2] That a fascination with nature and its exceptions prevailed at the imperial court is attested by the picture's collection and preservation. Roughly a decade after the artist painted it, the picture of the three-legged chick was cut, pasted and bound into a compendium of fifteenth-, sixteenth- and seventeenth-century animal studies and stored in Holy Roman Emperor Rudolf II's princely collection in Prague. Referred to

50 Arcimboldo, 'Study of a featherless three-footed chick', from Cod. Min. 42.

by scholars as Codex Miniatus (painted volume) 42 (Cod. Min. 42), the compendium is now housed in the Austrian National Library in Vienna.[3]

The three-legged chick is just one of many plant and animal studies Arcimboldo completed over a 25-year period while he was in residence at the imperial court, first in Vienna and then in Prague. Arcimboldo executed all the studies in watercolour; he dated some of them; he signed none. He gave two studies inscriptions, in which he described or identified the subject at hand.[4] Many of the artist's plant and animal studies are based on specimens that were painted from life, or 'ad vivum', while others were modelled on painted or printed images.[5] They are spread between four compendia, three in the Austrian National Library (Cod. Min. 42, Cod. Min. 129 and Cod. Min. 130) and one in the Print Cabinet in Dresden (Ca 213).[6] All of Arcimboldo's plant and animal studies were trimmed and pasted into the compendia at the end of the sixteenth century along with nature studies by other artists. In this way, Arcimboldo's works engage the nexus of early modern collecting, the pursuit of natural knowledge and imperial imagery in early modern Europe. Moreover, these animal and plant studies deepen our understanding of Arcimboldo's participation in and contribution to the burgeoning study of nature, or 'natural history', at the imperial court and beyond.[7]

Arcimboldo's plant and animal studies are equally noteworthy for the ways they evince different modes of portraying nature inside and outside the imperial court. While some of the works examined in this chapter exhibit Arcimboldo's skill at observing and rendering nature in all its particularities, others display his reliance on and adaptation of other artists' plant and animal studies. Additionally, the images reveal the diverse functions and trajectories of Arcimboldo's representations of flora and fauna.

COUNTERFEITS

All but one of Arcimboldo's extant nature studies were completed after he arrived at the imperial court in Vienna. The earliest mention of the artist in the imperial archive occurs on 29 March 1562, where his name appears in a report penned by the courtier Adam Swetkowyz for Maximilian II's father, Holy Roman Emperor Ferdinand I. Swetkowyz relayed to Ferdinand that Arcimboldo was copying portraits of the imperial family – presumably so that the copies could be sent to other courts. A year later, on 28 April 1563, Swetkowyz wrote to Ferdinand informing the emperor that he would be very pleased with Arcimboldo's portraits.[8] Given that Arcimboldo completed Maximilian II's Seasons in 1563, and given he completed the first series of the Elements in 1566, Arcimboldo must have finished several animal and plant studies early in his time at court while he was also hard at work copying portraits. The date '1563' appears beside an inscription on a study of a goat's deformed hoof in Cod. Min. 42. Lucilla Conigliello has attributed this and another study of two additional deformed goat hooves to Arcimboldo on the basis of these brief inscriptions (illus. 51).[9] We know that Arcimboldo continued to paint plant and animal studies after he completed the imperial allegories because many of the studies attributed to him bear dates in the artist's hand that span the 1570s and 1580s.[10] It was during this period that Arcimboldo studied animals that roamed the gardens of Maximilian II's residence in Vienna, including deer and more exotic animals such as Maximilian's elephant Suleiman.[11]

As of 1565, court documents refer to Arcimboldo as the imperial *contterfetter*. At the time the term *contterfetter*, or the more frequently used *contrafacteur*, was typically used to describe those capable of the faithful reproduction of nature. Thus, 'counterfeit' (to use the modern spelling) referred to a specific type of maker as well as a specific type of picture. The practice of painting, drawing or sculpting in which nature seemed faithfully observed and described was termed *ad vivum, nach dem Leben* or 'from life'.[12] Working and works made 'from life' acquired authority from the claim that the artist had mirrored nature. Because counterfeit pictures often asserted a high degree of mimetic veracity, they were considered able to convey visual information about what was being portrayed. This notion of transmissible visual information was bound up with the term 'counterfeit', whether it was applied to a portrait or to a study of flora or fauna. In this way, portraiture and animal and plant studies were manifestations of the period contention that both the human and the non-human 'could be read from the logic of their external signs'.[13] The primacy

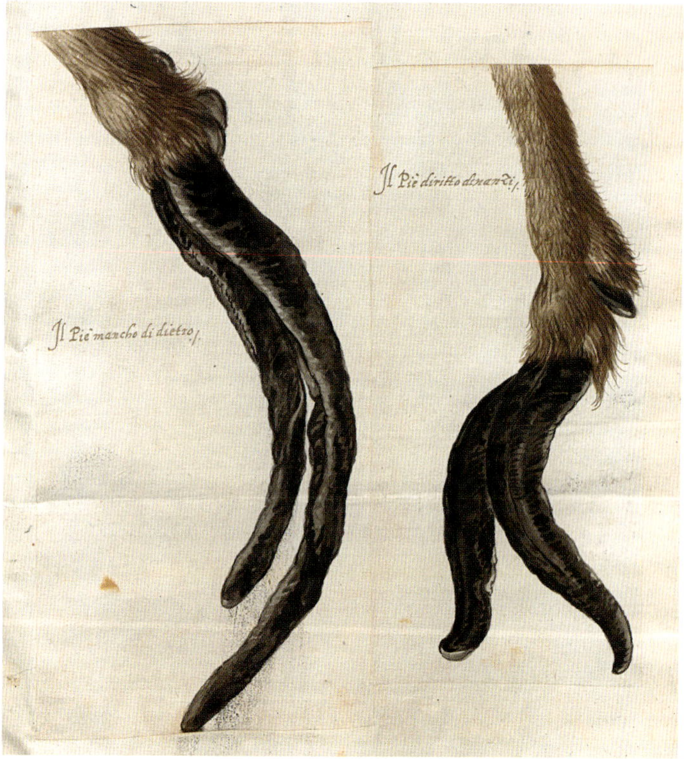

51 Arcimboldo, 'Study of a goat's deformed hoof (?)', from Cod. Min. 42.

of the exterior aligns portraiture and studies of flora and fauna epistemologically, and it may be one contributing factor to Arcimboldo's development of a hybrid form of the two genres in his imperial allegories and invertible paintings over the course of his career.

Beyond epistemological affinities, portraiture and plant and animal studies, or natural history illustrations, have structural similarities. For instance, both portraiture and nature studies share the act of posing. In the case of portraiture, the sitter is posed by the artist or by the sitter themselves. This pose – whether it is reading, praying or peering out at the viewer – was often intended to make the sitter appear unselfconscious. As Harry Berger asserts, the *sine qua non* of early modern portraiture is sitters posing as if they are not posing.[14] This avoidance of striking a pose is also at work in Arcimboldo's nature studies. Many of the animals Arcimboldo portrayed are depicted as behaving naturally, their bodily posture and facial countenance seemingly uncontrived. If a plant or animal study appears to be an objective representation, it is because the painter endowed the image with a sense of authoritative autonomy, by way of the picture's composition and degree of detail as well as the subject's position and context. However, as we will soon see, Arcimboldo's rendering of plants and particularly animals was in many cases not just posed but a subtle invention of the artist or a variation on another artist's posed image of a specimen.

There is a final affinity between portraiture and nature studies: like a sitter in a portrait, the animal or plant portrayed in a natural history illustration awaits a future viewer. Unlike a genre painting or a history painting, which are imagined representations of an event that occurred in another place at another time and in which figures engage with one another – and therefore are not rendered solely for someone outside the scene – both portraits and natural history illustrations are premised on an acknowledged and belated viewer who exists outside of the picture.[15] Who, then, is the intended belated viewer of Arcimboldo's plant and animal studies?

The circumstances that prompted Arcimboldo to make his animal and plant studies are mysterious. Were they solely preparatory studies for later works? Were they records of curious animals at the imperial court? Were the drawings collected to stand in for plants and animals, so they could be studied by naturalists at the imperial court and beyond? Since many of Arcimboldo's animal and plant studies share characteristics with sixteenth- and seventeenth-century natural history illustrations, I preface my discussion of his works with a profile of that context.

DISCOVERING NATURE

Early modern natural history took up the observation, description and investigation of nature. Informed by the Aristotelian view that nature was made up of a finite number of discrete entities that could be understood wholistically by way of collecting, ordering and systematizing them, it was practised by a wide range of individuals educated in an array of fields and crafts.[16] Approaches and methods to discern nature's components and to order them varied across time and place. The ends to which this knowledge was put were also diverse. Scholars, artisans and naturalists took up the study of nature to further medicine, to participate in alchemical pursuits, to make dyes, to excavate mines, to cultivate gardens, to breed animals and to understand nature's laws and nature's anomalies, among other reasons.[17] To do this, naturalists had to gain access to the elements of nature they desired to scrutinize. Once access was achieved, they observed, manipulated and documented nature. Frequently, the fruits of these encounters with nature were recorded in text and image either by the naturalist or by an artist in their or someone else's employ. These pictorial and textual documents of the naturalist's or artist's observations fostered the collection, ordering and systemization of nature. The documentation also permitted the circulation of knowledge about nature as well as creating ersatz specimens for those that were difficult to acquire or were susceptible to destruction and decay.

Natural history illustration was critical to recording and concretizing nature's ephemera. But what distinguishes natural history illustration from other representations of flora and fauna? Generally speaking, natural history illustration is distinguished from other representations of nature on the basis of its function – the transmission of particular visual information about nature to an interested viewer.[18] The belief in the direct transfer of information from the picture to the interested viewer contributes to the sense, in the past and today, that the specimen on the page is identical to the model upon which it is based. In other words, the image claims to depict the details of an object as they existed and were seen by the individual who crafted the image. Behind the natural history illustration, often, is the intention of the artist to make the viewer a first-hand witness to the thing portrayed. In many cases, natural history illustration was the sole means of examining a plant or an animal. In other cases, it was one of several. We know of examples where natural history illustrations reproduced specimens of plants and animals that were stored in the imperial collection.[19] Perhaps, before it was trimmed and pasted into Cod. Min. 42, Arcimboldo's painting of the three-legged chick was found alongside its model in the imperial collection. Alternatively, it is possible that Arcimboldo's study was executed to stand in for the specimen after its decay. Whatever the case, the study not only documents the chick's appearance but establishes the specimen outside of a point in time, by omitting what happened to the specimen over the years, just like a portrait might.

THE ARTIST'S NATURE

When looking at many of Arcimboldo's plant and animal studies, it is evident that he trained himself to record visual information and that over time he developed skills at representing nature. However, it is not always immediately clear what he was trying to demonstrate with his images or for exactly whom. Unlike his other paintings discussed in the chapters that follow, Arcimboldo did not sign his plant and animal studies. Had he signed them, he would have proposed a different model of the images' value, function and relationship to the viewer; this is because he would have not just explicitly placed himself in the role of a talented mediator of nature but made a claim about the object's status as a collectible object, in part or fully on account of who made it.

Scholars have rightly suggested that many of Arcimboldo's plant and animal studies were initially intended to be preparatory studies for future compositions. Indeed, several of his extant studies have been directly connected to Earth in his Elements series.[20] If this was the sole purpose of many of the artist's plant and animal studies, we might say that they only became natural history illustrations when they were cut, pasted and categorized into bound compendia at the imperial court during the last years of the sixteenth century, perhaps even after Arcimboldo died. Whatever the case, it is apparent that these works by Arcimboldo represent a junction between preparatory study and natural history illustration.

The works examined in this chapter also testify to the complex processes in making and collecting natural history illustrations. As we will see, Arcimboldo's studies were generated by the artist working from living and dead specimens as well as painted, drawn and printed models. The works also show that in some cases Arcimboldo adhered to his models and that in others he veered from them. Taken together, Arcimboldo's plant and animal studies make clear that these diverse practices were not

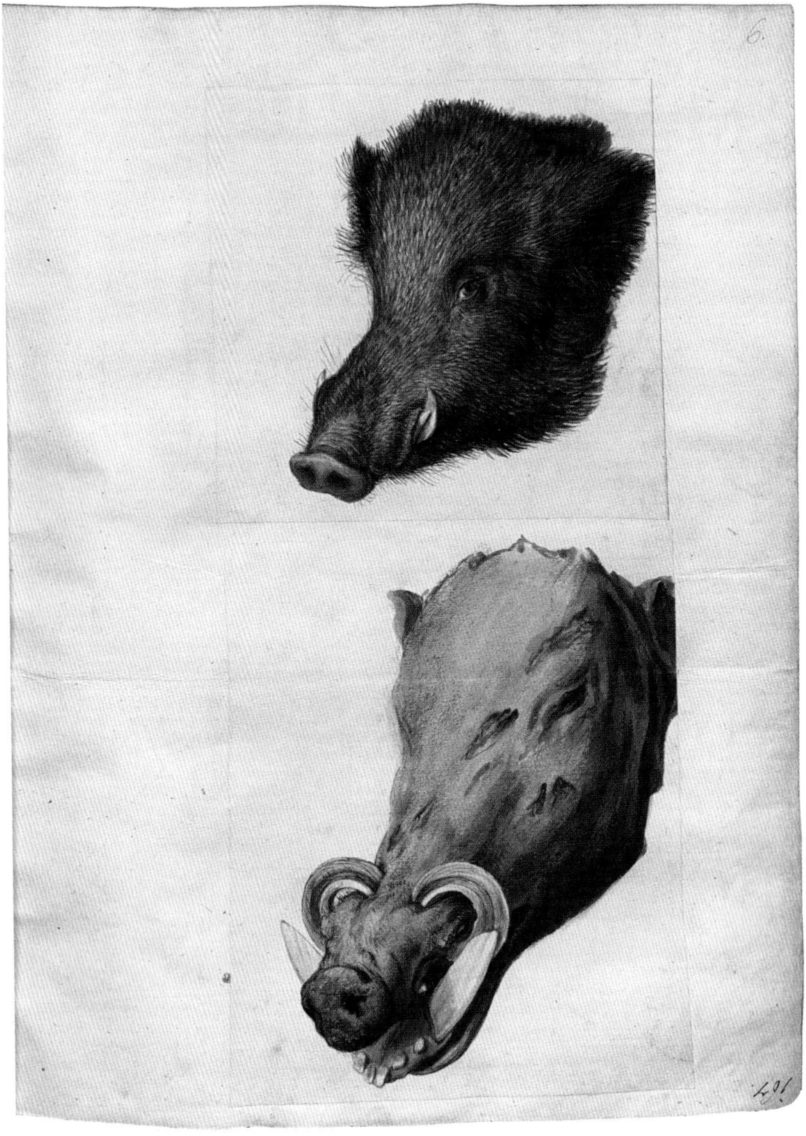

52 Arcimboldo, 'Boar and head study of a boar', from Cod. Min. 42.

at odds but coexisted comfortably at the imperial court in Vienna and Prague.

Consider, for example, a sheet that contains Arcimboldo's study of a wild boar's head, which is placed directly above his rendering of a mummified head of a monstrous boar (illus. 52). The 1607–11 inventory of the imperial collection lists '1 boar snout and skeleton, where the upper tusks with their tips over the snout have penetrated the flesh and crookedly grown into the bone', so we can be fairly confident that the head done in a light wash at the base of the sheet was modelled on the specimen from the imperial collection.[21] Interest in nature's aberrations was widespread at the time. Accounts and images of two-headed cows, conjoined twins and hirsute people were printed on cheap broadsides, discussed in books like Ambroise Paré's *On Monsters and Marvels* (1573) and depicted in portraits like Lavinia Fontana's *Portrait of Antonietta Gonzalez* (*c.* 1595) (illus. 53). The combination of the boar's misaligned teeth and its mummified state made it doubly monstrous. That Arcimboldo coupled his study of the head from the imperial collection with the study of a normative boar's head suggests that the head at the top of the sheet allowed the artist to show just how peculiar the imperial specimen was. In addition to the difference between their respective states (alive/dead, preserved/unpreserved) and anatomy, the two heads also differ in execution. Whereas the mummified head was rendered in a loose manner, with an emphasis on modelling, the head floating above it is highly finished: the artist has painstakingly articulated countless individual boar bristles. Such a degree of finish is not characteristic of Arcimboldo's animal studies, which typically exhibit an economic use of brushstrokes, as seen, for instance, in his representation of a reindeer pasted six folios after the heads of the boars in Cod. Min. 42 (illus. 54). The careful attention to the normative boar's bristles, snout and tusks could be attributed to the fact that Arcimboldo based the boar's head behind

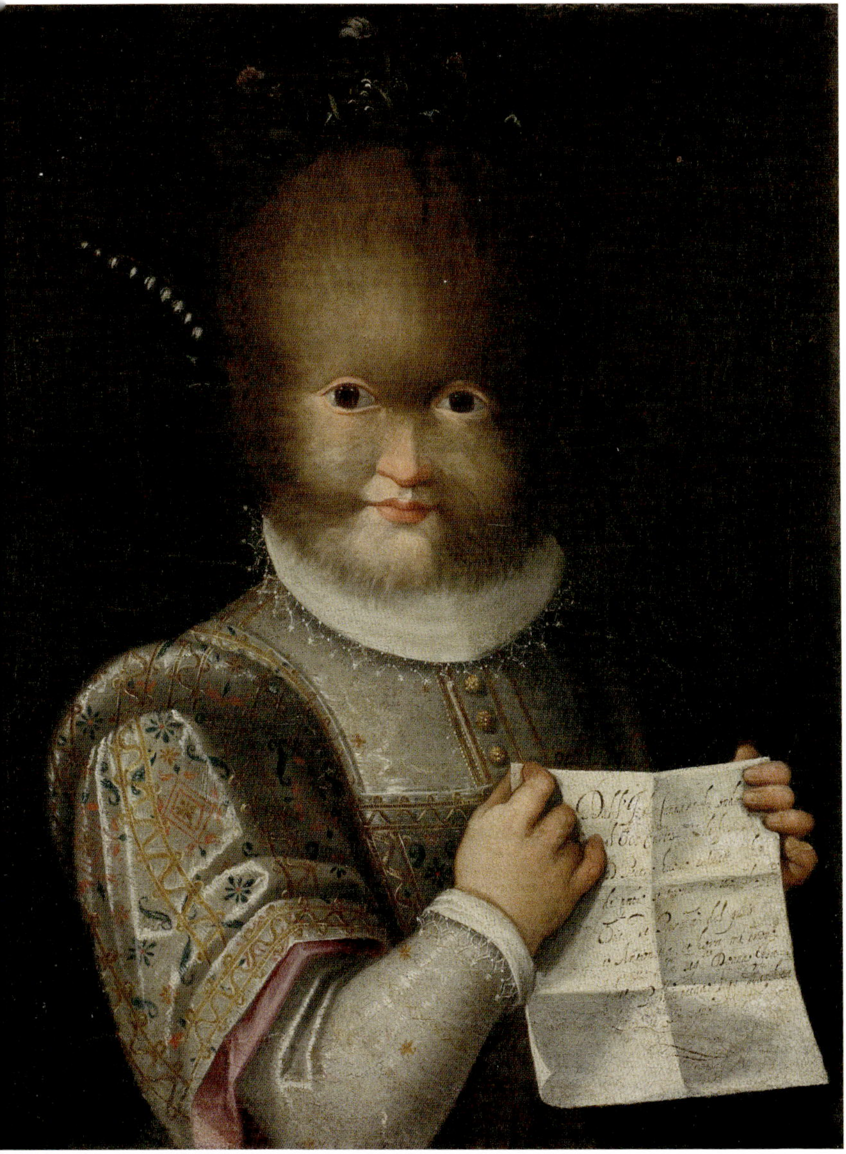

53 Lavinia Fontana, *Antonietta Gonzalez (or Gonsalvus)*, *c.* 1595, oil on canvas.

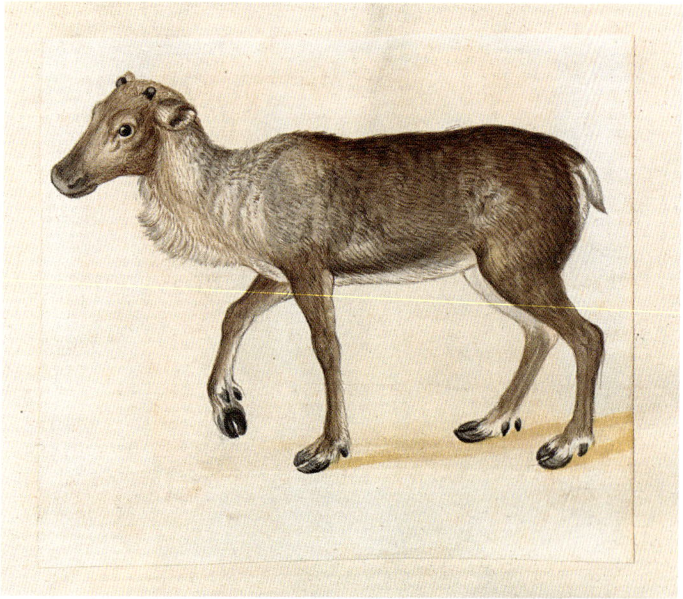

Earth's right ear on this study. Yet even though these features of the boar suggest that Arcimboldo had access to either a living or dead specimen, the human quality of the boar's eyes belies the study's claim to mirror nature.

Anthropomorphic features in natural history illustrations were sometimes the consequence of the circumstances of rendering a dead specimen, the eyes of which might have been removed, or because the artist was working from a live creature on the move. This must have been case with the artist's representation of a red duiker (illus. 55), probably based on a red duiker that roamed the imperial gardens in Vienna.[22] The comparative lack of attention lavished on the red duiker's coat may reflect the artist's inability to observe the features of a mobile animal up close. Rather than delineating each individual element of the animal's coat, Arcimboldo emphasized the animal's variation and subtle change of colour.

54 Arcimboldo, 'Study of reindeer', from Cod. Min. 42.

Minute detail is also absent in Arcimboldo's representation of the animal's horns and snout. However, albeit lacking copious detail, the study of the red duiker does provide the viewer with a sense of the animal's colour, form and texture.

Like Arcimboldo's boar's head, the red duiker reappears in artworks produced inside as well as outside the imperial court. A reversal of Arcimboldo's red duiker watches as Adam and Eve are expelled from Eden in a painting in Vienna dated to circa 1580 (illus. 56). Two and a half decades after Arcimboldo's red duiker appeared in Eden, it flanked Venus and Bacchus while nuzzling a bunch of grapes in Bartholomeus Spranger's *Venus and Bacchus* (1597–1600), now in Hannover (illus. 57). Another watercolour of the red duiker, portrayed above a mountain coati and attributed to Arcimboldo, was part of Ulisse Aldrovandi's collection of natural history illustrations (illus. 58). The same watercolour, according

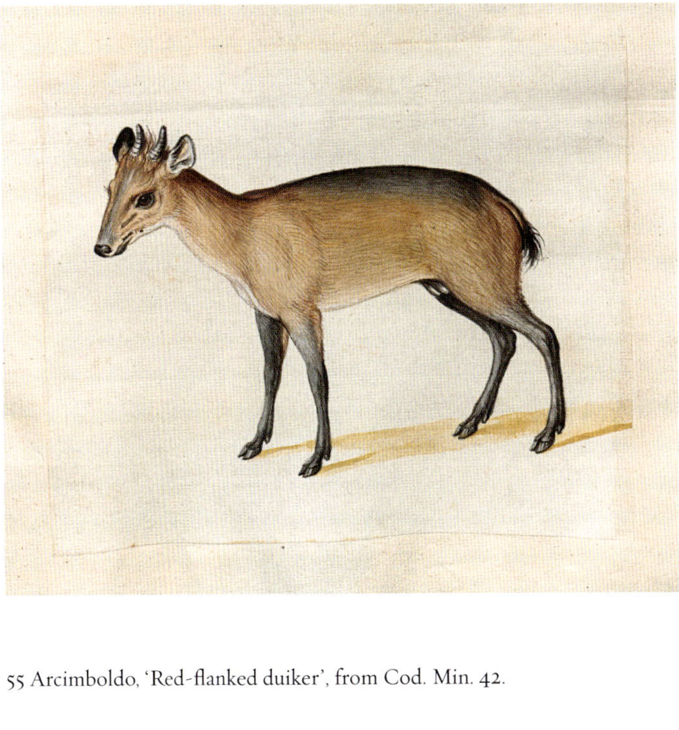

55 Arcimboldo, 'Red-flanked duiker', from Cod. Min. 42.

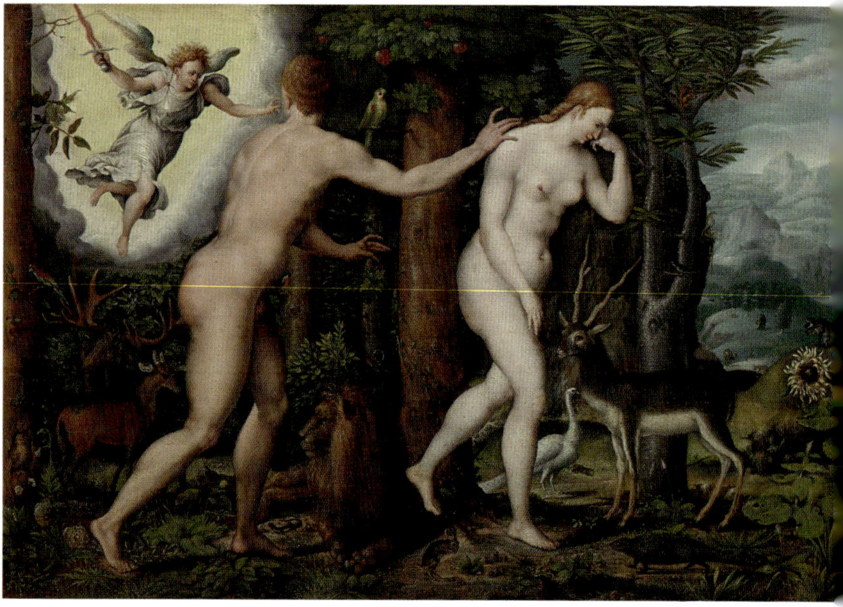

to Manfred Staudinger, served as the model for a woodcut in Aldrovandi's posthumously published *Paralipomena* (1642) (illus. 59 and 60).[23]

Copying the plant and animal studies of other artists for larger compositions as well as additional animal studies was 'ubiquitous' in the late sixteenth century.[24] Arcimboldo not only provided material for other artists to work from but copied works himself. His study of an elk cow is a case in point (illus. 61). Here, Arcimboldo has based his study on a watercolour by Albrecht Dürer (illus. 62).[25] Though the sex of the elk in Dürer's watercolour contrasts with Arcimboldo's elk, the position of the legs corresponds almost exactly. Another feature that tethers Arcimboldo's elk to Dürer's is the skin lappet on the animal's neck. The fidelity to Dürer's study ends here, however.[26] In addition to altering the sex of the animal, Arcimboldo has darkened it, shortened its fur

56 Hans Hoffmann, *Fall of Man*, *c.* 1580–90, oil on panel.

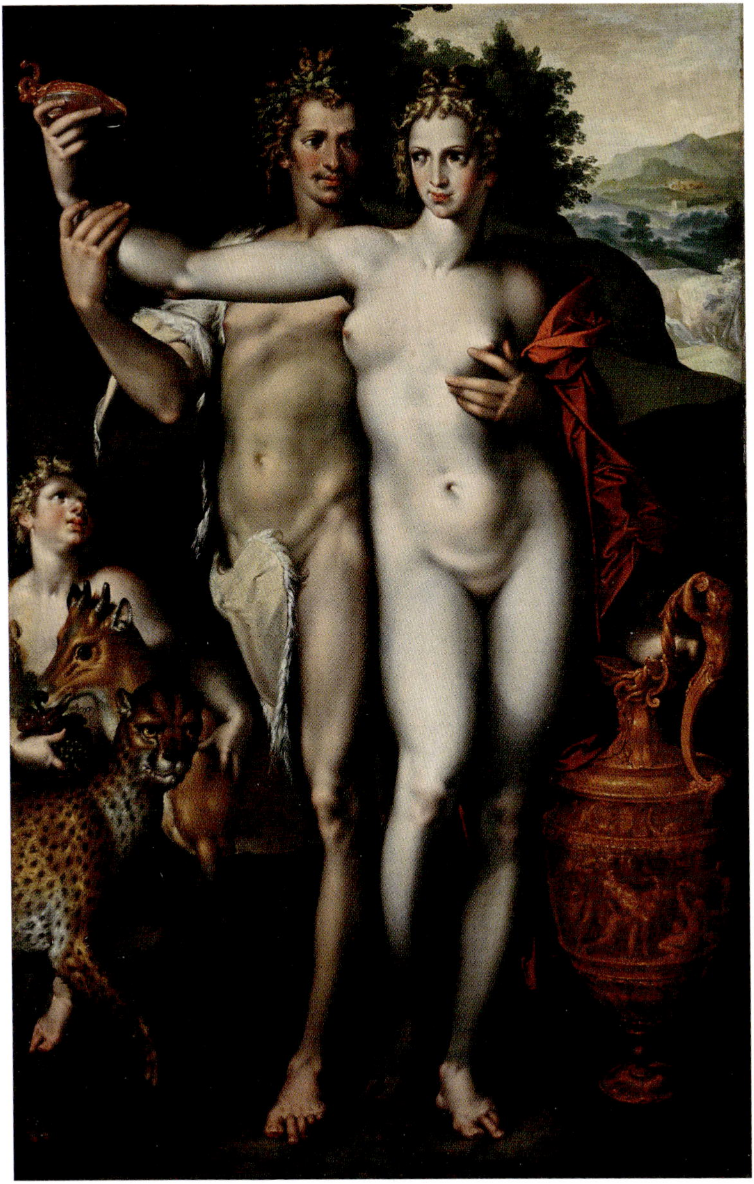

57 Bartholomeus Spranger, *Bacchus and Venus*, 1597–1600, oil on canvas.

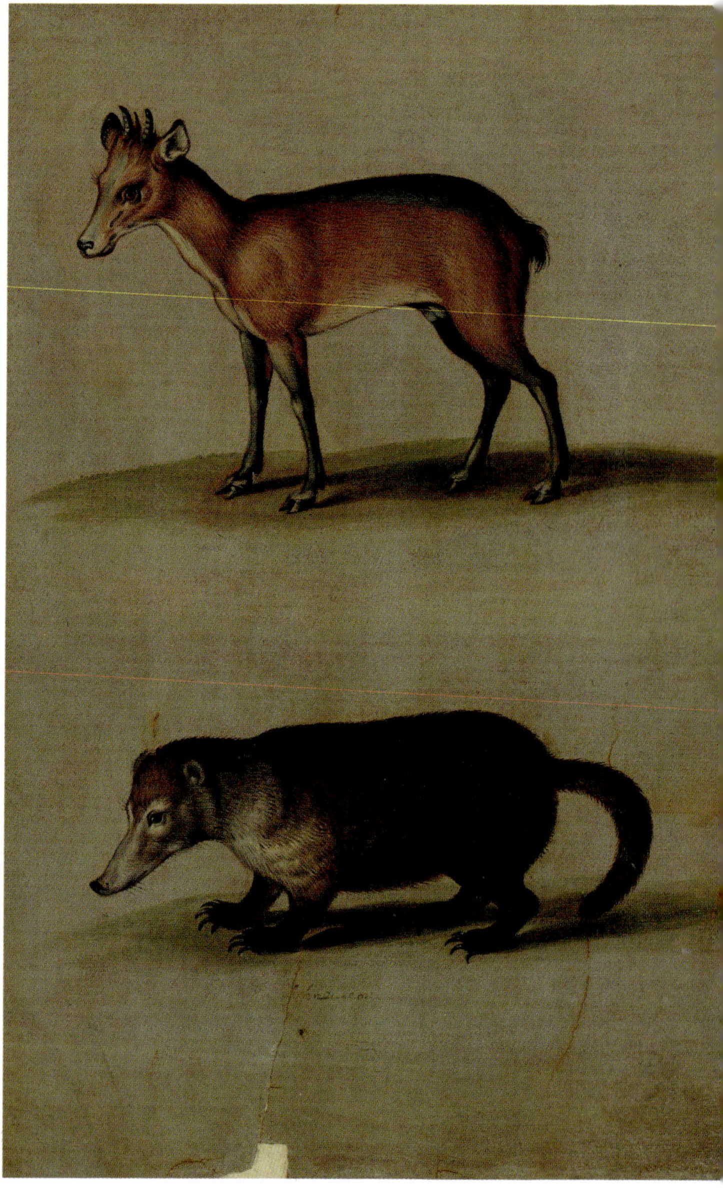

58 Arcimboldo, 'Red-flanked duiker and mountain coati',
in Ulisse Aldrovandi, 'Tavole di animali', end of the 16th century.

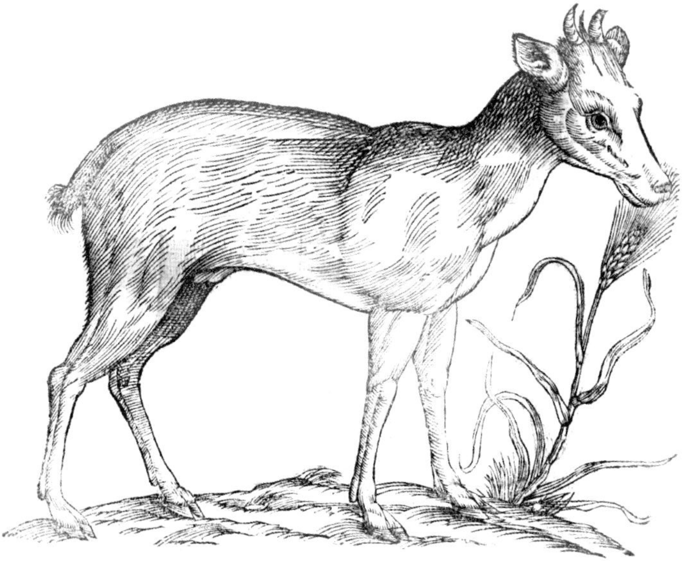

and portrayed a fuller shadow. He also hung a study of a bull elk's skull and antlers above the cow and portrayed flower studies adrift on the page. Just like the artists who relied on Arcimboldo's red duiker for their compositions, Arcimboldo used his source as a guide that could be altered, supplemented and radically recontextualized. With this example, we can see that natural history

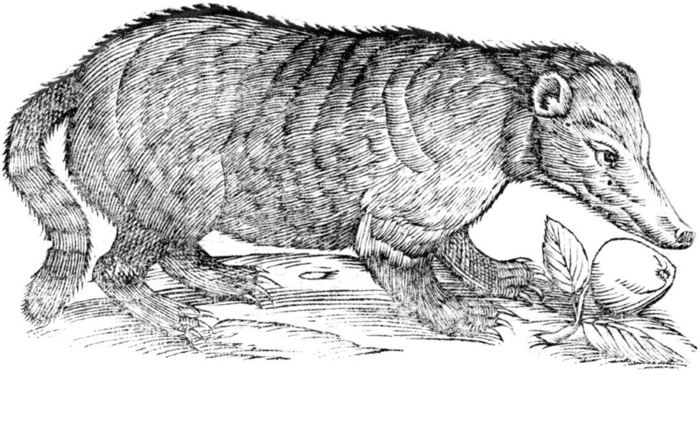

59 'Red-flanked Duiker', in Ulisse Aldrovandi, *Monstrorum historia cum Paralipomena accuratissima historiae omnium animalium* (1642).
60 'Mountain coati', in Ulisse Aldrovandi, *De quadrupedibus digitatis viviparis*, vol. II (1645).

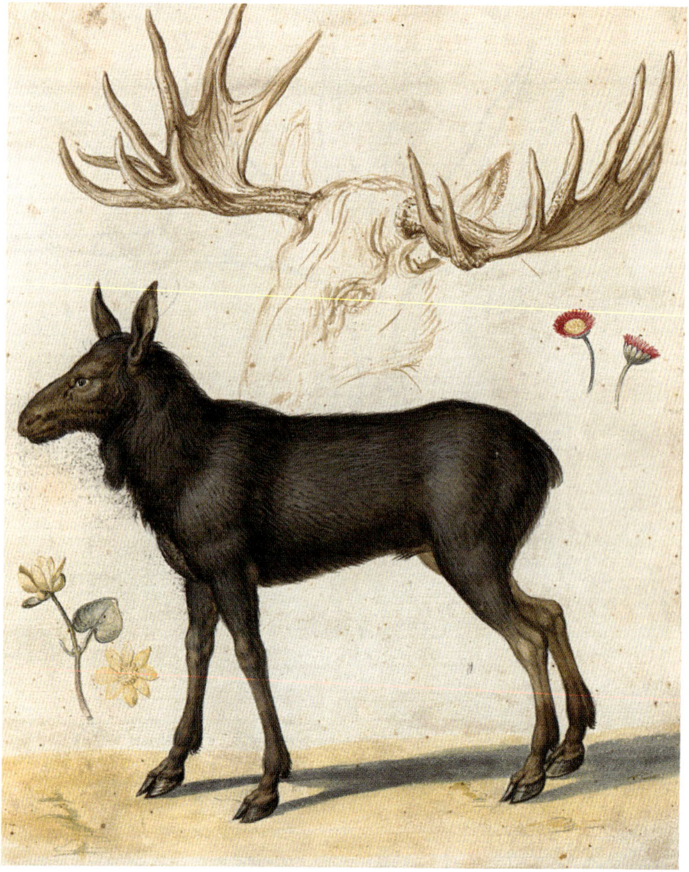

illustration was formed by artists studying animals or specimens in the flesh, as it were, as well as shaped by the adaptation of pre-existing images. These images were in turn manipulated by artists for imaginative history paintings as well as published materials in widely read treatises. What mattered was not whether an artist like Arcimboldo encountered the actual living and breathing creature; what mattered was that the artist made a picture that had the effect of having done so.

61 Arcimboldo, 'Study of elk', from Cod. Min. 42.

Exactitude was clearly not paramount for Arcimboldo. We can see this in watercolours that were pasted into a compendium currently housed in the Print Cabinet in Dresden. Take, for example, a watercolour of a lioness (illus. 63). Her body, ears, whiskers and toes are composed of a few thick, suggestive lines and her face has been anthropomorphized. These elements of the picture can hardly be considered descriptive. In fact, descriptive representational aims in this image are of a second or third order. Often, such rudimentary images were the result of an artist working from woodcuts published in natural history treatises, such as Conrad Gessner's *Historiae Animalium*.[27] Gessner's book became a standard against which representations of animals were judged, as it gained authority on account of its ubiquity.[28]

Though the boar heads, the red duiker, the elk and the lioness differ in terms of their models, degree of detail, accuracy and function, they evidence Arcimboldo's proclivity to describe the

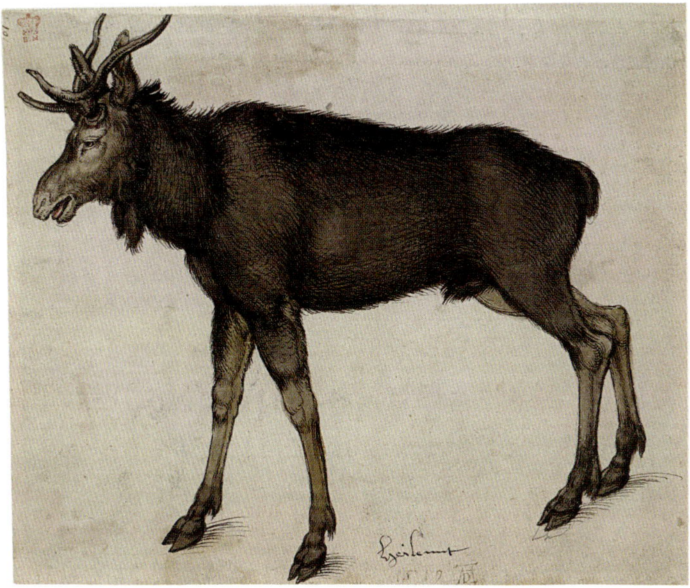

62 Albrecht Dürer, *Study of an Elk*, 1501–4, pen and ink on paper.

superficial appearance of the subject at hand. Arcimboldo did not go beyond looking at the subjects of his animal studies. He would take in and repeat the basic form of the specimen along with some detail. Consequently, there were commonly features of the subject that never made it on to the page, such as the parts of the animal's mouth, its reproductive anatomy or the precise quality of its fur, feathers or hair. The stages of life were not taken up by the artist either. With just a few exceptions, Arcimboldo's animal studies portray the subject full grown and in good health, unencumbered by age and disease, not unlike his portrayal of Rudolf II as Vertumnus (illus. 14).[29] Arcimboldo does not show the specimens from a variety of angles. Instead, he renders them in profile or three-quarter view. The specimens are also never anatomized, and the works rarely carry inscriptions. Never are the habitats of his subjects recorded with any exactness. What is not depicted in Arcimboldo's animal studies means that what facts are being represented are in no way conspicuous. Despite these vagaries, Arcimboldo did make meaningful contributions to the study of natural history.

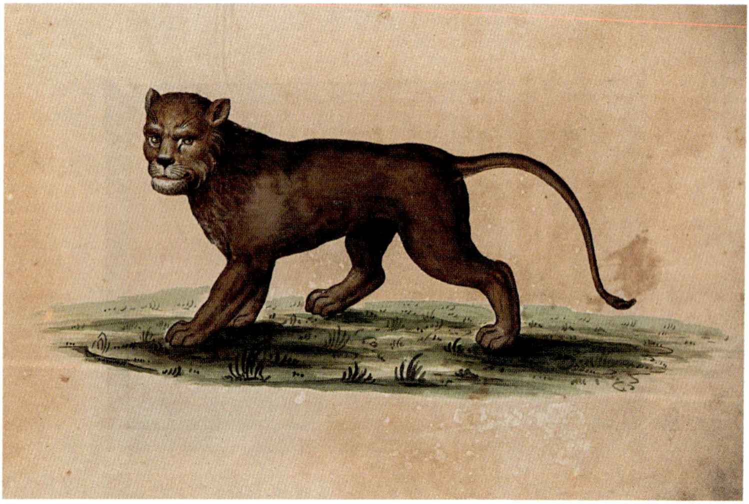

63 Arcimboldo, *Study of Lioness*, c. 1600, watercolour.

ARCIMBOLDO AND ALDROVANDI

Twenty years after Arcimboldo began to appear in the imperial court records, his name emerged in a correspondence between a physician and a naturalist. On 11 September 1582, Franciscus Paduanus, a physician at Rudolf II's court in Prague, wrote to the renowned naturalist Ulisse Aldrovandi (1522–1605) in Bologna. The letter reads:

> Today I received from Giuseppe Arcimboldo of Milan, the emperor's principal painter, colored pictures drawn after nature of several exotic birds and quadrupeds . . . But as I said before, I am forced to avail myself of the help of a painter who harrows and tries my patience. For he was careless to the following extent: when a nobleman a few days ago brought to the emperor the plant that Carolus Clusius calls Tulsai or Persian Lily in the first chapter of Rariorum aliquot stirpium . . . luckily I managed to get a hold of it when it was still fairly fresh. I immediately brought it to be painted; he [Arcimboldo] promised to do so, but did not keep his promise. He travelled off to a wedding. He stayed away for some days and meanwhile the flower yellowed, the leaves fell off and the plant withered and died. And though you surely will have seen the plant elsewhere, I was fairly vexed by his callousness.[30]

Putting aside Arcimboldo's alleged carelessness and Paduanus's indignation, it is surprising that the good doctor was 'forced' to avail himself of Arcimboldo's talents to illustrate the Persian lily. Rudolf II had a deep bench of painters and naturalists at the Prague court who were just as, if not more, capable of mirroring nature (more on this shortly). Whatever the circumstances, Paduanus's letter to Aldrovandi makes clear that Arcimboldo produced animal and plant studies to be used in his paintings as well as for others to examine, collect and store for their pursuits in natural history. Arcimboldo's animal and plant studies were just as easily the building blocks of fantastical allegorical imagery that he conjured in his mind as they were the foundations of a body of empirical knowledge.

Aldrovandi was deeply devoted to acquiring, commissioning, collecting and publishing almost anything nature had to offer.[31] And even though Arcimboldo foiled Aldrovandi's chance to acquire a depiction of an exotic (but by Paduanus's own admission well-known) plant, we know, thanks to Manfred Staudinger, that Arcimboldo had been or eventually became more reliable. Staudinger's meticulous work has linked six images by Arcimboldo to Aldrovandi's own collection of images and to the naturalist's voluminous publications.[32] Staudinger was able to make these connections because the studies in Aldrovandi's collection and publications were based on Arcimboldo's studies, which were collected and compiled at Maximilian II's and Rudolf II's courts. These studies are Arcimboldo's watercolours of a blue-headed quail dove, a sheet containing studies of a red hartebeest and a black buck, and a sheet by Arcimboldo in which a red duiker shared the page with a mountain coati (illus. 58), all of which were pasted into Cod. Min. 42. So, to be clear, in addition to producing new plant and animal studies upon request, Arcimboldo produced multiple copies of several of his animal studies that were housed in the imperial collection. Paduanus (and probably others at the imperial court) sent Aldrovandi several of these original and copied animal studies by Arcimboldo. Aldrovandi, in turn, also collected Arcimboldo's studies and modelled printed images published in his various publications on them as well.

NATURE AND THE IMPERIAL COURT

Arcimboldo was not the only artist with ties to the imperial court whose watercolours of flora and fauna were shipped to, collected and published by Aldrovandi. Sometime in the 1590s Fra Francesco Malocchi (d. 1614), a Franciscan friar and superintendent of the Orto Botanica in Pisa, dispatched a watercolour of a cardinal by Daniel Fröschl (the future imperial miniature painter and compiler of the 1607–11 inventory of Rudolf II's imperial collection) to Aldrovandi, who later published a woodcut based on Fröschl's study in his *Ornithologiae* (1600).[33] It is no shock that painters who excelled at representing nature, such as Fröschl and Arcimboldo, found themselves in the employ of the imperial court. Beginning in the fifteenth century, the Habsburgs turned to nature to legitimate their claims to rulership; to cultivate learnedness (or the look of learnedness); to provide a site for contemplation and play; and to flaunt access to and command of things costly and exotic.[34] Philip the Good of Burgundy (1396–1467), Maximilan II's great-great-grandfather, maintained a menagerie at his chateau at Hesdin. It harboured a wolf, a lynx, a fox, an ibex, wild boar, stags, monkeys and deer. Holy Roman Emperor Charles V, Maximilian II's uncle, became an avid gardener after he abdicated the throne and retired to the monastery of Yuste. Charles V's sister, Isabella of Austria (1501–1526), who married Christian II of Denmark (1481–1559), was also known for the gardens she cultivated in the grounds of Copenhagen Castle.[35] The Flemish botanist and physician Rembert Dodoens dedicated the first edition of his *Cruijde Boek* (1554) to Charles V's other sister, Mary of Hungary (1505–1558), and Mattioli, publisher of Dioscorides's *Materia Medica* was supported by Charles V, Ferdinand I and Archduke Ferdinand of Tyrol (1529–1595).[36] Giorgio Liberale, an Italian artist at Rudolf's court in Prague, painted sizable and exhaustibly described watercolours on parchment of Adriatic sea creatures that formed the basis for woodcuts illustrating Mattioli's luxury edition of Dioscorides.

Liberale also made sumptuous studies of sea creatures for Rudolf's uncle, Archduke Ferdinand of Tyrol.[37]

Arcimboldo's first imperial patron, Maximilian II, was celebrated in the Holy Roman Empire and beyond for his curiosity about the natural world. After visiting Maximilian's court in Vienna, the Italian marquis Guglielmo Malaspina wrote:

> After the dispatch of his business His Imperial Majesty attends to a garden he is newly planting and it seems that he spends as much time there as he can spare from business in which he is involved, for he doesn't care about wind or rain, but continuously goes to that place; the Duke of Ferrara has sent him several crates of trees and likewise Archduke Ferdinand considers this is his [the emperor's] [principal] pastime.[38]

Maximilian's devotion to his plants is further attested to by the fact that the court gardener Carl de Seiniß compiled itemized lists of the contents of the garden for Maximilian's daily perusal.[39] Animals also took hold of Maximilian's attention. The 1598 inventory of the Ducal collection in Munich lists a vivarium of artificial animals that were said to have been cast by Maximilian.[40] It was Maximilian who invited both Carolus Clusius and Dodoens to Vienna. According to court records, Clusius was even given a place among the emperor's Gentlemen of the Chamber – a rare honour.[41]

Whereas Maximilian II immersed himself in nature, Rudolf stood apart from it. Rudolf supported a myriad of painters celebrated, then and now, for their breathtakingly naturalistic plant and animal studies. Joris Hoefnagel, Jacob Hoefnagel, Roelandt Savery, Pieter Stevens, Paulus van Vianen, Anselmus de Boodt and Daniel Fröschl all claimed the emperor as their patron. At the same time Rudolf was cultivating natural history painting at his court, he was also seeking out plant and animal studies by the eminent early sixteenth-century German artist Albrecht Dürer. In 1588, shortly after Arcimboldo departed the imperial court to retire to Milan, Rudolf acquired hundreds of drawings and nature studies by Dürer that had been collected by the Nuremberg patrician Willibald Imhoff (1519–1580). Around the same time, the imperial ambassador to the Spanish court, Hans Khevenhuller, acquired 250 sheets by Dürer from the estate of Cardinal Antoine Perrenot de Granvelle (1517–1586) in Madrid.[42] Along with his quest to collect images of flora and fauna, Rudolf also sought out actual plants and animals, living and preserved. To this end, he relied on diplomats like Khevenhuller and merchants, such as Hans le Tor and Emanuel Sweerts.[43]

Most of these pictures and specimens were stashed away in albums, drawers and boxes in the imperial collection.[44] The collection contained all sorts of natural specimens – rhinoceroses' horns, boar tusks, bezoar stones, stuffed birds of paradise, deer antlers, pressed plants, dried seeds and roots. Like Arcimboldo's watercolours of the three-legged chick, the boar heads and the red duiker, many of the plant and animal studies that were made at the imperial court, and which were incorporated into the collection, documented things that were already part of the imperial collection, doubling it, in a sense. Despite this redundancy, the imperial collection and other princely collections (remember that several of Arcimboldo's nature studies were part of the Electoral collections in Dresden) were considered appropriate venues for the study and storage of nature studies, indicating that there was an identification between the study of art and the study of nature.

Compendia in Rudolf's collection, such as Cod. Min. 42, make clear this identification as many of the nature studies collected by Rudolf were bound into albums with other types of study, such as preparatory drawings for mythological paintings.

The compendia served multiple functions – at once storage, protection, a means of organization, a reference or a model, documentation of the collection, a store of different artists' hands, and descriptions of things lost due to death, time, infestation or climatic conditions. The 1607–11 inventory of the imperial collection in Prague lists at least fourteen *Zaichnusbücher* or 'drawing books', any of which could be describing Cod. Min. 42.[45] However, in almost every such entry, Daniel Fröschl lists the name of at least one artist whose work appeared in the compendium he was documenting. Arcimboldo's name does not occur in these entries, perhaps because, as stated earlier, his nature studies remained unsigned and unattributed until recently.

READING THE BOOK OF NATURE

Though we cannot confidently connect Cod. Min. 42 to a specific inventory entry, we do have a general idea when it was compiled. Based on the pages' watermark, Fritz Koreny has dated the onset of compilation of Cod. Min. 42 to 1579, just three years after Rudolf was crowned emperor and roughly nine years before Arcimboldo departed the imperial court in Prague.[46] Notably, folio 161 of the compendium also carries the inscription '1579 . . . in Praga'. Kaufmann suspects that the studies in Cod. Min. 42 were brought together before Rudolf's reign.[47] In sum, the compendium numbers 170 folios, on which pen and ink drawings, watercolours and tempera paintings have been affixed. It contains representations of plants, birds, wild animals, insects, fish and several landscapes. Very few of the works are signed; however, many were inscribed with dates, mostly ranging between the 1570s and the 1580s, with a few exceptions – notably a study of a deformed goat's hoof dated 1563 by Arcimboldo and another study of lizards by Arcimboldo, dated 1553. Arcimboldo's studies are collated among works by Simon Marmion, Hans Hoffmann, Hans Verhagen, Hans Bol and Daniel Fröschl. The studies by German and Dutch artists are more detailed and finer than Arcimboldo's studies in Cod. Min. 42, which are looser and sketchier by comparison.

Cod Min. 42 contains 23 watercolours that have been attributed to Arcimboldo.[48] All the watercolours have been cut down and pasted into the compendium, by whom we do not know, but it forever altered not only the look of the works but their purpose. Sylvia Ferino-Pagden has proposed that the cutting and pasting of Arcimboldo's studies transformed them from private, personal studies used for the production of paintings into 'natural history illustrations'.[49] The fact that Arcimboldo's watercolours on folios 8, 6, 11, 20 and 21 seem to have served as models for his painting *Earth* supports Ferino-Pagden's view. Whatever the case, once Arcimboldo's watercolours were trimmed and pasted into Cod. Min. 42, they became models for other works of art that were produced at court. Recall that Arcimboldo's red duiker appeared in two paintings produced at the imperial court.[50]

Strikingly, despite the disparate styles, degrees of finish, dates and origins of the works in Cod. Min. 42, such representations of the natural world could coexist within the compendium's system of image management; a system that allowed nature to be read like a book. In addition to making nature appear readable, the codex's format scales nature to the human body and permits side-by-side comparisons of the studies therein. The cut-and-paste quality to the folios of Cod. Min. 42 also enables one to consume the pictures as tactile objects that could, in theory, be moved, situated anew and recontextualized.[51] The journey from the original sheet upon which the studies were placed to their new cut-and-pasted reconfiguration was a thoughtful one. The compiler(s) isolated the image on the page, determined the width of a border, trimmed the image and relocated it into the compendium, and by doing so gave the image a new function and a new constellation of meaning. Treating the studies as three-dimensional objects that can be handled and manipulated helped transform them from a private preparatory study (as was the case with Arcimboldo's highly finished boar's head) into a collectible artefact.[52] But unlike the collectible natural specimens, which were not systematically organized in the collection, the fragmented images are notably integrated with one another in the compendium. To be sure, the material uniformity of the fragments fosters the sense that the fragments possess a conceptual uniformity as well.[53] This harmonization of the disparate elements of the compendium should not, however, obscure the fact that Cod. Min. 42, like the natural world, is also a warehouse of fragmentation. Neither completely unified nor entirely disintegrated, Cod. Min. 42 lies somewhere between natural harmony and natural chaos, just as Arcimboldo's studies lie somewhere between preparatory study and natural history illustration.

Thus far, this examination of the production, collection and compilation of Arcimboldo's plant and animal studies at the imperial court has proposed that these works share structural affinities with portraiture; it has also teased out the differences in style and finish in his nature studies; and it has thrown into relief the various functions of Arcimboldo's studies of flora and fauna at the imperial court. For them to serve such a variety of purposes, Arcimboldo's studies of plants and animals had to acquire authority in the eyes of the artist, in the eyes of naturalists and in the eyes of other artists. Artists' reliance on Arcimboldo's nature studies speaks to their authority in terms of both their close imitation of nature and their capacity to nourish the production of artwork at the imperial court. That Arcimboldo spurred on the imagination of other artists with his nature studies runs counter to many of the accounts of his impact on the history of art. Frequently, accounts of Arcimboldo's effect on other artists centre on imitators of his composite heads. Yet Arcimboldo's plant and animal studies were smuggled into the work of naturalists, artists and collectors alike.

They helped fill a void of knowledge, a void in the collection and void in a pictorial composition. Perhaps the relationship between invention and documentation in his work, and in late sixteenth-century Europe, is less tense or agitated than we have heretofore understood it to be. It is clear Arcimboldo believed in the usefulness of studying and representing flora and fauna for documenting what he saw, for disseminating information and for building his earliest composite paintings, which in many instances were, as we will see in the next chapter, impossible portraits.

THREE

Nature and Empire

On 9 March 1569, Holy Roman Emperor Maximilian II paid Arcimboldo 13 gulden and 8 thaler. Whoever recorded this payment in the imperial account books neglected to specify what it was for. Thomas Kaufmann has proposed that the payment was a form of gratitude (*aus Gnaden*) for a gift.[1]

The gift, or gifts, in question are two series of paintings in oil on panel by Arcimboldo. Each series contained four paintings. In the first series, completed in 1563, each painting represents an individual season – Winter (illus. 2), Spring (illus. 3), Summer (illus. 4) and Autumn (illus. 5). In the second series, completed in 1566, each painting represents one Element – Earth (illus. 6), Air (illus. 7), Fire (illus. 8) and Water (illus. 9). Unlike previous artists' representations of the Seasons and the Elements, which portrayed multiple figures in elaborate landscapes, Arcimboldo's eight paintings for the emperor take up the conceit of portraiture. Each individual season and each individual element is portrayed as a close-up bust-length figure in strict profile against a dark ground. Two profiles in each series face right, and two in each series face left. However, in a break from conventional portraiture of the period that claimed to reproduce the likeness of a specific individual at a particular moment in time, Arcimboldo's figures depart from the humans upon which they were modelled. Rather than composing a person made up of the stuff of humans (skin, teeth, hair, clothing and jewellery), Arcimboldo built his figures out of nature's bounty (flowers, plants, fruits and vegetables) and the animals and things that partook of or lived in her elements (fish, mammals, birds and weapons).

With these paintings Arcimboldo introduced the conceit of the composite image to the imperial court, and in doing so he challenged what period viewers expected of an imperial allegory, an imperial portrait and a mimetic image. Perhaps the paintings' novelty was one reason why they were accompanied by a poem by Giovanni Battista Fonteo (1546–1580), a Milanese humanist and friend to Arcimboldo, when they were presented at court on New Year's Day in 1569. The 309-line panegyric claimed that the composite figures were modelled on members of the imperial family (though at times it is difficult to know who is being represented in which painting).[2] More importantly, Fonteo's poem explained that both series amounted to an elaborate and laudatory political allegory, which hailed the Holy Roman Emperor as the master of nature.[3] Before diving into this novel imperial cosmology that the two series propose, we must first focus on the paintings themselves, and the paradoxical way they attempted to glorify the House of Habsburg by reducing its members to mere matter.

THE SEASONS

Let's begin with *Summer* (illus. 4). Here a young male figure faces right against an inky ground.[4] The figure's face, though, is no longer a face. Instead, it is a carefully composed harvest of summer fruits and vegetables. Rather than the bridge of a nose, we see a small cucumber, and instead of a flaring nostril, an apricot. Two glossy cherries stand in for a swollen upper lip. A pod of five green peas reads as teeth, while the bulbous end of a pear takes the place of a chin. Round and flush, a peach is a cheek. Garlic and onions form a jawline. His powerful neck is made up of a parsnip and a large radish; his throat, an apple; his ear, an ear of corn. Crowning this visage is an elaborate diadem of wheat, plums, berries, grapes, an aubergine and a burst melon, all of which are carefully interspersed with leaves and stems of the trees, bushes and vines from which they were plucked. Human craft, or something akin to the human craft, appears in the figure's 'clothing'. As an alternative to a luscious textile of silk or satin, the figure's garment is woven from summer wheat and adorned with an artichoke that seems to burst forth from his breast. Stitched in his high collar, in a measured and clearly rendered Roman majuscule, is the name 'Giuseppe Arcimboldo'. Below this 'signature' on his sleeve we read '1563', the year this painting and its three companions were completed. Like the figures in *Winter*, *Spring* and *Autumn*, the figure in *Summer* is situated in a contextual void, and like his counterparts he turns away from the viewer, allowing us the time and the freedom to inspect his features closely.

Arcimboldo's 'gift' to Maximilian II of the four Seasons and the four Elements was freighted with imperial significance.[5] The Seasons are part of a learned allegorical programme developed by Arcimboldo and others to claim that the Habsburg emperor is the sovereign of the world and the master of nature. As such, the paintings are part of an extended metaphorics of sovereignty and were created, in part, to account for the new and complicated relationship between Church and Empire following the Peace of Augsburg in 1555.[6] This new metaphorics of sovereignty promoted a shift in the representation of the empire and its rulers. These representations are still centred on Habsburg bodies, but rather than human bodies which have been given the authority to rule by an external power, such as the Electors of the Holy Roman Empire or the Pope, Arcimboldo makes the Habsburgs inaccessible to worldly politics by way of the figures' transgression of normative corporeal codes.

Consider Summer's opposite, Winter. *Winter* (illus. 2) is at once an allegory and a portrait of the recipient of Arcimboldo's 'gift', Holy Roman Emperor Maximilian II.[7] Arcimboldo used a thick and gnarly tree branch to approximate the emperor's neck. We are afforded a glimpse inside the branch at the figure's throat, inside of the figure's ear and inside the top of the figure's nose. Instead of the green interior of a young and vital tree, we see the dried and moribund wood of a tree that supports only the growth of foreign organisms – the moss which evokes tufts of beard and the cock-eyed fruiting shelf mushroom which forms lips. These exogenous elements contribute to the figure's grotesque countenance, so too the stumps on the emperor's chin, which put one in mind of the tumours of a systemic disease.[8] In contrast with the other Seasons, Winter's eyes do not gleam, but are lifeless voids over which extends a small branch, both an eyebrow and a horn. Though Maximilian was only 42 when the work was presented to him, the picture is of an aged man, the knots of the tree and the rough bark calling to mind the growth and wrinkles of the flesh of someone who has walked the earth for many years. All, however, is not decay. Behind the mass of interwoven branches that crown Winter, we see green ivy springing forth. Indeed, the ivy appears not just to be alive but grows as the small yellow leaves on the curling tips of the tendrils attest. Arcimboldo invested a similar vibrancy in the lemon and the orange that dangle from a twig sprouting out of Winter's sternum. It is clear from the ends of the fruit's branches that they have been recently harvested, their juice the closest thing to blood in this entire picture. Akin to Summer, Winter is clothed in a sumptuously woven garment of wheat or perhaps straw. The garment draped around Winter's shoulders evokes a king's mantel, which would have been worn on ceremonious occasions, such as a New Year's Day feast. That the garment was intended to conjure an image of the sovereign is also clear from the crown woven into the mantel and situated on the figure's shoulder in the centre of the picture.[9] Arcimboldo's desire to mirror Maximilian by presenting him with an image that corresponds to him and at once invents another version of him is a tactic that the painter will employ again, though with a different sovereign patron.

Among the most significant elements of *Winter* is the way in which the emperor appears unaware that he is bark and branch, and not flesh and blood. Behind this reading is the figure's minimal expressiveness. He provides no physiognomic or gestural cues to signal to the viewer that his extraordinary body is anything but ordinary. And while Maximilian's lack of awareness of his singular corporality manifests his steady mind and sovereign presence, it also affords Arcimboldo the opportunity to flaunt his powers of mimesis and poesis. There is more, however, to the painting's mutual affirmation of sovereignty and artistic virtuosity; there is also an allusion to classical imperialism. In his poem Fonteo conveyed that Maximilian was portrayed in the guise of Winter because, according to ancient sources, Winter was the first of the seasons and thus the 'head' of the year.[10] Fonteo also connected *Winter* to Livy's and Dionysius of Halicarnassus's accounts of the origins of the foremost temple in ancient Rome, the Temple of Jupiter Optimus Maximus on the Capitoline Hill.[11]

In their histories of Rome both Livy and Dionysius of Halicarnassus recount the tale of a severed human head that was discovered in the foundation of the Temple of Jupiter Optimus Maximus when it was being built during the reign of Tarquin the Elder (615–578 BCE).[12] In each author's version the head, miraculously, did not display a single sign of putrefaction. Dionysius of Halicarnassus reported that the head continuously bled, and Livy claimed that although the head had been buried for some time, all the features remained perfectly intact. According to both foundation myths, upon its discovery the preternatural head was taken to the temple's oracles, who interpreted it to be an omen that Rome would become 'the head of Italy' or 'the head of the world', the *caput rerum*. Add to this that Ovid, in his *Fasti*, tells us that the Temple of Jupiter Optimus Maximus had a ritual centrality in the empire, as it was the temple where sacrifices were made at the beginning of the new consular year. Moreover, Ovid declared the day of the sacrifice to be a feast day for those who had universal power.[13] It goes without saying that in the case of Arcimboldo's *Winter*, these classical allusions were far from obvious. In fact, it required that Arcimboldo and Fonteo provide a supplemental text to accompany *Winter* and the other seven paintings, so that the deep pictorial, historical and literary complexity to the works was not lost when the paintings were presented to Maximilian II on New Year's Day in 1569.

Of the four seasons Arcimboldo painted for Maximilian in 1563, only two remain in Vienna – *Summer* and *Winter*.[14] A version of *Spring* (illus. 3), currently housed in Madrid's Real Academia de Bellas Artes, might have been part of the original series.[15] When compared to *Winter* and *Summer*, *Spring* elicits something different from the viewer. This difference is a consequence of multiple factors. Perhaps the most salient is the composition of the female figure in profile. Rather than turning and twisting singular and independent plants, fruits and vegetables to approximate a chin, a nose, a lip or a brow of the figure and then juxtaposing and fitting it beside a different plant, vegetable or fruit which was itself manipulated by the artist to resemble an adjacent facial feature – which demands that the legibility of each element is dependent on another – in *Spring* Arcimboldo filled in the human form with leaves, stems and flowers. In essence, *Spring* is a different type of pictorial composition from those paintings we have encountered thus far in this chapter. Rather than being built up out of a variety of nature's diverse products, Spring's form is stuffed with Spring's bounty.

Consider Spring's flesh, which is a mass of sweet briar, save her chin (an apothecary rose), her nose (an orange lily), her eye (a pansy), her brow (lavender) and her ear (a peony). Though the features just listed give the figure's face a sense of depth, it is not nearly as sculptural as Summer's face with his peach cheek and pear chin. Contributing to this difference in depth is the lack of painted optical effects. Nowhere in *Spring* do we see light reflecting off a surface as we do in the cherries of Summer's lips, or the peas in Summer's mouth (which may only convincingly evoke teeth due to the way Arcimboldo made light glint off them). Nor in Spring do we see as many elements modelled with light and shade as we do in the bark of Winter's neck or the fungi that are his lips. The light in Spring is flat, except for when it falls on her shoulder of romaine lettuce, the iris ornamenting her chest, or the white lily extending away from the crown of her head and dramatically assigned a position against the painting's dark ground. Another feature that distinguishes *Spring* from *Summer* and *Winter* is the construction of the figure's garment. Both Summer and Winter are clothed in garments which appear to have been woven and then stitched together. Look at Summer's sleeve and collar. Or consider the trim of Winter's mantel, which has been carefully finished. Spring's dress betrays none of this human manufacture. Instead, her clothing is composed of nature's variety, specifically leafy greens. And there is quite an assortment. Spinach, betony, purslane, violet, feverfew, columbine, wormwood, purple dead-nettle, Echinophora, sage, dandelion and several other species were all plucked from the earth and arranged together to create a mass intended to suggest a shoulder, a breast and a neck.[16]

Some specimens received more attention than others. For example, the dark leaf of columbine parallel to the base of the ornamental iris is meticulously described, whereas the purple dead-nettle leaf just above it is less so. Might this difference in description be due in part to the artist's method in creating this work? Throughout this entire discussion of *Spring*, I have omitted two fundamental aspects of this work. First, the plants and flowers portrayed in *Spring* bloom at different times of year. This means that when Arcimboldo was painting Spring he was very likely working with nature studies that he compiled over a series of months and years. Second, the artist privileged the look and effect of the painting over accurate content, and he presumed that others would too.

Even though few, if any, of the botanical studies upon which *Spring* is based survive (surprising given that there must have been scores of them), it is important to try to conceive of the process by which this painting came to be. The artist required direct access to the living natural specimen. If he did not have access to the living plant, then he must have had access to another artist's rendering of the living plant. Given that all the blooms, stems and leaves that make up *Spring* are not wilted or ravaged, it is plausible that Arcimboldo had access to the imperial gardens in Vienna, where it is likely many of the plants were cultivated. Arcimboldo studied these specimens (or drawings and water-colours of the specimens) with great care, and he spent a good deal of time visually documenting their intricacies – every vein, every jagged edge, every yellow stamen, every curled petal. This undertaking must have required time and planning. Therefore, upon completing the studies of each individual plant Arcimboldo must have stored them away for later use, as we know he did for *Earth*, in the Elements series.

How Arcimboldo arranged the drawings on the page is unknown – as we saw in the previous chapter, the artist occasionally composed his natural history drawings unconventionally, as was the case with his study of the elk cow (illus. 61) and boar heads (illus. 52). However he arranged the studies on the page, it seems probable that determining how the studies would relate to each other in the final composition of *Spring* required less cognitive dexterity than composing *Summer* or *Winter*. The labour involved in composing *Spring* must have been largely devoted to preparing and ordering the necessary studies. Indeed, Sam Segal accounted for at least eighty different species of plants in *Spring*.[17] The only painting by Arcimboldo that comes close to this natural diversity is *Water* from the Elements, which contains 62 aquatic animal species.[18]

At this juncture, it is important to state that I am labouring the nuts and bolts of the composition of these composite heads for a reason. Once we begin to see how the artist composed the heads, we can also begin to see how the heads can be just as easily decomposed. To put it another way: to understand the paintings is to take them apart. In a certain respect, they demand dismemberment. This exercise of dismemberment, I want to suggest, can also be extended to the paintings' allegory. For though the paintings attempt to make a claim about Habsburg bodies, Habsburg sovereignty and the mastery of nature, the paintings simultaneously undermine that claim and reveal Habsburg sovereignty to be both fraught and entirely artificial.

Unlike *Spring*, Arcimboldo's *Autumn* (illus. 5) required that the artist not merely fill the form of the figure but conceive of it as comprised of individual units removed from external variables. Determining which unit would come to represent which body part required that Arcimboldo carefully manipulate, control and order the image of the unit he was working with. The original 1563 version of *Autumn* is now lost. A version of *Autumn* dated 1573 that Maximilian II gave to Elector August I of Saxony (1526–1586), and which is now currently housed in the Louvre, must stand in as our surrogate.[19] Though *Autumn* contains less variety than *Spring*, it is exemplary of some of the cognitive dexterity required in composing the composite heads. At the most basic level the artist, through his handling of nature's products, affords the viewer the opportunity to see one thing – a fruit or a vegetable – in terms of another, a facial feature or a body part. The order of the process is not evident, but it involved either first determining the form of the facial feature or body part – an eye, a chin, an ear, a nose, a shoulder or a clavicle – and then seeking out a fruit or vegetable that visually corresponded to it, or simply vice versa. Undoubtedly this required physically exploring the component – turning it around, flipping it over, viewing it like a sculpture from all angles. Another element of the process must have involved assembling several pieces of fruit or vegetables together to get a sense of the vegetable's or fruit's likeness to a body part when viewed in the company of other components. When viewing the composite heads, one cannot help but wonder if the artist attempted to manufacture the heads out of actual specimens and then paint from the model. I doubt this, given the way the composite heads defy gravitational laws. How, for instance, did the white pumpkin crowning Autumn's head not force, by its weight, the components of the figure's face to tumble? What force is keeping in place the upside-down pomegranate, which forms Autumn's chin?

The thwarting of physics is not the painting's only unexpected element. Take, for instance, the husk of a berry which is both eyelid and eyelashes, or the split fig, spilling forth; its seedy centre functions as the ornament of an earring. Indeed, the longer one looks at the broken fig, one notices that it is not the only component open for inspection. Look again at the chestnut, which is at once thin lips, moustache and the glistening tip of a tongue. Or turn your attention to the cracked, green walnut carefully suspended from the foreshortened pumpkin stem. The walnut's precarity calls attention to the right corner of the painting. Like the white lily in *Spring*, the walnut's careful description and modelling stands out against a dark ground, and calls attention to Arcimboldo's powers of illusionism, his craft and another human element of the work, the pumpkin's harvest, which from the look of the stem was cut with a sharp knife. Still, there is more. The stem of the pumpkin cannot help but evoke the plant it was harvested from and the pumpkin's connection to the earth, a displacement that is picked up again by the scraggly roots of the carrot and the radish of the figure's thick neck.[20] These wispy roots tellingly exceed the confines of the pieces of wood which, bound together by a grape vine, serve as the figure's costume. It is no accident that this sartorial choice recalls a wine barrel, given the intensity of the viticulture on Autumn's head – the grape leaves an excellent stand-in for a crown fit for Bacchus.

That some of the grape leaves have begun to lose their crisp, green colour is, of course, apropos of the season. But they suggest something beyond the time of year. For what is a yellowing leaf if not a sign of pending death and degeneration? The large, yellow grape leaves so carefully counterpoised with the cracked walnuts are one of the most striking elements of the painting. However, when *Autumn* is considered in the context of the whole series (as it was intended to be) we are assured that nature's demise is never permanent, but merely part of a seemingly endless cycle of birth, bloom and decay – a reassurance of eternal renewal. What is so remarkable about Arcimboldo's series of the Seasons and Elements is the way the paintings bind this new pictorial language of the eternity of the Habsburg empire with artistic skill and ingenuity.

It would be remiss if I did not mention one more critical and peculiar element in *Autumn*: the snail creeping across the ridge of the pumpkin. It would be remiss because this snail forms a bridge between this painting and another by Arcimboldo. Let me explain. In the second half of the sixteenth century, naturalists like Hadrianus Junius (1511–1575) believed that snails, like mushrooms and other fungi, were spontaneously generated from the damp and dark soil of the forest floor when it was warmed by an external heat source.[21]

That Arcimboldo went to an effort to bring the earth to the viewer's mind should not come as a shock, for in addition to being part of the series of the four Seasons, *Autumn*, like the other paintings in the series, was paired with one of the paintings from the four Elements. The pairs are as follows: Winter/Water, Spring/Air, Summer/Fire and Autumn/Earth.[22] There might still be another reason why the artist conspicuously placed the snail. Towards the end of the sixteenth century and at the beginning of the seventeenth century, painters of nature and still-life painters often seized upon animals that were thought to have been spontaneously generated to refer metaphorically to their ability to create works *ex nihilo*.[23] We will never know for certain if Arcimboldo was investing the snail in *Autumn* with such an allusion, but as we will see later in this book, Arcimboldo was adept at cultivating an image of himself as an artist unsurpassed in his abilities to conjure pictures from the fertile fields of his mind.

THE ELEMENTS

Snails do not appear in Arcimboldo's *Earth* (illus. 6). Currently in a private collection, *Earth* is a mesmerizing conglomeration of living and dead mammals. The roughly forty eyes, some in pairs, others not, that gleam from within the picture are a major force behind its ability to immerse the viewer; they eye us as we eye them. With its evocation of its components' vitality, this painting departs from the allegories of the Seasons because, rather than the facial features being composed from inert matter, in *Earth* we have a picture of a face that is made up of faces. Another difference: Earth is composed of moving parts. For not only was the artist tasked with portraying the faces of a wide assortment of earth-bound four-legged animals, but he had to contend with their flexible limbs, spines and tales. On one hand, these features provided Arcimboldo with more opportunities to manipulate the shape of the component parts of his composition. On the other hand, it meant that he had more to obscure. The bull which forms Earth's neck is an excellent example of Arcimboldo's ability to see an animal in a particular position and liken it to a specific body part that happens to connect two other body parts.

The bull is exemplary of yet another distinguishing feature of the Elements: the playfulness with which the artist handles the scale of the parts that make up the whole. Look at Arcimboldo's treatment of the figure's 'chest' and 'shoulder'. Compare the size of the skin of the ram to that of the bull above it. If the ram were to be refilled with its entrails and life, and if it were to rise, it would tower over the bull. Maybe this is fitting: after all, the ram skin is clearly intended to reference the Habsburg chivalric order, the order of the Golden Fleece.[24] The ram skin was often portrayed on or near the Holy Roman Emperor in portraits dating back to Maximilian II's grandfather, Holy Roman Emperor Maximilian I. The intertwining of the ram's limp hind leg with the tail and leg of the lion skin is also imperially freighted. The toothless lion that form's Earth's shoulder is intended to conjure the Nemean lion that Hercules slew with his bare hands.[25]

Long before Arcimboldo painted Earth's lion skin, Hercules and the Nemean lion had converged in representations of imperial rule. In fact, the entwined limbs at the base of Earth's neck recall the flaccid and knotted lion paws draped over the shoulders of an ancient Roman bust of Emperor Commodus, made sometime between 180 and 193 CE. It makes good sense that both Commodus and Earth don the skin near their neck and torso, as the Nemean lion's skin made the individual who was wearing it invulnerable to attack (as if the life-force which had been drained from the lion was divinely transferred to the one who wore its carcass). It is evident that Arcimboldo delighted in rendering the remains of the lion and the ram which, vacant of vitality, differ from many of the components of the composite heads we have so far encountered. In addition to the mythological beast, the toothless maw and the eyeless sockets of the lion put one in mind of early modern taxidermy. As we know from the previous chapter, it is very likely that Arcimboldo was afforded the chance to study Maximilian II's collection of preserved animal bodies when he was making preparatory drawings for *Earth*. Arcimboldo's decision to place the lion's slack jaw on Earth's shoulder is intriguing. On one level, the lifeless void calls attention to the indomitable animal's trouncing. On another level, by defanging the animal, the representation does the same. Moreover, the empty mouth at the base of the painting forms a void. Thus, even though the lion skin is intended to convey the imperviousness of Earth's (and by extension the emperor's) body, it leaves the body of the figure open to penetration. Earth's eye is a mouth of a wholly different sort. Here Arcimboldo has staged a drama. The mouth, fangs and tongue which read as Earth's eye belong to a snarling wolf, whose teeth verge on piercing through the flesh of a distracted hare, whose back and hindquarters have taken the shape of Earth's notably hooked nose.

Though *Earth* is assembled out of an assortment of mammals – an antelope, an elk, an elephant, a warthog and a leopard, to name just a few – those that possess either fangs, horns or tusks make up the bulk of the figure's head. Maybe these types of animal dominate the picture because Arcimboldo had access to the emperor's collection and menagerie. We know that King John III (1502–1557) of Portugal and his wife, Catherine of Austria (1507–1578), gave Maximilian II an elephant named Suleiman in 1552, when Maximilian was archduke.[26] Though Suleiman only lived for eighteen months in the imperial menagerie, during that time Maximilian had images made of the animal, from which Arcimboldo could have worked. Or perhaps these beasts were chosen because their teeth, tusks and horns were thought to have apotropaic or prophylactic value, making Earth's head full of magic and medicine. It is also conceivable that many if not all the animals were hunting trophies. None of these possibilities were mentioned by Gregorio Comanini when he discussed Earth in *Il Figino* (1591), his treatise on painting.[27] Instead, Comanini explained that the placement of the animals on Earth's face and body was derived from Pliny the Elder's ideas on physiognomy, which the ancient Roman author laid out in his *Natural History*. This may be true. But it also may be a tactic to bolster the learned persona that Arcimboldo was busy cultivating towards the end of his life.

I would like to point out that *Earth* is a painting in which occlusion plays a starring role. In the entire composition we are permitted to see the bodies of only three animals – the hare and wolf as well as a monkey who looks out at us from the back of Earth's head. The rest of the animal bodies are entirely omitted. This may be because, by occluding the bodies, Arcimboldo was able to include a greater number and diversity of animals. However, we cannot overlook the possibility that the artist, or the patron, wished to have the head of the Earth composed out of the heads of the earth's most majestic, or dangerous, or nimble beasts. In other words, the painting proposes that the ruler of the earth reigns because he has absorbed or incorporated these noble and powerful animals into himself. If this was the case, it would not be the only time when the paintings played around with 'heads' and their association with rulership. Just think back to the ways in which *Winter* evoked the Temple of Jupiter Optimus Maximus and the 'head of the year'. The allusions are both learned and witty.

There is yet another correspondence between *Earth* and *Winter*, namely the ingenious ways in which Arcimboldo composed the head so that specific features of particular components create a 'natural crown' – in the case of *Earth* the crown is made up of antlers' tines and in *Winter* with tangled branches. It is as if nature herself has crowned these figures, and therefore it follows that these figures are natural rulers – not rulers chosen by men or anointed by a pontiff. This notion of natural sovereignty is crucial to the rhetoric of both the Seasons and the Elements;

the processions and tournaments Arcimboldo devised at the imperial court, which will be addressed in the next chapter; and his portrait of Rudolf II as Vertumnus, examined in Chapter Five. In the imperial allegories, the processions and tournaments and *Vertumnus*, Arcimboldo articulated the power of the Habsburgs through a decidedly artificial symbolic system that endeavoured to codify the relationship between the House of Habsburg and the cosmos.

Yet even though the imperial allegories draw upon the cosmic splendour of the House of Habsburg, the paintings still challenge what the viewer expects of an imperial allegory, an imperial portrait and a mimetic image. Take the painting of *Water* (illus. 9), for example. Water is a figure magnificently composed of 62 slippery aquatic animals. In this painting, as in *Earth*, Arcimboldo has sacrificed the naturalistic proportions of the vertebrates and invertebrates that make up Water, for the sake of creating facial features that are in proportion to one another. Arcimboldo has additionally anthropomorphized several of Water's component parts. This is most apparent in the walrus that throws its head back to reveal its bright canine tongue and in the sun fish whose large wet eye convincingly takes on the task of standing in for the eye of the composite figure. The sun fish's eye differs from all other eyes in the Seasons and the Elements, not just because an eye has come to represent an eye, rather than an inanimate object or a void, but because the eye of the sun fish has the viewer in its sights. In no other painting from either series is the viewer addressed. Another anomaly is Water's mouth, teeth and tongue, which are the mouth, teeth and tongue of a bullhead shark that has been rotated on to its right side. Yet another distinguishing feature is the jewellery, clearly not entirely natural, that hangs from Water's ear and neck. Aptly made of pearls, the jewellery's reflection of light calls our attention to it. Our eyes lingering over the pearls in the painting produces two results. First, it creates the sense in the viewer that

Water has adorned him or herself (in my view the gender of the figure is far from clear) as a beautiful woman might. Second, it makes clear the potential optical effects sea creatures can provide for a painter.[28]

I want to linger over the way Arcimboldo selectively exploits his mimicry of the shiny and wet surfaces in the painting. Several components of *Water* appear as if they have just emerged from the sea. The belly of the pike with supernumerary gills to the left of the octopus and underneath the string of pearls has lustre. So too does the blood clam, which stands in for the figure's ear and from which dangles the tear-shaped pearl. Another shiny element is the tongue of the bullhead shark, which appears moist and slick. Yet the more one looks for the reflection of light off wet surfaces, the more one finds oneself disappointed because there is, given the subject matter, a lack of lustre. Moreover, this lack of lustre denotes a lack of water.

Fittingly, I cannot stop wondering about the circumstances under which this painting was made; I cannot avoid summoning the stench of the dead fish; and I cannot help recalling a story about Leonardo. In his biography of Leonardo, Giorgio Vasari recounted that when he was a boy, Leonardo desired to paint something 'that might be able to terrify all who should come upon it, producing the same effect as once did the head of Medusa'.[29] And so, the young painter decided to paint this painting in a cave into which he permitted no one entry. According to Vasari, upon securing his chthonic studio Leonardo smuggled in:

> Lizards . . . crickets, serpents, butterflies, grasshoppers, bats and other strange kinds of such like animals, out of the number of which, variously put together, he drew forth a most horrible and fearful beast that poisoned and enkindled the air with its breath . . . And so long did he labor over making it that the stench of the dead animals

> in that room was past bearing, but Leonardo did not notice it, so great was the love that he bore towards art.[30]

Clearly Vasari (and Leonardo) are entangling putrefaction, odour and ugliness with fright. I suspect something akin to Leonardo's Medusian enterprise is afoot in Arcimboldo's *Water*. Through its naturalism, the painting makes the claim that Arcimboldo painted the components from life. Individual components suggest that he might have, and if this is the case, he must have been inundated with rotting fish. And the more we concoct this noxious odour as we look at the work, the more we notice (more so than in the other paintings in either series) the figure of Water is ugly. But perhaps more importantly, it appears that the figure of Water is not aware of his or her ugliness.

If *Water* evokes the mingling of putrefaction and unsightliness in Leonardo's cave, Arcimboldo's *Fire* (illus. 8) recalls Leonardo's monster's enkindled breath. Just look at the lit wick of a lamp in the figure's mouth! Though this intimation of breath is perhaps the most lifelike element of the picture, one wonders what would happen if the parted lips closed and the flame ignited Fire's upper lip, which is comprised of two bundles of kindling. The figure of Fire is on the verge of total combustion. His blazing hair (which remarkably emits no smoke) is dangerously close to the wound-up fuse standing in for the figure's forehead. Once the four-wicked candle that appears to be feeding the figure's head melts down, the ignited wicks could easily tumble into the shovel full of gunpowder that forms part of the figure's upper torso. It is as if *Fire* is an intricate booby trap, set for self-destruction. The unlit candle peeping through a space in the firestone that takes the place of the figure's ruddy skin seems to register the painting's insinuations of self-annihilation.

Of course, understanding Fire as a figure of self-immolation is not how most scholars have interpreted this work, and understandably so. The Golden Fleece, carefully draped over the double-headed imperial eagle, tells us that we need to consider the relationship between the element of fire and the House of Habsburg. The chain of the order hanging from the neck of the figure is both an example of goldsmithing (fire put to use) and a barrier between the roaring fire in the top register of the painting and the firearms in the lower register. Might the chain of the order signify the imperial control of fire and control of the instruments of war, which form the foundation of the figure? Remarkably, the painting can generate two interpretations which seem to oppose each other. On one hand we can read the work as a warning against self-destruction, and on the other we can read it is as a paean to Maximilian II's ability to bend fire to his will. As we will see in Chapter Six, Arcimboldo was masterful at pondering, inventing and painting invertible paintings that contained two different pictures and two different meanings. And is the entire conceit of the composite heads not also playing with two opposing modes of representation – mimesis and poesis?

Situating the House of Habsburg in the two series was crucial to Arcimboldo's task. It is clear that the artist not only strove to insert pictorial references to the Habsburgs seamlessly in a handful of the works, but strove to place that pictorial reference consistently across the two series. Often, he references the House of Habsburg on the figure's heads or on the chest or both. Take a copy of the now-lost 1566 version of *Air* (illus. 7), which is currently in a private collection in Switzerland. Here the peacock (an emblem of the House of Habsburg) fans its tail on the shoulder of the figure, facing right, who is made entirely out of birds. The imperial eagle that looks in the same direction as the figure is situated on Air's chest. Thus, just as in *Fire*, what was considered to have the most force, or perhaps to be the most dangerous element of the composite head, forms the base of the composite figure.

We cannot be certain if this version of *Air* is a faithful copy of the original 1566 work. Unlike all the other paintings discussed in this chapter, scholars agree that *Air* is not a product of Arcimboldo's hand.[31] Accordingly, I do not want to spend too much time discussing the work's particulars. However, it is important to note that even though it is difficult to identify many of the birds that make the flock that forms the figure's hair, all of them have the capability of flight. Thus, unlike the chickens and turkey which form the lower-half of the figure's face, the birds which make up the figure's hair engage the element of air twice over because they not only occupy the air but can appear to our earth-bound eyes to be lighter than it.

If there is one thing the Seasons and the Elements afford the contemplative viewer, it is the opportunity to ponder the relationship between man and the Seasons and man and the Elements. But of course, they do more than this. They allow one to consider the pictures' claims that the Seasons and the Elements are under the influence of the emperor (and by extension all the Habsburgs) to such a degree that they take on each other's forms. And yet, I have tried to show throughout this chapter that there are instances in which the paintings undermine or throw into question that Habsburg mastery of nature. Perhaps in addition to their feats of mimesis, and their ingenious and fantastical composition, it is the oscillation in meaning that keeps us looking. Beyond this, all eight paintings afford one the opportunity to ruminate on an unprecedented shift in the representation of the empire and its rulers, which is deeply dependent on Arcimboldo's unprecedented entanglement of mimetic and fantastic imagery as well as his wit and virtuosity.

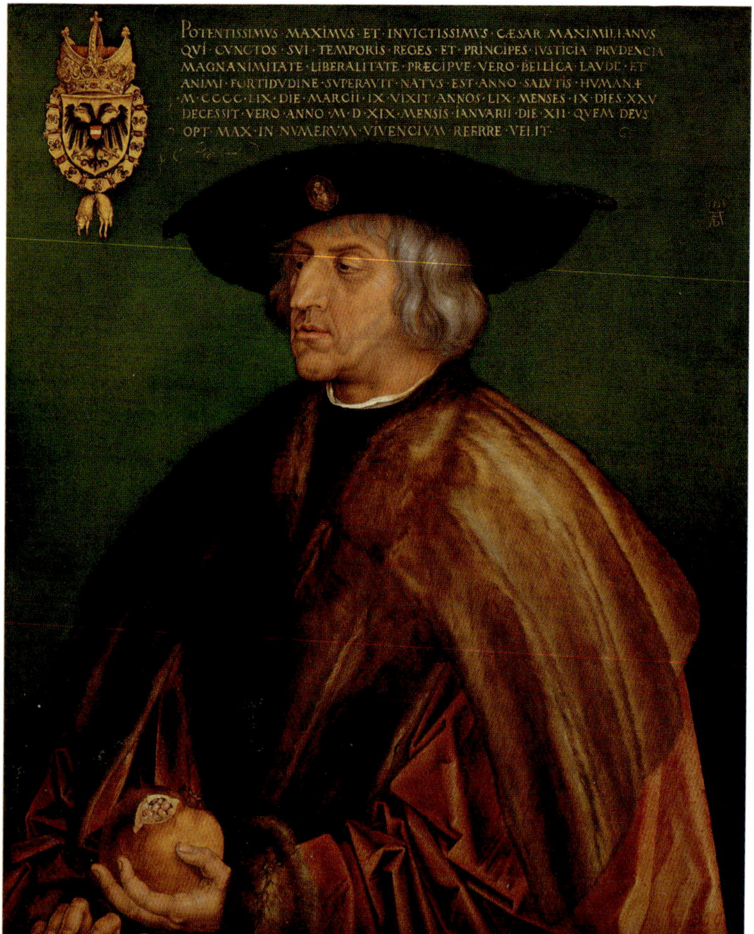
POTENTISSIMVS · MAXIMVS · ET · INVICTISSIMVS · CÆSAR MAXIMILIANVS
QVI · CVNCTOS · SVI · TEMPORIS · REGES · ET · PRINCIPES · IVSTICIA · PRVDENCIA
MAGNANIMITATE · LIBERALITATE · PRÆCIPVE · VERO · BELLICA · LAVDE · ET
ANIMI · FORTIDVDINE · SVPERAVIT · NATVS · EST · ANNO · SALVTIS · HVMANÆ
· M · CCCC · LIX · DIE · MARCII · IX · VIXIT · ANNOS · LIX · MENSES · IX · DIES · XXV
DECESSIT · VERO · ANNO · M · D · XIX · MENSIS · IANVARII · DIE · XII · QVEM DEVS
OPT · MAX · IN NVMERVM · VIVENCIVM · REFRRE · VELIT ·

FOUR

Harmonious Bodies

When Arcimboldo completed the Seasons (1563) and the Elements (1566), he became the first artist to conceive of and portray time, nature and the House of Habsburg as if they were one. Since the reign of Holy Roman Emperor Maximilian I (1493–1519), the Habsburgs had self-consciously and overtly associated the dynasty with nature's plenitude. Take, for example, Albrecht Dürer's 1519 *Portrait of Maximilian I* (illus. 64). Here against a luscious dark-green ground the ruler of the Holy Roman Empire holds his personal device, a pomegranate, a section of which has been split open to reveal its seedy centre. In his youth Maximilian recognized a metaphorical resemblance between himself and this ancient fruit of the *Punica granatum*. Regarding this correspondence, the emperor is rumoured to have said, 'Though the pomegranate lacks a particularly handsome skin and a particularly lovely smell, its interior is full of munificence and shapely seeds.'[1] Whereas Maximilian seized upon the promise of bearing fruit, his grandson Charles V fixed with intensity on nature unfurled and in full bloom. In Willem de Pannemaker's tapestry series (illus. 65), executed between 1540 and 1555, the emperor's coat of arms hovers over a superior specimen of a field of flowers.[2] Here in the tapestry's concatenations of spontaneous and unpredictable growth we see plenitude unleashed in its ornamental mode. The tapestry's web of flowers functions to connect the House of Habsburg to nature's pure and unchecked bounty.

64 Albrecht Dürer, *Maximilian I*, 1519, oil on panel.

Arcimboldo was not the first artist to extend this bountiful metaphor to Maximilian II's reign in his paintings of the Seasons and the Elements. The Flemish composer Jacobus Vaet (1529–1567) wrote a motet for Maximilian II's coronation in Frankfurt on 24 November 1562.[3] The polyphonic choral music heralded Maximilian II's ascension to the imperial throne as the inauguration of a new Golden Age during which peace would reign and nature would flourish. For the emperor's royal entry into Vienna on 16 March 1563 the imperial antiquarian, Wolfgang Lazius (1514–1565), had the streets of the imperial capital lined with trees from which low-hanging artificial fruit hung – as if the emperor's reign created the conditions for nature's fruition. Hugo Blotius (1533–1608), Maximilian II's imperial librarian, likened the emperor's growing collection of books and the systematic ordering of them to a burgeoning garden. He wrote to the emperor, 'Here the garden of the library which I cultivate is always pleasant and flourishing, always useful and delightful. It constantly produces flowers in the full bloom of the mind and spirit. It does not die in spring, summer, fall, or winter nor is it exposed to stormy weather.'[4] In his letter to the emperor, Blotius neglected to mention that the library had been taken over by mould, spiders and mice, all which left the books ravaged.[5]

The fantasy of the imperial control of nature's fecundity also found its way into the emperor's art collection. In the late 1560s the imperial antiquarian Jacopo Strada (1507–1588) (Lazius's replacement and nemesis) worked with the famed goldsmith Wenzel Jamnitzer to design a fountain 3.7 metres (12 ft) tall for the emperor's table.[6] Now mostly destroyed, the fountain's base was made up of four gilded figures: Flora, Ceres, Bacchus and Vulcan. Each mythological figure corresponded to a season: Spring (Flora), Summer (Ceres), Autumn (Bacchus) and Winter (Vulcan). A lion bearing the coat of arms of Burgundy (the house of Maximilian II's paternal grandmother) and Austria was placed in the centre of the figures that formed the base. Atop the base rested a three-tiered platform. The first tier represented Earth, the second tier Air and the third tier Ether – the fiery substance believed to exist between Earth's atmosphere and the celestial sphere. This cosmologically and figuratively intricate platform supported the fountain itself, which was in the shape of Maximilian II's imperial crown, thus standing in for the emperor himself. If the base established Maximilian's position as the head of nature and the cosmos, the superstructure situated him in both historical and eschatological time. It held aloft the figures of Ninus the Assyrian, Cyrus the Persian, Alexander the Greek and Julius the Roman. Each of these rulers stood for an empire that – according to interpretations of the biblical prophecy in the Book of Daniel – had to rise and topple before the inauguration of messianic time – the time, according to the fountain, of Maximilian II's reign.

In a very simple sense, Arcimboldo's allegories of the Seasons and the Elements, Dürer's portrait, Pannemaker's tapestries, Lazius's entry and Strada and Jamnitzer's fountain are linked together because they were cultural artefacts, commissioned, designed and executed for a Holy Roman Emperor, and their mission was to associate the emperor with all of nature's most benevolent powers. Yet, if we take a deeper look, Arcimboldo's paintings differ in two regards. First, in Arcimboldo's paintings nature's connection to the power of the emperor is integrated into a fully represented and ordered scene rather than acting as an addendum or a supplement to a representation, symbolic or otherwise, of the ruler. We find the supplemental element in Dürer's portrait and Pannemaker's ornamental tapestries. Second, in comparison to Vaet's motet and Jamnitzer's fountain, Arcimboldo's imperial allegories are less mythological and less expressly historical. They are not anchored in human time; they are anchored in cosmic time, which is cyclical and eternal rather than teleological.

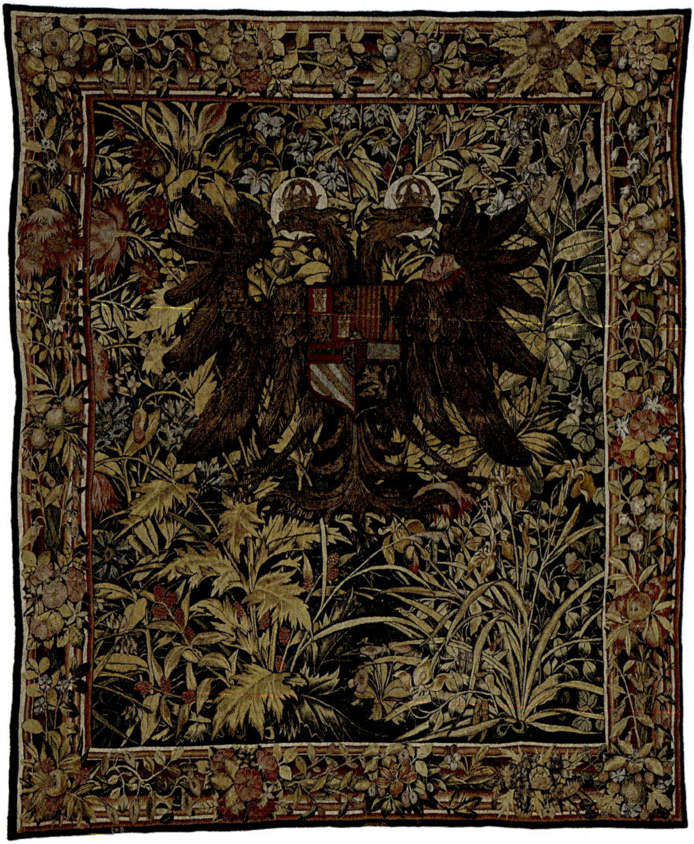

Couching the imperial allegories in the quaternary system of the four Seasons and the four Elements allowed Arcimboldo to skirt historical time and avoid the question as to who bestowed imperial authority on to the emperor and when. As far as the allegories were concerned, Maximilian II was a natural ruler. However, in the allegories it is not entirely clear over what or whom Maximilian rules. This is why Fonteo's poem was necessary to spell out the conceit that Maximilian was portrayed in the paintings as the ruler of the universe. In doing so, the poem itself made

65 Willem de Pannemaker, *Tapestry with Arms of Charles V*, *c.* 1540–55.

evident that even though the components of the allegories were by and large naturalistic, once situated in the composition of the composite head they became, paradoxically, less legible and could, therefore, be interpreted incorrectly. Thus, it is possible to understand Fonteo's poem as balm that eased Arcimboldo's anxiety around the paintings' ability to convey a clear meaning.

In 1571 Arcimboldo elaborated on his cosmic system to address geopolitics more explicitly. However, rather than using *representations* of bodies to embody nature and the Habsburgs' position in it, he used actual bodies to demonstrate the Habsburgs' role within the broader cosmos. The bodies made up a procession that introduced a tournament. The tournament was one of several events put on by the imperial court to honour the marriage of Maximilian II's brother, Archduke Charles von Steiermark, to Maria Anna von Wittelsbach of Bavaria, which took place on 24 August 1571, in Vienna. In designing the procession Arcimboldo built upon longstanding cosmologies to invent an idiosyncratic and expanded representation of a harmonious universe.[7] Within this harmonious universe Arcimboldo superimposed the Habsburg dynasty, their global imperial ambitions and the cosmos. The procession, with its symbolic bodies moving through space and time, also provided Arcimboldo with the occasion to articulate a vision of political power in largely secular terms, thus, as we will see, skirting thorny confessional tensions within the empire and between individuals who were present at the wedding.

FESTA

Courtly festivals, like allegories and portraiture, were part of the official language of politics in early modern Europe. The events – which encompassed a ruler's triumphal entries and processions for the coronations, weddings and funerals of rulers and their family – were conceived, choreographed and performed for large audiences made up of other nobles, political dignitaries and the population of a given location. In addition to conveying the prosperity, prestige, skills and virtues of the individual(s) being honoured, these events were also audacious displays of the humanistic learning and logistical prowess of the people who designed them. Almost always sponsored by the state, a municipality or both, early modern festivals of the sort Arcimboldo designed were arguably the *sine qua non* of soft power.[8]

Designed to include performance of multiple bodies in space and time, these events were ephemeral and could have been easily forgotten if not for extant programmes drawn up by the designers of the events before they took place and, in certain instances, illustrated descriptions which were published after the fact. By the time Arcimboldo devised the tournament procession for Charles of Steiermark and Maria Anna of Bavaria in 1571, Maximilian II was fluent in such courtly revelries. Ferdinand I was the centrepiece of several such occasions. On 8 November 1558, Ferdinand triumphantly entered Prague as the recently crowned King of Bohemia. As Ferdinand wound his way around Prague, he passed through several triumphal arches that had been erected for his visit. These ephemeral architectural structures were loaded with allegorical and mythological imagery which heralded the newly crowned king. An arch erected by Prague's Jesuits featured personifications of Peace and Justice in addition to a figure of Mars. Ferdinand commissioned an arch which featured the biblical giants Samson and Gideon along with personifications of Faith, Religion, Justice, Temperance, Nobility, Power, Magnanimity, Goodness and Piety. A third arch featured a personification of Concord as well as an inscription that described Ferdinand as the second Jupiter.[9]

In the spring of 1560 Maxmilian II organized a month of tournaments in honour of his father and his uncle, Duke Albrecht V of Bavaria (1528–1579). These tournaments took place in Vienna and were supplemented by several highly choreographed events – a mock sea battle on the Danube, a siege of an ephemeral fortress and fireworks. During the festivities, Giovanni Bonna, the Habsburgs' house giant, dressed as a Wildman. A 'magic hill' belonging to the obscure goddess 'Isabella of Carthage' was also noted.

Perhaps the most elaborate Habsburg entry was organized for Maximilian II himself upon his election to King of the Romans. This coronation ended a protracted dynastic dispute between Maximilian and Philip II of Spain. Organized by the imperial antiquarian Wolfgang Lazius in 1563, this triumphal entry (mentioned above) primarily centred on dynastic succession.[10] One triumphal arch designed by Lazius even portrayed Ferdinand I handing the empire to Maximilian II. As in Ferdinand's entry into Prague, personifications of princely virtues were incorporated into the festival's imagery as well as references to Jupiter. Red and white, the colours of the House of Habsburg, took on sacramental significance when red and white wine flowed from wells situated next to St Stephen's Cathedral.

THE IDYLLS OF THE EMPEROR

The 1571 tournament procession that Arcimboldo designed took on a very different character from the Habsburg festivals and processions that preceded it. A revival of medieval chivalric practices, tournaments were elaborately choreographed martial games that took place at courtly celebrations.[11] Typically, tournaments foregrounded hand-to-hand combat such as a joust or a mêlée. Behind these skirmishes was a longing for the chivalric past and noble combat against a worthy and equal foe. As staged violence, they provided a thrill and the chance to witness brutality and agility. Tournaments were also occasions where one could steal a glimpse of the court's guests in attendance, and they were proceedings that generated gossip, which was frequently conveyed by way of a letter to another dignitary or courtly gentleman who could not make the journey to Vienna or who was just simply not invited. Tournaments also allowed the hosts to show generosity and magnificence. As such, they were ideal sites to premiere ideologically loaded political messages that were intended to be understood by the valued and politically influential guests.[12]

As far as we know, Arcimboldo had little to do with orchestrating the combat at the tournament in August of 1571. He was tasked with devising the opening act – the procession. If the tournament harked back to a bygone medieval past, the procession evoked and idealized classical antiquity. The parading bodies moved through crowds like Julius Caesar and his army after throttling Gaul, or Trajan and his legions brandishing the booty they had taken from the temple in Jerusalem. Yet, whereas Caesar and Trajan had waged war elsewhere and returned victorious with prisoners, slaves, weapons and goods, the participants of Arcimboldo's procession were at a wedding and they were in costume. It was total theatre.

Gian Paolo Lomazzo (1538–1592), the Milanese eccentric, painter, art theorist and rabble rouser, recounted Arcimboldo's procession in his *Trattato* as a means to laud his friend and fellow Lombard. He wrote:

> In fact this man was truly unique in his inventions and more than anything for the conception of masked pageants, so that he was assigned the task of designing the whole festivities on the occasion of the celebrations of the wedding of His Highness, Archduke Charles, Maximilian's brother. For the first tournament in which the Emperor himself took part, he had the happy and unusual idea of having three kings appear, who stood for the three parts of the world Asia, Africa and America, to honor the

> princes of the Austrian dynasty. Asia was represented by Archduke Charles, the bridegroom, Africa by Archduke Ferdinand [Maximilian's brother] and America by the commander of the Archduke's calvary. These happening to find themselves in the appointed place when they heard of the coming wedding festivities, they joined together and offered their services as tournament stewards. Arcimboldo then had Europe meet them, under the guise of four figures representing her four most important provinces, namely Italy, France, Spain, and Germany. Archduke Ernst [Maximilian's son] stood for Italy, Archduke Rudolf [Maximilian's son] for Spain, the Emperor's calvary major for France, and the Emperor himself for Germany. The cloths, insignia, symbols and accompaniers of these persons indicated and signified their respective provinces, and I shall not here count up all the devices, constructions, wonders, and glories of this tournament since that would fill an entire volume.[13]

There is much to say about this lengthy quotation. For our purposes, I want to emphasize just a few of Lomazzo's statements before describing a part of this procession in more detail. First, it is important to keep in mind that it is probable Lomazzo only knew the details of the events he reported on because Arcimboldo relayed them to him personally. Therefore, it is conceivable that the elements of the procession Arcimboldo considered the most important and those he took the most pride in were those presented by Lomazzo.

Lomazzo's description of the 1571 procession recounts only a fraction of the event's content. Classical deities such as Juno, Iris, Diana, Athena, Venus, Neptune and Bacchus made appearances. So too did individuals outfitted as woodsmen and amazons. Other participants in the procession portrayed the cardinal virtues, while still others were garbed in the clothes of Victory and Gluttony. Sirens were also part of the event.[14] Seven of the emperor's chamberlains participated, each dressed as one of the Liberal Arts. Each Liberal Art was accompanied by two illustrious ancients. For instance, Geometry was joined by two men, one in the guise of Archimedes, the other Archytas. It is believed that seven drawings now housed in the Uffizi's Gabinetto dei disegni e delle Stampe are Arcimboldo's original designs for the Liberal Arts, or that the artist based the drawings in Florence on his original designs for the 1571 tournament procession.[15] Unfortunately, beyond these seven drawings the whereabouts of the other designs for the 1571 tournament are unknown.[16] They may never have re-emerged from the tailor's workshop after the costumes had been fabricated.

The extant drawings of the Liberal Arts give us a sense of both what Arcimboldo imagined each figure would wear and what attributes would identify them. The drawings executed for the 1571 procession are uniform in size, roughly 30 × 20 cm (12 × 8 in.). Each displays a single full-length figure, standing frontally or just slightly turned. All the drawings are inscribed at the top in a clean humanist hand. Each inscription identifies the Liberal Art and the Liberal Art's two representatives. Brown ink and blue wash was used in the execution of all the extant drawings. In comparison with Arcimboldo's natural history illustrations, the level of detail is minimal. The style is antiquarian in nature with Arcimboldo placing emphasis on the specificity of the costume rather than on the figure wearing the garment. Take, for example, Astrology (illus. 66). Here the figure dons a full-length belted tabard over a long-sleeved tunic. The tabard carries a border on which Arcimboldo rendered the most schematic of stars. The inscription at the top of the drawing reads, 'Astrology, led by the Alexandrian Ptolemy and the Roman Julius Hyginus. White garment bordered in red with golden stars.'[17] Nothing in the annotation mentions

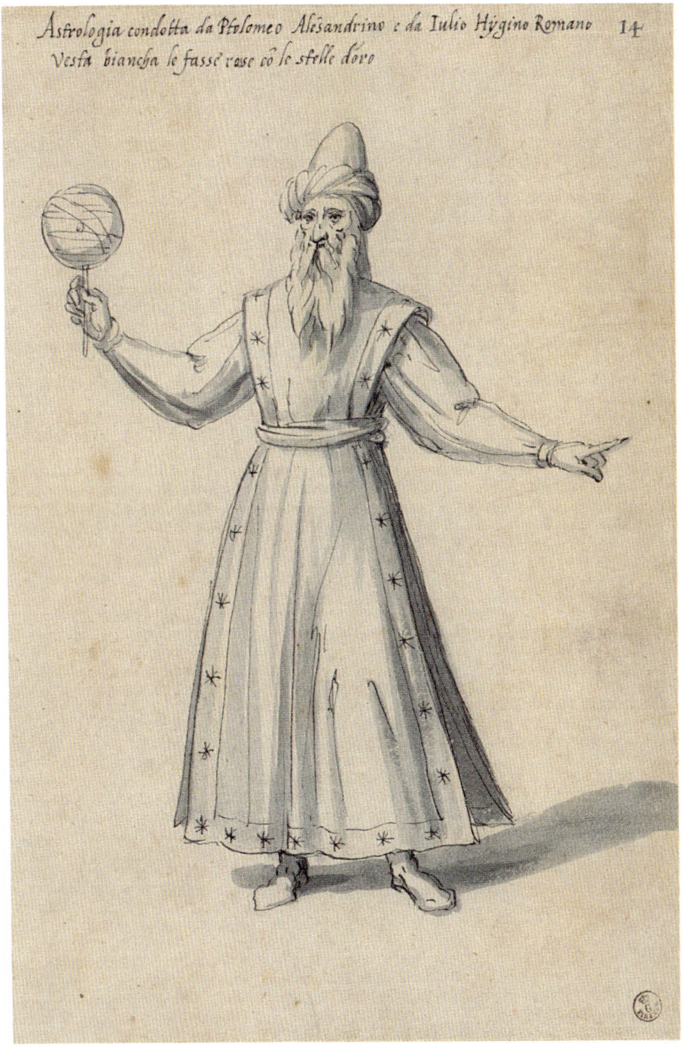

66 Arcimboldo, costume for the allegorical figure 'Astrology', from 'Drawings of Tournaments dedicated to Rudolf II', 1585, pen and watercolour on paper.

Astrology's conical hat, the (presumably) celestial globe or the figure's voluminous facial hair.

FABRICATING CELESTIAL AND TERRESTRIAL HARMONY

Given the time, research and intellectual energy Arcimboldo put into the figures of the Liberal Arts, it is surprising that Lomazzo makes no mention of them. Arcimboldo and, by extension, Lomazzo were markedly proud of the incorporation of the Habsburgs, especially the emperor, into the performance. They also boasted of the originality of the roles the Habsburgs played. The procession afforded Arcimboldo the opportunity to overlay the dynasty and the world. As we will see in a moment, the aspects of space (the continents) and time (dynasty) were central to the entire event and to the political message of the procession. However, before we dive headlong into the particulars, I want to call attention to the fact that Lomazzo goes out of his way to state that Arcimboldo was 'assigned the task of designing the whole festivities'. This claim of authorship is consequential because it attempts to annihilate any trace of collaboration between Arcimboldo and other festival designers. Lomazzo doubled down on this point at the end of his account of the festival. He wrote:

> And all this was the idea and the invention of the inimitable painter, even though a certain Fonteo introduced into the court and assigned by the latter to work on the program of festivities, was so shameless as to claim he was the author of one of these compositions. The Emperor was much amazed when he heard this, as he knew well that the idea came from Arcimboldo with whom he had often discussed.[18]

What a tangled web! I am not concerned with whether Arcimboldo or Fonteo fabricated his role in designing the tournament procession. What is important, in my view, is Lomazzo's and Arcimboldo's desire not only to assert that Fonteo was a liar but to declare that Maximilian deemed Fonteo a storyteller as well. It is not just that Lomazzo, Arcimboldo and Maximilian are of the same mind regarding the true authorship of the procession but that Lomazzo seized upon an opportunity to flaunt publicly the proximity, intimacy and intellectual exchange between the artist and the emperor. How far Arcimboldo has come from his humble days working alongside his father in Milan Cathedral!

Even though Arcimboldo and Lomazzo denied Fonteo's role in the festivities surrounding this celebration of the wedding of 1571, most of what we know about the processions, the pageants and the balls that were organized for the nuptials of Charles of Steiermark and Maria Anna of Bavaria is based on a cartel, or programme, penned by none other than Fonteo. Moreover, a second cartel in Fonteo's handwriting has also been uncovered. In this second document Arcimboldo is listed as the tournament's *fabricator* and Fonteo as the tournament's *coordinator*.[19]

THE NATURE OF A HABSBURG POLITICAL UNIVERSE

Arcimboldo's Seasons and Elements were an adumbration of the tournament procession of 1571. The marriage of Archduke Charles of Steiermark and Maria Anna of Bavaria provided Arcimboldo with the occasion to reconceptualize imperial imagery and the cosmos with profound political significance. The procession itself shows that Arcimboldo strove to invent a new and expanded representation of the early modern European macrocosm and corresponding microcosm. When we consider the 'main cast' of the procession, for lack of a better phrase, it becomes evident that Arcimboldo could easily imagine members of the imperial family and court officials as cosmological actors to amplify their claims of political power.

Arcimboldo orchestrated the event so that it shored up the contention that the Habsburgs oversaw and orchestrated global politics. Both the beginning and the end of the procession functioned as framing devices. Opening the event was the bridegroom himself, Maximilian II's younger brother Archduke Charles, costumed as 'Asia'. He was accompanied by the emperor's other younger brother, Archduke Ferdinand II, who was dressed as a personification of 'Africa'. Charles and Ferdinand were joined by 'America', who was being performed by the commander of the archduke's calvary.[20] So already at the start, the three largest and most (from the perspective of Europe) enigmatic locations on earth are portrayed by three men subordinate to the emperor politically, and two out of the three were subordinate to the emperor by virtue of their birth order. These subsidiary figures were met by other performers personifying the planets, who carried minerals associated with each individual planet. They were also joined by people costumed as the Winds, believed to inhabit the realm between the air and the cosmos, known as the ether. The elements, who were portrayed by imperial administrative figures, came next. The seasons, three of whom were members of the imperial family, followed. The procession concluded with various individuals in the guise of European rivers.

All the figures who met Asia, Africa and America were divided into four groups that represented the four pre-eminent provinces of Europe. That Europe was divided into four parts is understandable, given that Arcimboldo was working with a schema that made sense of the world by organizing it into quaternaries.[21] Arcimboldo was, of course, working with the same schema when he devised the paintings of the Seasons and the Elements. The first of the four groups represented Italy. It was led by two persons dressed as the two easterly winds, Vulturnus and Eurus. Imperial counsellor Wolfgang Rumpf attired as the element Air came next. Air was followed by an individual dressed as Mars and carrying a piece of iron. Maximilian's son Ernst (1553–1595), who was eighteen and Archduke of Austria, came afterwards. It is important to note that Arcimboldo cast the imperial family as the Seasons. Given that Ernst was the youngest of Maximilian's two sons who participated in the procession (Maximilian had a total of six sons and six daughters), it was fitting that he donned the trappings of Spring, since Spring corresponded with the youngest age of Man. Arcimboldo's casting of Ernst also makes sense in the context of a dynastic argument. It is the opening gambit of an explicit dynastic component to the procession; a component that was initially only implicit in Arcimboldo's paintings of the Seasons and the Elements. The River Po was the conclusion of the first group. The inclusion of the rivers helped to signal the geographic locations of the four European groups in the procession.

The second group of processors represented Spain. This time the westerly winds, Africus and Curus, were the ushers. They were tailed by Fire, who was played by Adam Dietrichstein, Maximilian's Supreme Prefect. The Sun, wielding gold, followed behind Dietrichstein. Archduke Rudolf, Maximilian's eldest son, costumed as Summer came next. Rudolf's presence was freighted; this was his first public appearance having returned to the Habsburg German-speaking lands, after spending much of his young life at the Spanish court of Phillip II.[22] The River Hiberus was the last personification of this group, and surely functioned both as a reminder of Rudolf's sojourn as well as a key link to the Spanish line of the Habsburg family.

France was third in the line-up. The southerly winds, Eurus and Notus, headed up the group. The element of Earth was behind them. Jupiter, holding tin, followed. After him came a middle-aged French knight who was cast as Autumn. The end was brought up by a personification of the River Rhône.

The fourth and final group was the most consequential. It represented Germany, the realm of the Austrian Habsburgs. Arcius and Boreas, the northerly winds, heralded the finale. They were followed by an individual dressed as Water. Luna, a personification of the Moon, holding aloft silver was fourth in line. Holy Roman Emperor Maximilian II, in the guise of Winter, followed. The River Danube rounded out the fourth symbolically laden group.

It makes perfect sense why Maximilian II garbed as Winter concluded the procession. Situating the emperor at the end suggested that his time had come. It is also important to keep in mind that by placing Maximilian at the end of the procession, Arcimboldo was suggesting that Maximilian was both a part of the cosmos and the head of the cosmos. It is the same position the artist placed Maximilian in the imperial allegories. This time, however, he stationed Maximilian at the head of a far more comprehensive and complex cosmos.

PROCESSION AS PROGNOSTICATION

To articulate this expanded cosmos, Arcimboldo adapted a conventional neo-Platonic schema of the macro/microcosm.[23] This adaptation not only extended the imperial allegory that he initiated in the paintings of the Seasons and the Elements but allowed Arcimboldo to represent the cosmos and the imperial family in a more complex harmony. For instance, according to a theory of cosmological correspondences going back nine centuries to the writings of the indefatigable scholar and cleric Isidore of Seville (d. 636), the four seasons were considered in conformity with the four cardinal directions.[24] Winter corresponded with the north, and from the perspective of the participants in and spectators of the 1571 procession it was logical that Winter and the northerly winds be grouped under the rubric of 'Germany'. The same can be said of Autumn, the westerly winds and France, and of Summer, the southerly winds and Spain. Italy was the odd man out. Spring and the easterly winds follow the pattern, but Italy is not to 'the east' of any of the European kingdoms represented in the procession. Although slightly awkward, the grouping of Italy with 'the east' does not belie Arcimboldo's ambitious plan to invent, organize and set into motion a universalizing schema of all space, all time and all matter on earth and in the heavens.

The harmonic interaction of the earth and the heavens is of the utmost importance to the procession's imperial message. According to the rationale of Arcimboldo's schema, if the planets, the elements, the seasons and the cardinal directions are not at odds with one another, or in other words, if like is drawn to like, material existence on earth will remain in balance.[25] Evidence of a balanced cosmos is the flourishing of peace and prosperity on earth. And by placing Maximilian at once inside and at the head of the harmonious system, the procession argues that it is the emperor who provides peace and prosperity and will continue to do so. At the same time, however, the procession asserts that this harmony not only allows for the emperor's legitimate rule over Europe but lays the groundwork for the imperial rule of other earthly places and peoples, namely Asia, Africa and America, who initiated (and perhaps were initiated into) the cosmological structure of the procession.

Obviously, like Arcimboldo's paintings of the Seasons and the Elements, the representation of the cosmos presented by the procession does not correspond to one's everyday experience of the world. This is because the procession, as well as any representation of the macro/microcosm, endeavours to capture aspects of the universe that are imperceptible. Without familiarity with the neo-Platonic universalizing schema, it would have been a visually absurd event. Arcimboldo's adaptation of the original schema makes these elements of the universe perceptible; it demonstrates the complexity of the universe; it attempts to make it available to human understanding; and it endows it with an explicit political message. To do this, Arcimboldo asserted an independence of thought in determining what to include and exclude in his schema for the procession of 1571. There are certain elements of the quaternary schema that he entirely omitted, namely the four qualities (hot, cold, dry and wet), the four humours (black bile, yellow bile, blood and phlegm) and the four senses (hearing, seeing, tasting and touching). Arcimboldo takes up only what serves the imperial message and then he supplements it with precious and semi-precious metals carried by the personifications of the planets and the four rivers – all of which situate each quaternary in a geographic space and a political realm.

At this point I want to call attention to a conspicuous fact: even though the procession is a representation of nature, the natural world is expressed in unnatural terms. Thus, like the imperial allegories, Arcimboldo's procession does not have a mimetic relationship to nature. Both projects are artfully artificial. In many ways the procession is a sequel to the imperial allegories. Even though, like the allegories, the procession substitutes human figures for nature's elements, seasons, products (the metals) and geography, it veers away from the conceit of portraiture that was central to the allegories. Instead, the procession operates within the idiom of conventional personification – the bestowal of human form on an abstract quality, place or idea. The painted allegories did this too, but the personifications portrayed in the paintings were unconventional on account of their composite nature, and though they were in some sense personifications, the painter treated the representations as if they were portraits. The bust-length figure in strict profile emphatically associates the allegories with portraiture, specifically ancient Roman imperial portraiture. (Call to mind any coin issued by the Roman Empire with the head of the emperor in profile.)

Despite the difference between the procession and the allegories, it is important to remember a shared feature between the two projects: neither attempts to convey a narrative. Arcimboldo does not set out to convey how the cosmos came to be; the allegories and the procession strive to display the cosmos as Maximilian wanted it to be. Yet the 1571 procession, as stated above, is far more expansive than the painted imperial allegories and made a more explicit dynastic claim. The procession argued that the House of Habsburg controlled, partook of and could mete out the power of the cosmos, and that it would do so for generations; hence the privileged position accorded to the Seasons (three of which were played by Habsburgs) in the procession.

The form of the procession is an apt one to convey the dynastic element of Arcimboldo's cosmos, as it requires that the participants move through space over a period of time.[26] As such, it allows for the representation of the future succession of rulers without falling back on a narrative. Moreover, the procession removes the Habsburg dynasty from the human world twice over. It sets them apart from the other dignitaries and other rulers, who are positioned by Arcimboldo as a passive audience, and the procession also incorporates the Habsburgs into the cosmological order. But as I stated earlier, this is not just any order. It is a stable and consistent order that will be as eternal as the sun and the seasons.

The portrayal of the stable order relies on the omission of the process by which the Habsburgs gained their political position – election and coronation – and it papers over the part played by the electors of the empire, most of whom were guests at the wedding. Most importantly, it was Arcimboldo who facilitated this erasure. The procession also excludes other signs of rulership. The ruler's shrewdness, honour and deliberateness have no place here. Nor do the emperor's subjects and the empire's vast network of bureaucracy. Indeed, the administrative apparatus of the empire is either in disguise or nowhere to be seen. Additionally, the procession lacks religious imagery or a representation of religious authority. As such, it is possible to see the procession as an elaborately choreographed, ritualized performance that omits God's role in the cosmos.

It is no surprise that Maximilian may have wanted to avoid explicitly religious or overtly confessional imagery during this period and on the occasion of this particular marriage. The procession was designed during a stretch of confessional tension in the Holy Roman Empire. Fears of the empire being torn asunder by fighting Protestant factions or distrust between Catholic and Protestant leaders was pervasive. At the centre of questions about how or where one worshipped, as well as questions about the reality of any metaphysical or divine basis of political power, stood Maximilian II, who had very early on in his reign attempted to walk the middle path between his Catholic and Protestant subjects. As a matter of fact, Maximilian II sought compromise between the religious factions and laboured to rule over an empire that was becoming ever more religiously pluralistic.[27] Maximilian threw himself into establishing compromise by inviting an assortment of Protestant and Catholic advisers, physicians, scholars, military commanders, artists and humanists to his court. He also worked to make the Habsburg hereditary lands sites for the settlement of Protestants and Protestant communities. This spirit of compromise, however, was frowned upon by Maria Anna of Bavaria's family. The Wittelsbachs, who ruled over the Duchy of Bavaria, were staunch orthodox Catholics, deeply entangled in the politics of the Church and contributors to Jesuit missions at home and abroad.[28] They also fancied themselves as the right arm and sword of the Counter-Reformation in German-speaking lands. Some of the measures they took to ensure the flourishing of Catholicism in their realm included forbidding Protestants from living and working in Bavaria and criminalizing the sale of books published by Protestant presses.

As Arcimboldo's procession was a supplement to the celebration of the alliance between the Habsburgs and the Wittelsbachs at a time when Maximilian was attempting to establish and maintain strong ties with Protestant electors, it makes good sense that the procession avoided explicit religious imagery. In its place Arcimboldo positions the claim not only that the Habsburgs were the supreme rulers of Europe and America, Asia and Africa, but that Habsburg sovereignty was cosmically ordained and therefore entirely natural. This brings us back, full circle, to the Habsburgs and nature's plenitude. Whereas we opened this chapter with images and objects that claimed nature's plenitude was something external to the dynasty but bestowed on the Habsburgs, we close the chapter with Arcimboldo's claim that the Habsburgs doled out nature's plenitude.

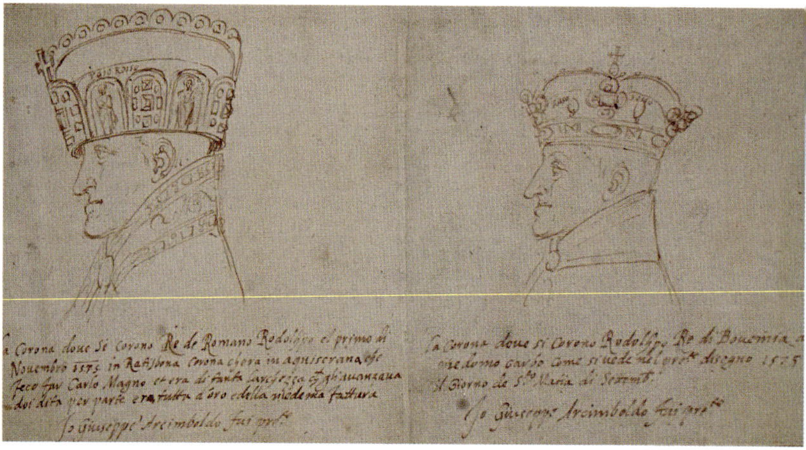

FIVE

Impossible Desires

If the Seasons and the Elements were an adumbration of the 1571 tournament procession then Arcimboldo's portrait of Rudolf II as Vertumnus (illus. 14), the Roman god of the seasons, was the culmination of the Lombard artist's undertaking to naturalize sovereignty by portraying, in unnatural terms, the sovereign as nature. That this was a protracted process is evident when we examine two drawings Arcimboldo put down on paper in 1575. Currently in Prague, the two pen and ink drawings are displayed as a pair, though it is doubtful that they were intended to be viewed side by side (illus. 67).[1] Both drawings portray Rudolf II donning the Habsburg imperial regalia for a coronation. The drawing on the left purports to record the young and remarkably thin Rudolf on All Saints Day (1 November) 1575; the day he was anointed Holy Roman Emperor and given Charlemagne's crown in the Free Imperial City of Regensburg.[2] The inscription beneath the right drawing states that Rudolf is wearing the crown of Wenceslas, which was bestowed upon him on St Matthew's Day (21 September) in 1575, the day he took the Bohemian throne in Prague. Each of these coronations took place after the untimely death of Maximilian II, Rudolf's father, earlier that year.

In each drawing Arcimboldo leaned on one of his favoured portrait formats – the bust-length profile. In both renderings the artist had a light touch, sketching the outlines of the crowns,

67 Giuseppe Arcimboldo, *Two Portraits of Rudolf II with Crown*, 1575, pen and ink on paper.

the mantels and this subject's prominent Habsburgian features. Rudolf's ample, jutting chin and his canine underbite were carefully captured by the artist, as were the emperor's thin lips and heavy eyelids. Rudolf's youthful and slender face seems not to have provided Arcimboldo with folded or furrowed skin to capture. Perhaps the artist made up for this lack of specificity by showering attention (and maybe a little frustration) on Rudolf's left ear. The focus of each drawing is a crown coming into contact with the subject's head. On the left that contact is precarious. Arcimboldo comments on the crown's size in the inscription beneath the drawing. He writes: 'The crown that is located in Aachen was so big that on the sides it has a two-finger-wide gap and was totally made of gold.'[3] Upon reading this statement one cannot help but wonder if Arcimboldo had the honour and the pleasure of measuring with his own fingers the gap between crown and head. I suppose we will never know. We do know the artist made sure to convey that Rudolf was swimming in his coronation attire – Rudolf's sloping shoulders, his minimal neck and the way the crown and mantel almost come to touch at the back of the freshly crowned emperor's head make this apparent to the viewer. Perhaps the regalia's heft contributes to my sense that Rudolf is here portrayed as if seized by despair. The emperor's crown was clearly a heavy one. This was due in large part to the 288 precious stones and pearls that were set into the 'hoop crown', which was made up of eight golden plates hinged together and adorned five hundred years earlier for the coronation of Holy Roman Emperor Otto I (illus. 68).[4]

The drawing on the left makes clear that Arcimboldo attempted to render a detailed likeness of the size and shape of the imperial crown. It is also clear that Arcimboldo was interested in recording the placement of the stones and pearl on the 'hoop' and on the front-left and rear-facing plates. The artist strayed from his model when he drew the 'figure plates'. On the crown itself these

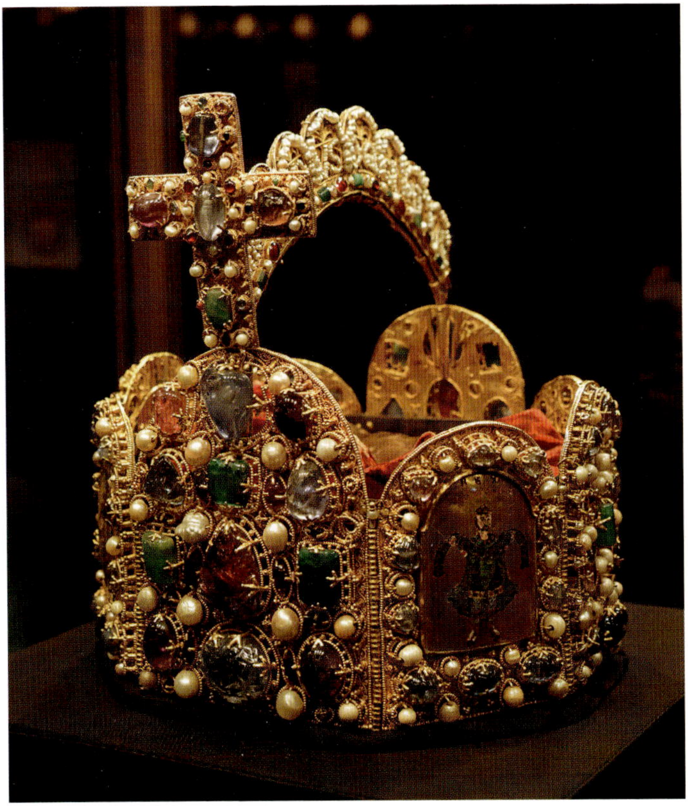

figures – King Solomon and King David from the Hebrew Bible – are cloisonné and executed in a Byzantine style. In no way do the figures of David and Solomon on the crown resemble the classicized figures in Arcimboldo's drawing of the crown. Arcimboldo gave the Wenceslas crown on the right-hand figure a similar amount of attention. Why these drawings were made remains uncertain.[5] Whatever is the case, the drawing of Rudolf on the left is singular in its portrayal of the dissonance between man and crown.

Compare Arcimboldo's drawing of Rudolf attired in regal trappings to Albrecht Dürer's fantastical 'portrait' of Charlemagne

68 The Imperial Crown of the Holy Roman Empire.

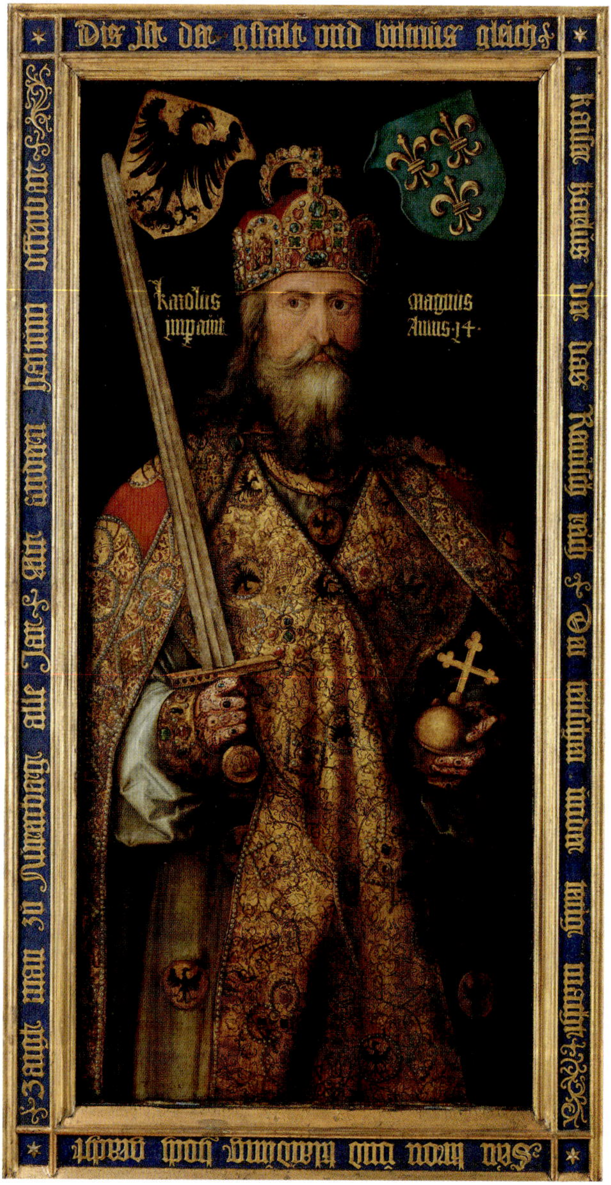

69 Albrecht Dürer, *Emperor Charlemagne*, *c.* 1511–13, oil on panel.

(illus. 69). Dürer's 'portrait' of the founder of the Holy Roman Empire, completed at the request of the Nuremberg city council, was one of a pair of portraits. The other, also painted by Dürer, was of Emperor Sigismund, who ruled the empire from 1433 to 1437. Both paintings were displayed in the Schatzkammer of the Schopper House in Nuremberg where the regalia of the emperor was housed before its annual procession through the streets of Nuremberg, on the Friday following Easter. Dürer's painting of Charlemagne portrays the emperor facing frontally and in three-quarter length, which, as Christopher Wood has shown, harked back to medieval representations of emperors.[6] Emerging from a dark ground, the first 'German' emperor is enveloped in the sacred attire of empire. His brocaded mantel is peppered with imperial eagles and encrusted in gems. He brandishes the imperial sword with his right hand while his left grasps the imperial orb. Charlemagne's broad body exceeds the frame on which is inscribed 'Charlemagne ruled for 14 years. He was the son of the Frankish King Pippin, and Roman Emperor. He made the Roman Empire subject to German rule. His crown and garments are put on display annually in Nuremberg, together with other relics.'[7] Out of this frame the emperor peers solemnly as his long hair and beard at once announce his wisdom as well as his correspondence to Christ. The emperor was, after all, considered to be Christ's vicar on earth. How strikingly different is Dürer's painting of Charlemagne from Arcimboldo's drawing of Rudolf II? Dürer's painting makes it appear as if the regalia was made precisely for the Frankish emperor; Arcimboldo's makes the sitter look as if we have caught him amid a child's game.

It is remarkable that Arcimboldo's first-known portrait of Rudolf II conjures up an image of the emperor toying around in someone else's wardrobe, because the portrait of the emperor the artist executed fifteen years later portrays Rudolf in the guise of a Roman deity who was infamous for his mastery of disguise. I am, of course, referring here to the artist's Rudolf II as Vertumnus. Completed in 1589 in Milan, the portrait was shipped to the emperor along with an explanatory poem by Gregorio Comanini in early 1590. By this time, Arcimboldo's portrait of Rudolf II as Vertumnus was an idea whose time had come. At its core, *Vertumnus* is a painting that redefines the sovereign's body by annihilating it.

CHANGELING

The name 'Vertumnus' is derived from the Latin verb *vertere*, which means 'to change'. Since Vertumnus was deemed the god of the seasons by the ancient Romans, his name was rather fitting. And given his name and his penchant for transformation, it is easy to understand why Ovid cast him as an agent of deceit in the *Metamorphoses*. The Roman poet features Vertumnus along with Pomona, the goddess of gardens and orchards, in the fourteenth book of the *Metamorphoses*.[8] As told by Ovid, Vertumnus is a figure who seduces and destroys as well as a figure who controls time and sparks generativity. The tale opens with Pomona sequestered (of her own volition) from persistent suitors in a walled garden. Attracted to and challenged by the renunciate, Vertumnus sets his mind on possessing her. To do so, he employs his powers of transformation. He attempts to gain entry to the garden by taking on the form of a fisherman, then a fowler and then a hunter.[9] All these attempts fail, as Pomona bars each of Vertumnus's manifestations entry into her garden. After these consecutive failures, Vertumnus tries a different tack. Instead of a gentleman bearing gifts, possessing practical knowledge or displaying physical brawn, he cloaks himself in the guise of a lame crone. He gains Pomona's trust and entry to her garden by offering her the advice of an old, wounded woman. The advice, like its proponent, is disguised. Vertumnus tells Pomona the tragic tale of Iphis, a lowly shepherd whose love was refused by the young Princess Anaxarete. After being spurned, Iphis could not see a way out of his grief, so he hanged himself on the threshold to Anaxarete's house. This humiliation, however, was not enough for Anaxarete, who mocked the deceased shepherd at his own funeral, causing Venus to turn her to stone. To Vertumnus's chagrin, this tragic tale does little to convince Pomona of the merits of her suitors. Finally, Vertumnus (still in disguise) takes a more direct approach and encourages the young goddess to wed so that Pomona's fate will not be that of Anaxarete – petrified forever. Sensing Pomona's deep scepticism, Vertumnus becomes enraged, removes his disguise and begins to ravage Pomona. At first, she struggles against her attacker, but upon seeing Vertumnus's face, upon encountering his true and divine form, she falls in love and transforms a one-sided love into one that is mutual and generative.

This is a rather fitting story for Arcimboldo's portrait of Rudolf as Vertumnus because it centres on a god who reveals himself by showing his true face. Such a divine revelation, in the words of Jean-Pierre Vernant, 'implies a relationship of parity between partners who look one another in the eyes'.[10] He explains that in classical mythology such an encounter could not occur between a god and a mere mortal without the mortal's immediate annihilation or transformation. To avoid Actaeon's fate (being torn limb from limb by his own hounds) when confronted with the deity, mortals must practise 'Looking away, lowering one's eyes to the ground, covering one's head: mortals have no other way to acknowledge their unworthiness and avoid this risk of confronting the unequaled unbearable splendor of the divine countenance.'[11] It seems to me that Arcimboldo's painting of Rudolf as Vertumnus tries to create the sensation in the viewer that we are confronting a form of divine splendour, and we cannot look away.

NATURE'S PERFECTION

In Arcimboldo's *Vertumnus*, the emperor peers out at us through blackberry eyes, breathes through a pear nose and bears pomegranate teeth. His body, presented by the artist in the form of a bust, is composed of a vast assortment of fruits, vegetables and flowers that ripen and bloom at different times throughout the year. A pumpkin takes the place of his chest, an artichoke stands in for his left shoulder, a radish protrudes from his throat and a chestnut marks his chin. A garland of flowers, all in full bloom, is draped across the emperor's torso. Crowned with a spray of wheat and bunches of grapes, Rudolf is likened to Christ.

> Jesus took the bread, and after blessing it broke it and gave it to the disciples and said, 'Take, eat: this is my body.' And he took a cup, and when he had given thanks he gave it to them, saying, 'Drink of it, all of you, for this is my blood of the covenant, which is poured out for many for the forgiveness of sins.' (Matthew 26:26–8)

Of course, Christ gave his own body so that humanity could be born again from their graves. Arcimboldo's portrait argues that Rudolf and his reign will never come to an end.[12]

What is this eternal body that looks out at us from the portrait? It is not a mortal body. It is a body that is associated with nature's peak productivity. By its very nature, it is a body that is life-giving and nutritive. It is also a body that does not require self-maintenance or self-preservation. Irregularities and mutations have been excluded. Parasites are nowhere in sight. Diseases, too, are absent. Waste has been eliminated. Filth has been washed away. Putrefaction banished. As such, Arcimboldo's portrait of Rudolf II is an eager, virtuosic and imaginative denial of the loss or deterioration of the sovereign body. Arcimboldo has also constructed a body completely closed off to the world and to the bodies of others. In the guise of Vertumnus, the body of the emperor is expunged of any orifices or openings. Vertumnus cannot tune his ear to anything or anyone. There are no lines of communication, and none could be forged without piercing Vertumnus's body of abundance. This was not the case with Arcimboldo's painting of Maximilian II in the guise of Winter, where the artist lavished attention on the gnarly and knotted bark surrounding a void stuffed with dead wood that reads as Winter's ear. Perhaps Arcimboldo recognized that to portray a sovereign's bodily openings would entail carving out a space in the body that would always be empty; that would always be lacking.

It is possible to see this composite portrait of the emperor as Arcimboldo's effort to mask and repress the vulnerability and finitude of the sovereign body. However, this desire to portray the sovereign body as an everlasting font of life has, in the end, created an image more akin to death than life because Arcimboldo has created a body that is resistant to time and impervious to change. It follows that this articulation of the sovereign body heralds a departure from that which the artist put forth in the imperial allegories and procession of 1571. To be clear, the imperial allegories, the procession of 1571 and the portrait of Rudolf as Vertumnus argue that the Habsburgs do not stand apart from nature, and by dint of being part of nature they partake of nature's powers. This distinguishes them from all other humans and legitimates their claim to rule the Holy Roman Empire and even the world. The differences between *Vertumnus* and the imperial allegories and the 1571 procession centre on the early works' recognition of the passing of time as well as the emperor's progeny. In the portrait of Rudolf as Vertumnus, the passage of time has been halted and the need for heirs has been eradicated.

This figure of eternal self-sufficiency emerges from the darkness of the picture's ground. It is here where we encounter the emperor's body embodying the bounty of the world, all at once.

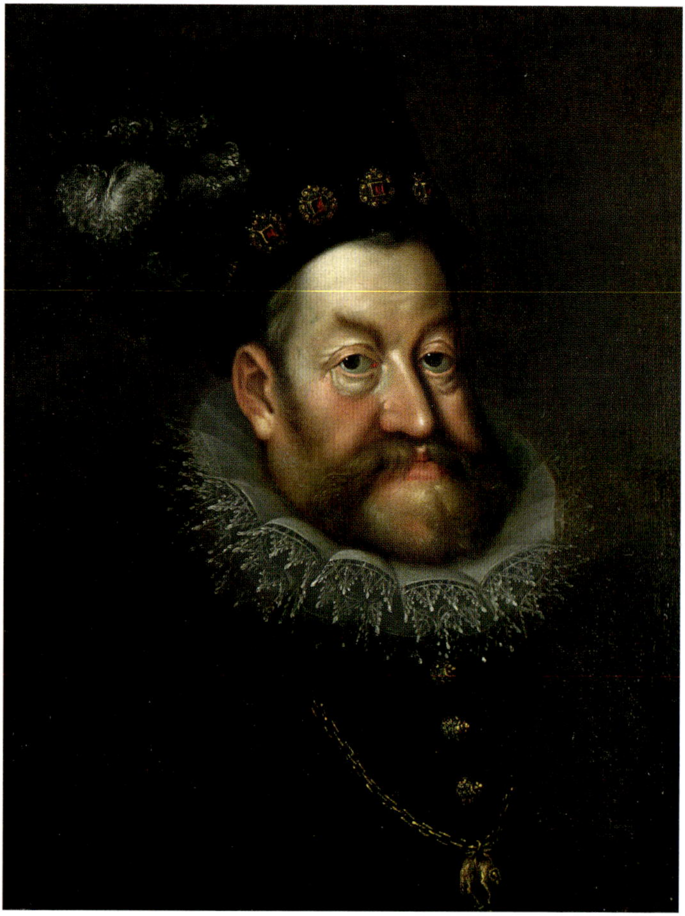

'This undifferentiated conjunction of seasons', writes Kaufmann, 'suggests that they form one undifferentiated season: this is the mark of the Golden Age that has come with the reign of Rudolf. This Holy Roman Emperor is thus shown as the ruler of a new Rome that will enjoy the eternal domination of the world.'[13] According to Arcimboldo's painting, this mastery has not been bestowed on the emperor by God or bloodline or the worldly

70 Hans von Aachen, *Rudolf II*, *c.* 1606–8, oil on canvas.

powers who elected him. Instead, Rudolf's mastery, and by extension his power, is presented as inherently natural, as evidenced by the total lack of imperial trappings, such as regalia or heraldry; and the variety of the earth's bounty, so carefully rendered and situated in the portrait, signals that Rudolf's power will be eternal. As I have written elsewhere, in Arcimboldo's painting of Rudolf II as Vertumnus, portraiture becomes an allegory hidden in plain sight, just as the allegory lightly conceals a portrait of the emperor.[14]

When compared to any other portrait of Rudolf II, Arcimboldo's rendering of the emperor teeming with organic life reads as if it were mask. Consider another portrait of the emperor, by the court painter Hans von Aachen, completed just a few years after Rudolf first saw himself as Vertumnus (illus. 70). Just as in Arcimboldo's portrait, the emperor is depicted in a conventional bust-length three-quarter view, and just as in Arcimboldo's portrait the emperor is in a contextual void against a dusky ground. He wears a black and weighty mantel that bears three buttons in the shape of rosettes, crafted from gold or gilded metal and a cobalt enamel. The chain of the Order of the Golden Fleece, with its eviscerated ram, dangles lifeless before the emperor's heart. A white ruff with a delicate and finely rendered lace envelops the emperor's neck. The open work of the lace strikes a contrast to Rudolf's wispy chestnut-coloured beard. Von Aachen's care in describing the details of Rudolf's countenance is perhaps most evident beneath the emperor's eyes, where the soft, thin skin both sinks and puffs. The eyelids too are described with the utmost precision as we see the papery skin folding in and over itself. Though Rudolf's eyes are trained on us, they show little sign of actually seeing; one even fails to find the world reflected in them. Perhaps this is why our eyes float upward to his expansive brow, which acts as a mount for his snug felt hat, embellished with rubies in ornate settings and a flurry of grey feathers.

Unlike when he gazed upon the von Aachen portrait of himself, when Rudolf II looked at Arcimboldo's *Vertumnus*, he contemplated a picture of an emperor who was more imperial than himself. Moreover, he saw himself overestimated and overvalued, and his power grossly exaggerated. What must it feel like to see yourself having powers to which no bounds can be set? The degree and the effect of this estrangement we will never know. Though Arcimboldo's painting is an example of the dissolution of the self into objects, it is also an attempt to portray the suffusion of the emperor throughout the world. Given that the painting proposes that the emperor and nature are one and the same, is the logical extension of the equation not that the emperor exists in every single element of nature; that Rudolf is everywhere and in everything? Or could it be that the work asserts that the emperor is otherworldly and remote? I think it is possible that the painting undermines its own message by successfully making both claims.

THE NECESSITY OF POESIS

This reading of Arcimboldo's *Vertumnus* is perhaps at odds with two poems deeply connected to the painting. The first poem is linked to the work's origin; the second, to its reception. Thomas Kauffman has shown the second poem in the fourth book of Sextus Propertius's *Elegies* was an important source for Arcimboldo's novel and idiosyncratic take on the Roman god of the seasons.[15] Written in the first century BCE, Propertius's elegy is an aetiological and archaeological account of a bronze cult statue of Vertumnus, the statue's placement in a temple on the Roman forum and the vegetal and floral offerings the people of Rome bestowed on to the deity. In addition to describing the placement of the temple on a bend of the River Tiber, the poem describes the appearance of the figure of Vertumnus morphing into a charioteer, a fisherman, a peddler, a shepherd and finally into horticulture: taking on the form of a rose, a cucumber, a squash, a mulberry and several other fruits and vegetables which make up and are prominent in Arcimboldo's portrait.[16] But there is still more the verse can teach us about the painting. In the elegiac distich, the bronze figure of the god who 'changed his appearance and yet always remained the same' stands in a small, unassuming temple on the Roman forum, where the Tiber had been forever diverted (*verso*) and where Romans offered the fruits of the ever-returning (*vertentis*) spring to the god of 'many manifestations' in autumnal harvest rites.[17]

In Propertius's account of the cult's permanent site and annual cult ritual, we have a confluence of two different types of change, one that is unalterable (the river) and the other, cyclical (spring's fruition). The wondrousness of such a union of stability and fluidity within a singular entity is presented as a conundrum by the elegy, which opens: 'The one substance, but many manifestations? A marvel for the clarification of which we may turn to the Tuscan god, Vertumnus, who changed his appearance and yet remained always the same.' As Thomas S. Suits has suggested, there are two ways to read the elegy. The first: a fabulous fable that afforded Propertius the opportunity to provide an account of the etymology of the name 'Vertumnus'.[18] Throughout the poem Propertius makes the god Vertumnus into a nexus of different types and degrees of change – diversion, reversion, aversion and conversion – to shore the god's status as a supreme changeling. There is another way to read the elegy: as a figuration of the interminability of change. However, it is important to note that, in contrast to Propertius's fantastic figure of constant becoming, Arcimboldo's Vertumnus is portrayed as unchanging or as pure being.

This fantasy, which is grounded on an unattainable desire, is not the same type of fantasy that Gregorio Comanini put forth in the poem he wrote to elucidate Arcimboldo's *Vertumnus* in 1589.

Comanini was interested in lauding fantastical images that are conjured in the mind of the artist – images 'of things that have no substance, like tritons, sphinxes, centaurs, and other fabulous monsters'.[19] The poem, which Comanini deemed a 'new type of poem', had two lives. The first iteration of Comanini's poem accompanied the painting on its journey from Milan to Prague in 1589 and was presumably read by or to Rudolf II upon his being presented with *Vertumnus* in early 1590. The second iteration was couched in the Milanese canon's treatise on painting, *Il Figino* (1591). Written as a dialogue between Father Ascanio Martinengo, Stefano Guazzo, a learned gentleman from Pavia, and Ambrogio Figino, a Milanese portrait painter, the treatise wrestles with painting's purpose – should painting be didactic or should it be pleasurable? In it, Comanini hails Arcimboldo as 'a tremendous ingenious fantastic painter, and one to be most highly commended'.[20] In the treatise, the poem comes to stand in for the painting, for as we are told, though bound for Prague, the painting remained in the artist's rooms, unseen by any of Comanini's interlocuters.[21] The poem is also a vehicle for Comanini to place praise for the artist into Vertumnus's mouth. Acclaim begins with a paradox. Consider the opening lines:

> Whoever you are looking at me,
> A strange and deformed image . . .
> If in looking you don't admire the ugliness that makes
>   me handsome,
> It's that you don't know that ugliness surpasses beauty.[22]

Following a description of Jove's transformation of chaos into the cosmos and after a litany of the myriad fruits, vegetables and blooms that form the body of Vertumnus, the poet returns to the heart of the matter:

But I pride myself
Most of all I delight in,
I arrogantly stretch myself to the sky,
In that I am like a Silenus, as
Dear to the young Greek as to the old one;
Esteemed by Plato, for on the outside
I seem a monster, and on the inside I
hide a kingly image and
a heavenly resemblance
Now tell me if it pleases you
To see what I have to hide
Now that I lift my veil
Holy invincible, supreme, august
And righteous Rudolf, honor of Austria.[23]

Just as Silenus's horrid appearance hides something beautiful and truthful within, so too does Vertumnus's monstrous appearance obfuscate something glorious. But before he concludes Comanini reminds us that this cosmic mask – which so effectively conceals and reveals the sovereign and which engendered the verse that animates and explicates the painting – was generated by the sovereign's most devoted painter.

Thus like a learned Egyptian Arcimboldo covered
Your royal face with a veil of lovely fruits
The most loyal, and the best servant
That consecrates his heart and work to your crown.[24]

It is obvious that Comanini wanted to convey the imperial significance of Arcimboldo's composite portrait, and the artist's utter devotion and submission to his patron. Remarkably, in *Il Figino*, at the conclusion of the poem Comanini praises the artist's skill, when he writes, 'Bear in mind that all the fruit and flowers in the painting imitate with the greatest possible accuracy.'[25]

It is important not to lose sight of Comanini's coupling of Arcimboldo's devotion to the crown and the artist's 'accuracy'. We will return to this pairing soon. Before we do, though, I want to draw attention to the fact that in Comanini's *Il Fígino* and in his poem that accompanied the *Vertumnus* painting from Milan to Prague, Comanini discounts the importance of the physical act of painting to the artist as well as to the emperor. In doing so, Comanini construes the painting of Rudolf as Vertumnus to be solely a product of the artist's unsurpassed ingenuity. Comanini even implies that the image of Rudolf as Vertumnus was formed whole, in the mind of the artist, as if Arcimboldo, like Jove, effortlessly ordered the cosmos of his picture. Thus, Comanini promotes the fiction, popular during the period in question, that the artist's initial imaginings of the subject corresponded exactly to the completed painting on panel. In *Il Fígino*, Comanini mentions Arcimboldo's 'skill', but this 'skill' is divorced from any mental or physical strain. Nor is Arcimboldo's skill taken to be the result of any form of training, practice, uncertainty or simple trial and error. In other words, Comanini's portrayal of artistic production is a fantasy in itself and suggests that the author either was unaware of artistic practices or wanted to omit discussion of those practices, so he could commend Arcimboldo's superiority in fashioning fantastic imagery.

Yet, even after an initial viewing of Arcimboldo's *Vertumnus*, one cannot help but register that both the intellectual and manual difficulty ranked high among things Arcimboldo cared about. Arcimboldo put a great deal effort into his paintings. Now is not the time to pinpoint every arduous task Arcimboldo was confronted with in producing *Vertumnus* and his other composite heads. It is, however, worth mentioning a few. Just consider what it took to gather the fruit, vegetables, plants and flowers necessary for the composition. Think about the amount of time throughout the growing season that Arcimboldo devoted to the raw materials of his picture. After procuring each of nature's products, he had to study intently and presumably draw each component. And the painting bears witness to the extraordinary lengths Arcimboldo went to in portraying each individual element naturalistically. He analysed each component's shape, texture and colour with care. He must have gone to great pains to draw equivalences between each component and each facial feature, each joint and each bodily bulge. This must have demanded that he manipulate every one of nature's products that he painstaking portrayed, so that he could assess it from every angle. After determining which portion of the fruit, vegetable or flower would stand in for a part of the sovereign's body, he had to ensure that it would still read as the chosen body part when adjacent to other components. In other words, every single component had to be minutely adjusted so that it could be placed into a totality that could have only come into being through uncertainty and then through trial and error. This process must have demanded intense self-correction. Imagine the minor alterations, the subtle emendations, the additions, the subtractions.

When considering all these procedures and the many others that went into the fashioning of *Vertumnus* and all of Arcimboldo's composite heads, it becomes evident that these allegorical paintings and his other composite portraits were not intended to appear effortless. These paintings demand that we will note and applaud the complexity of their execution. In some small way, even, an aspect of this strain that the artist exerted in producing the composite heads is transferred to the careful viewer. This is because the viewer must take multiple steps to begin to understand the content of the painting and how it was made. Must it not be the case that Arcimboldo yearned to engender recognition of his paintings' intricacy and adroitness in his intended audience? And must it not be the case that Arcimboldo hoped that this recognition would lead to his aggrandizement? Or, to put it slightly differently, the strenuousness of making the works was instrumental. Possibly, it was intended to impress and please the sovereign as well as to elevate the sovereign's opinion of and devotion to the artist. Or, perhaps, we might see Arcimboldo's exertion as a gesture of gratitude. Do not forget that roughly three years before gazing upon himself as a mythological being, Rudolf had bestowed upon Arcimboldo a noble title. It is conceivable that the effort Arcimboldo exerted was a gesture of reciprocity.

Whether or not Rudolf regarded the painting as a sign of gratitude, we may never know. We do know, however, that Arcimboldo's painting of Rudolf as Vertumnus makes apparent the contrived relation between objects of nature and the emperor. The painting also embodies two competing claims: that the sovereign was at once otherworldly and suffused throughout the world. In the end this painting reveals, like Arcimboldo's other imperial allegories and his 1571 tournament procession, the desire to desire the impossible.

SIX

To Make a Face

Though *Vertumnus* may have been Arcimboldo's ultimate portrayal of the imperial family, it was not his final work. After his departure from Prague and his return to Milan in 1587, Arcimboldo developed a new type of picture, which required a novel approach to viewing. This final chapter centres on three examples of this new work. Each painting represents (or seems to represent) two different subjects and fuses two opposing genres – still life and portraiture. Two of the three paintings are typically referred to as Arcimboldo's 'invertible paintings' because when oriented in one direction each is a conventional still life, but when turned upside down the still life morphs into a humanoid face. Now titled *The Vegetable Gardener* (1590) (illus. 10) and *Invertible Head with a Basket of Fruit* (1590) (illus. 15), the paintings are housed in Cremona and New York respectively.[1] The third work, *Flora* (1589) (illus. 16), resides in Stockholm. In *Flora* the double subject does not appear when the painting is turned on its head but rather depends on the viewer's proximity to the painting. From a distance, *Flora* appears to be the representation of a woman, but when seen up close the figure dissolves into an abundance of infinitesimal flowers.

Scholars have understood Arcimboldo's 'invertible paintings' to be products of the sixteenth-century craze for *lusus naturae* or 'jokes of nature'.[2] For sixteenth-century princes, naturalists and collectors of curiosities alike, nature was at her most jocular or most playful when she imitated herself and when she imitated man. Naturalists found nature mimicking herself when they stumbled upon a piece of jasper in the shape of a cobra or a lemon that looked like an eagle's beak, and they discovered her aping man when her products appeared like him – for instance, a coconut endowed with human physiognomy or a phallic mushroom that oozed milky fluid. Placed on shelves or tucked away in the drawers of cabinets, such singularities as well as their depictions were a mainstay of sixteenth-century collecting – noble, academic and mercantile. The anomalous and potentially accidental resemblance of one thing to another was key to the recognition of nature's play, as well as one of the premises of Arcimboldo's paintings addressed in this chapter, which were also once part of princely collections.[3] Yet, Arcimboldo was not merely manufacturing curiosities in his invertible paintings, nor was he merely set upon eliciting a chortle from his viewers. Kaufmann has demonstrated that Arcimboldo's invertible paintings were 'serious jokes' as they not only 'evoked delight' but pictorially demonstrated the similarities between nature's inventiveness, or caprice, and the caprice of art.[4]

IN JEST

According to early modern naturalists, nature betrayed her jocularity when she brought two different entities into harmonious coexistence, like when the root of a plant resembled Christ on the cross.[5] Arcimboldo's invertible paintings embody this playfulness twice over. On one hand, you have the concurrence of the human and the vegetal, and on the other hand, you have fusion of portraiture and still life. Arcimboldo was hardly the first artist to mimic nature mimicking man; take, for instance, Marcus Gheeraerts' *Allegory of Iconoclasm* from 1566 (illus. 71). Nor was Arcimboldo unique in his amalgamation of two genres or subjects in a single work. As Stephen Campbell has shown, Giorgione and other Venetians transformed Venetian painting through 'the combination, insetting, "grafting" of heterogeneous elements', such that a single work can be associated with more than one subject or with opposing forces, such as paganism and Christianity.[6] Titian's *Pope Alexander VI Presenting Bishop Jacopo Pesaro to St Peter* (*c*. 1503–6) (illus. 72) is one example. Here Pope Alexander VI augustly presents a kneeling Pesaro to an imposing St Peter, enveloped in heavy lustrous fabric, atop a classical carved relief bearing libidinous Bacchic rituals. Like Titian's painting, Arcimboldo's invertible heads also harmoniously embody a discontinuity of sorts. But whereas Titian's discontinuity, as Campbell has shown, is poetical, Arcimboldo's is epistemological. This is why: the paintings present themselves to be an artist's description of the world as it appeared before him. But in fact, they are carefully fabricated, artfully composed fictions. However, even though the works discussed in this chapter are neither imitative nor truthful, they manifest the truth of things – seeing is deceiving. As such, *The Vegetable Gardener*, *The Invertible Head with Basket of Fruit* and *Flora* are instructive. They teach rather than resemble, and they do so because the paintings work to sensitize the viewer to the subtle impact of what often goes unnoticed in a humanly arranged and ordered world. But before we dive headfirst into what and how these works channel one to see artifice, some context.

ARCIMBOLDO AND MILAN

All of the paintings examined in this chapter were conceived and executed around 1589, upon Arcimboldo's return to Milan and while he was sharing living quarters with the poet Giovanni Filippo Gherardini.[7] As you will recall, just prior to his homecoming, Arcimboldo had spent almost the entirety of the previous 25 years at the imperial court in Vienna and Prague contributing to Maximilian II's and Rudolf II's ever-expanding collections of

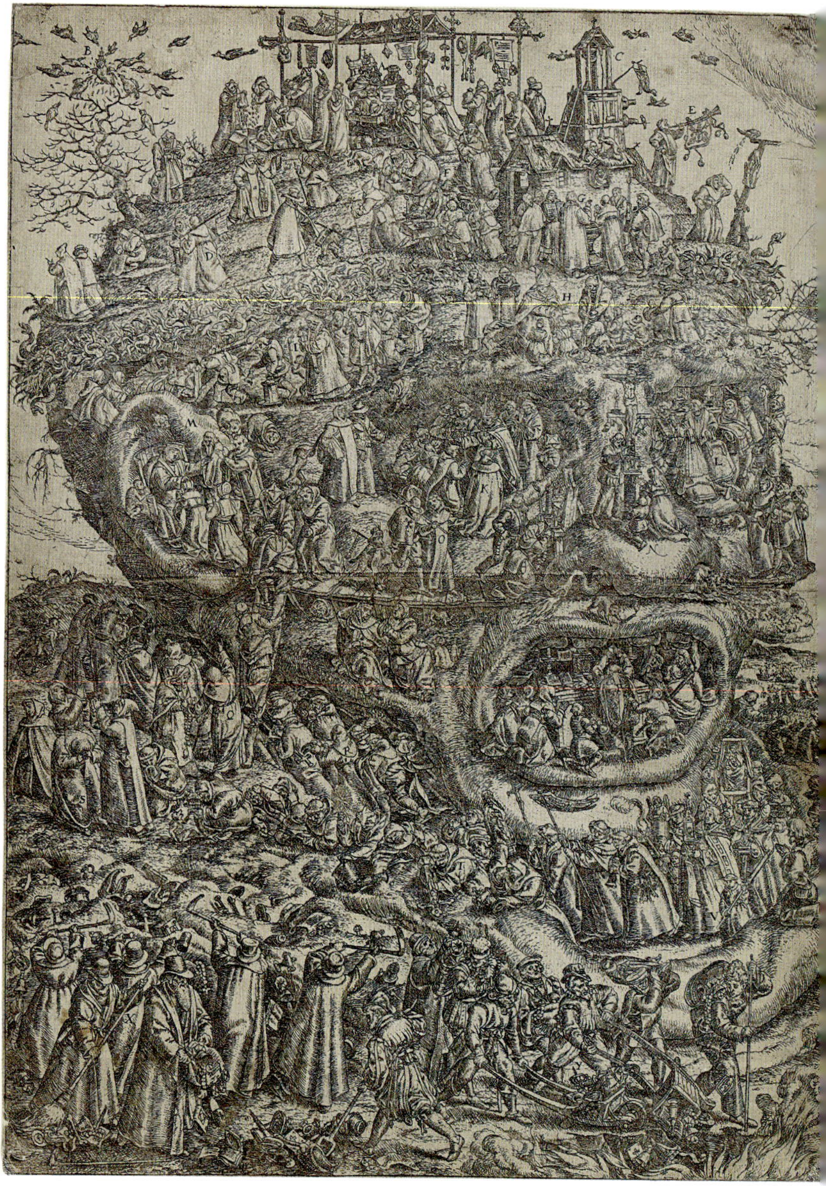

71 Marcus Gheeraerts, *Allegory of Iconoclasm*, 1560–70, etching.

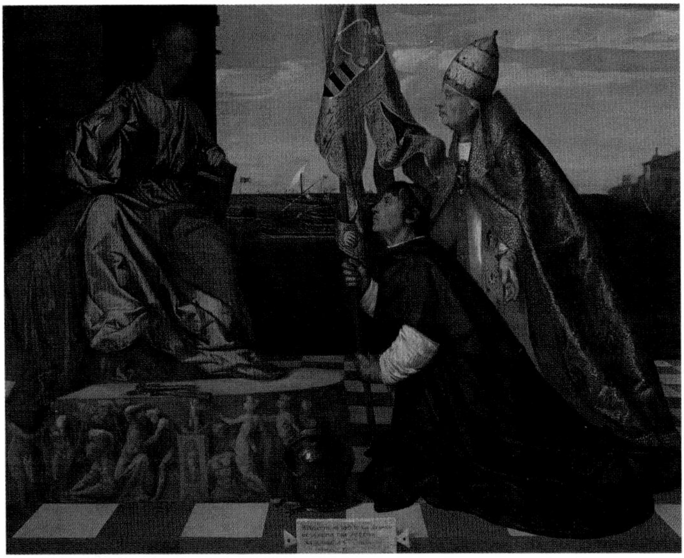

natural history illustration, devising and producing the imperial allegories of the Seasons and the Elements, and designing court spectacles, such as tournaments. For his tireless commitment to the imperial crown, Arcimboldo received a Letter of Patent from Rudolf II in 1592, which granted the artist and his progeny the pretensions of nobility.[8] Rarely given out, the honour was solely based on the emperor's esteem of the recipient.

Once settled in Milan, Arcimboldo set about relaying his many achievements and courtly acclaim to the local community of artists and intellectuals. Recall Gian Paolo Lomazzo's account of the tournament procession Arcimboldo designed for Maximilian II's brother, Archduke Charles, discussed in Chapter Four, which appeared in Lomazzo's *Trattato* (1584). In addition to Lomazzo, we know that Arcimboldo regaled the historian Paolo Morigia and the canon Gregorio Comanini with accounts of his life and accomplishments in Vienna and Prague.[9] Morigia even penned a fantastical genealogy of the Arcimboldo family in his

72 Titian, *Pope Alexander VI Presenting Bishop Jacopo Pesaro to St Peter*, c. 1503–6, oil on canvas.

La nobiltà di Milano (1595) to shore up Arcimboldo's new-found nobility. Comanini composed the poem that accompanied Vertumnus to the imperial court and republished it in his treatise, *Il Figino* (1591). In the same year Giovanni Filippo Gherardini published a booklet of poems in Latin and Italian in which another poem about *Vertumnus* appeared as well as a poem dedicated to *Flora*.[10] (Gherardini's verses on *Flora* were also republished in Lomazzo's *Idea*.)[11] Remarkably, a madrigal by a 'G. A. da Milano' which extolled *Vertumnus* was also published in Gherardini's booklet. The same publication also contained a sonnet praising all Arcimboldo's painting by the same 'G. A. da Milano'.

Given Arcimboldo's embrace by the intellectual community in Milan, it is no accident that sometime after arriving in the city, he portrayed himself as a man of letters (illus. 19). Currently housed in the Palazzo Rosso in Genoa, this drawing (briefly mentioned in Chapter One) is one of three self-portraits of the artist we know of.[12] In the extant drawing, the artist portrays himself staring vacantly into the middle distance. A thick and stiff collar of meticulously curled paper envelops his neck. The curls, which turn inward on themselves, strike a subtle contrast with the individual twisted strips of paper that make up the artist's full beard and moustache. Flat pieces of paper layered one atop the other take on the role of the artist's skin, their articulated edges reading as lines on Arcimboldo's surprisingly youthful face. A crumbled piece of paper, which stands in for the artist's left ear, is perhaps the most eye-catching detail of the whole self-portrait and looks as if it was plucked out of a dustbin. This wad is a pictorial evocation of the artist's seemingly fortuitous encounter with an accidental, though legible, form and is a testament to his skill at projecting representation on to an inchoate shape. It is notable that even though his ear is composed of a piece of debris, the artist's clothes appear courtly, which in turn casts him as someone learned. Indeed, it is Arcimboldo's intellect and bookishness that was praised in Comanini's *Il Figino*. In the dialogue, after Figino provides a meticulous and adoring description of Arcimboldo's painting of Vertumnus and Earth, Guazzo remarks:

> I don't recall ever before having seen such charmingly inventive paintings or such learned allegories as these. I know that a good painter needs to be as well read as the good poet because his knowledge enables him to become another Proteus, transforming himself into diverse forms and dressing in costumes of others, as is appropriate for a good imitator.[13]

According to Guazzo, it is not only the artist's creations but the artist who is made up of 'diverse forms'. Arcimboldo's recognition of his own protean qualities is laid bare by his own self-portrait. For what is it composed on and of? Why, the very stuff of books. Paper, a material whose sole purpose is to bear the mark of change, to be written and drawn upon, to be creased neatly, to be scrunched up, and whose function – letter, drawing, map, book – can be easily altered. Moreover, in Arcimboldo's drawing this very mutable material becomes something it is not – hair, skin, a collar – and by transforming bits of himself into paper he constructs himself out of the very material support of his self-portrait. Such a self-conscious play with his own image speaks volumes about the artist's desire to flaunt his power of intellect, imagination and ingenuity.

IMPOSSIBLE REALITIES

As we have seen throughout this book, Arcimboldo excelled at building his fantastical imagery out of mimetic components. His attention to the description of the natural world was like that of many of his fellow Milanese painters. Though sixteenth-century northern Italian painting was heterogeneous in style, function and content, at the end of the sixteenth century painters in Milan were invested in painting works whose naturalism was enhanced through the mastery of certain visual effects – the lustre or the sheen of fabric, the reflection of light off opaque solids and the portrayal of light moving through transparent objects.[14] Arcimboldo's late paintings, produced in Milan, partake of this tradition while literally turning it on its head.

Although Arcimboldo returned to his native home, it is evident that a long and deep experience of courtly art in Vienna and Prague made an important difference in his later works, particularly the invertible heads. His time at court, arguably, also had an impact on how he viewed himself at the time of his homecoming. Back in Milan, Arcimboldo was no longer a young artist among many, working alongside his father and others on large church frescoes, designs for stained glass and cartoons for tapestries, as he had been before he left for Vienna. Now he was a freshly minted noble, who had just returned from the imperial court where he had been named the official portrait painter to two consecutive emperors. As the previous chapters have shown, while he was at court Arcimboldo developed a radically new means for representing imperial power while displaying great ingenuity and skill in his establishment of the composite head as a new type of subject. The works he created in the last six years of his life would accentuate his imaginative prowess, build upon his painterly skills and bolster his intellectual persona.

As in the earlier composite paintings, in these late Milanese pictures Arcimboldo placed emphasis on individual figures against a dark ground. But to his composite mode the artist added the conceit of the invertible image. Oriented in one direction, an invertible painting reads as a still life – a bowl or a basket brimming with fruit and vegetables – but when turned upside down the painting resembles the head of a human. It should be noted, however, that

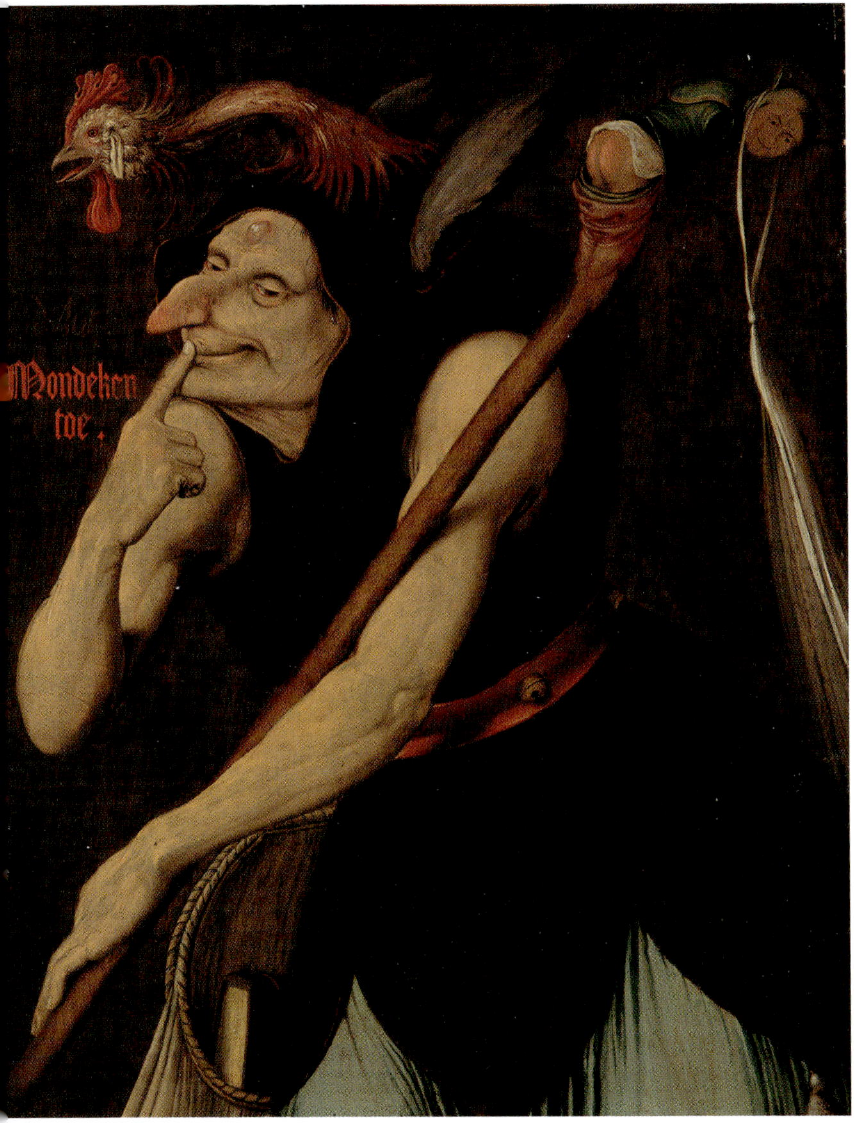

73 Quinten Metsys, *Keep Your Mouth Shut (Allegory of Folly)*, *c.* 1528, oil on panel.

the invertible paintings do not attempt to portray any particular human, which was the case in the paintings of the Seasons and the Elements, as well as his portrait of Rudolf II as Vertumnus. Thus, rather than a human figure taking on the character of a still life, in the invertible paintings a still life takes on the characteristics of a human, with exaggerated, though not specific, features. Consequently, unlike in Arcimboldo's earlier works executed at the imperial court, still life and portraiture coexist but not as easily. One might even go so far as to say that, on account of their lack of physiognomic specificity, the figures portrayed in the invertible paintings are more objects than persons. Indeed, the humanoid faces in the invertible paintings neither register any knowing looks nor convey any emotion. Furthermore, when Arcimboldo placed his paintings of the Seasons and the Elements in strict profile, so that hung together a Season and a corresponding Element would face each other, he conveyed an important element to the work beyond the physical limits of the frame. To put it another way, each Season and each Element was made with the virtual presence of another in mind. This is not the case with the invertible paintings, whose faces seek out nothing, but who encourage the viewer to seek out faces.

Whereas Arcimboldo's imperial allegories called to mind representations of Roman emperors, his invertible heads evoke representations of fools, such as Quentin Metsys's *Keep Your Mouth Shut* (*Allegory of Folly*) (*c.* 1528) (illus. 73). Like the fool in Metsys's work, the 'figures' in Arcimboldo's invertible paintings are placed almost against the picture plane, which contributes to their ironic monumentality.[15] The extravagant physiognomy of Arcimboldo's 'figures' is also like Metsys's – cheeks puff; eyes cross; jaws hang slack. As with representing the face of a fool, variety and variability are key. Indeed, when we look on Metsys's image of a fool or Arcimboldo's distorted visages, we are reminded of the fact that faces are mobile, fluid and able to morph into something else in the blink of an eye. Faces, as Lorraine Daston has pointed out, are as mutable as clouds.[16]

PICTORIAL FORTUITY

It is no wonder that Arcimboldo's invertible paintings call clouds to mind because when he was designing and painting them he was playing with a category of image that clouds exemplify – the accidental image or the image made by chance. Representations made by chance were considered representations that seemingly emerged, without the use of human hands, out of an inchoate form. By the time Arcimboldo painted his invertible paintings, accidental images had been extensively written about and discussed for over 1,000 years. Pliny in his natural history writes of nature tendering images of 'centaurs and faces of bearded kings in cracked blocks of marble', and Pliny as well as Aristotle, Lucretius and Philostratus wrote of images taking shape in clouds.[17] These ancient discussions also informed investigations into accidental images, which like the jasper cobras or the beaky lemons were considered 'jokes of nature' by students of natural history in the sixteenth century. Ulisse Aldrovandi's *Musaeum Metallicum* (1648), for instance, was full of accounts and pictures of stones that took on the form of something else: a human limb, a saint or a cross, for example. When writing about chance images, Renaissance artists added another actor to the discourse, namely the artist. For Leonardo or Alberti, chance images were representations that emerged from an inchoate form that came into existence by chance, without the intervention of human hands, but that were discernible by an imaginative artist. In Renaissance art theory, the material out of which a chance image appeared varied widely, from clouds, stains on a wall and striations in stone, to the shape of tree. What representations materialize from these contingent and amorphous shapes depends on what the artist chooses to see in them – an elephant, a landscape or a sleeping baby – whatever the case, the possibilities, at least in theory, are endless. Leonardo instructs:

> Look at walls splashed with a number of stains or stones of various mixed colors. If you have to invent some scene, you see there resemblances to a number of landscapes adorned in various ways with mountains, rivers, rocks, trees, great plains, valleys, and hills. Moreover, you see various battles and rapid actions of figures, strange expressions on faces, costumes and an infinite number of things.[18]

The incipient forms Leonardo mentions could help an artist generate anything and everything – each accidental mark is a veritable 'mother stain' in which there is a sequential generation of representational imagery. A major distinction between Leonardo and Pliny and Aldrovandi is the necessary role of the artist. If the artist does not give the random form the status of a representation, it is nothing more than a modelled surface or a misshapen mass. In giving the forms within the random form representational meaning, the artist exercises their imagination, which is considered productive work. Take note that, according to Leonardo, the artist has to strive actively to see the accidental images. This is not a passive undertaking. It requires real mental effort. Yet this effort can change something's entire identity. Alberti surmised that sculpture itself was born from an artist's effort to see into or beyond nature's accidental forms. His *De statua* (published 1568) begins with this passage:

> The art of those who tried to reproduce in their works the image and likenesses of bodies created by nature came about, in my opinion, in the following way. By examining a tree trunk, a clump of earth and other similar objects, they must one day have noticed certain features, which

> slightly transformed, could be made to resemble completely real natural shapes. After observing this, they then made attempts, with necessary care, to see if they could complete, by addition or removal, what seems to be lacking for the true likeness of a particular shape. So insofar as the object itself indicated, by correcting and perfecting its lines and surfaces, they arrived at their aim, and not without pleasure.[19]

As in Leonardo, Alberti portrays 'tree trunks, clumps of earth, and other similar objects' in possession of, or containing within, a multitude of coexisting objects and images *in potentiis*.[20] Moreover, Alberti imbues these particular and contingent natural forms with the capacity to convey to the artist that they are statues in waiting. There is a sense in Alberti's aetiology of sculpture that both nature and the artist have a certain degree of agency, and that sculpture 'in the likeness of bodies created by nature' came about through a form of cooperation between maker and material. Nature or artist, who should be attributed authorship? If the authorship is not evident, can we consider Alberti's account an illustration of an image made by chance, in a strict sense?

I am spending time questioning the degree to which certain 'accidental images' can be considered truly accidental because Arcimboldo's invertible paintings play with their own intentional structure.[21] They seem to be chance images – a still life that happens to resemble a face if flipped on its head. But the invertible paintings are in fact contrived to appear that way. Did Arcimboldo want his viewer to think that the intention behind his invertible paintings was in question? To put it another way, did Arcimboldo want the person or persons standing before his paintings to wonder if the artist had manufactured the face? Or did he want them to come away from the work thinking that the artist was particularly adept at perceiving and describing nature's playfulness? It's hard to say.

So, even though the accidental image is a model for Arcimboldo's invertible heads, we need to keep in mind some important differences between the two. First, Arcimboldo's invertible paintings are not the result of a chance event. They were calculated works made to appear contingent. Second, Arcimboldo's forms are not merely suggestive of other forms; another form actually appears when the painting is reoriented. Hence, it is very tempting to view the invertible paintings as an instance of man imitating nature imitating man. To do so, however, would require that we ignore the fact that Arcimboldo's invertible paintings do not represent raw nature; they depict nature that has been cultivated twice over. They depict products of nature that have been assembled and displayed together by someone for the sake of someone else, and that assemblage has in turn been altered so that when inverted it resembles a human face. In pretending to be presenting a likeness that was already in the world, the rhetoric of Arcimboldo's invertible paintings is this: 'What you see before you might not have been, or it could have been otherwise.' Arcimboldo's virtuosity lies in his ability to pose as a projective interpreter of a seemingly random basket of fruit. Rather than capturing and capitalizing on nature's randomness, Arcimboldo made an image that had a purpose and an order.

COURTLY REGIMES OF VISION

The invertible paintings operate within a regimen of vision proposed by the imperial collections of Maximilian II and Rudolf II.[22] Like Aldrovandi's *Musaeum Metallicum*, cabinets, boxes and drawers within the imperial collections were stuffed with 'nature's jokes'. In his inventory compiled between 1607 and 1611 of Rudolf's Kunstkammer in Prague, the court antiquarian and miniature painter Daniel Fröschl lists a piece of white stone that takes on the shape of a branch of coral, three little stones in the shape of penises and a root in the shape of a crucifixion, among many other *lusus naturae*.[23] Like Arcimboldo's invertible heads, collectible objects such as these were magnificent instances of something seeming to be two things at once, but on a different level they exemplify, in the words of Paula Findlen, 'the ability of polarities to exist within a category and, in fact, create a separate category through their coexistence'.[24]

In addition to undermining categories, objects like a stone that contained 'effigies of men and other animals' could also confirm nature's delight at her own imagination and ability to diversify ceaselessly.[25] Works of art in Rudolf's collection played with nature's playfulness. Take, for example, Hans von Aachen's painting *The Fall of Phaeton* (1600) (illus. 74). Painted on alabaster, the work associates nature's mimetic proclivities with Ovidian metamorphosis. Von Aachen not only portrays the transformation of Phaeton's sisters into poplar trees with ossified tears but makes the alabaster, the surface of the painting itself, look as if it transmutes into nebulous and mutable substances. A chance image painted by nature on to stone becomes in *The Fall of Phaeton* inchoate images of clouds and water, which the artist, flaunting his powerful transformative capacities, converted into the sky from which Phaeton tumbles and headwaters which a river god bridges with his heroic right leg. Thus, in *The Fall of Phaeton* von Aachen veers from Leonardo's advice to look at stone 'of various mixed colours' but not Leonardo's desire to 'see an infinite number of things'. Instead of exercising his imagination in discerning images in the clouds and water that the alabaster provided, von Aachen paints figures – Phaeton and the river god – on top of nature's images, and by doing so he thematizes the stone's resemblance to clouds and flowing water. Perhaps it was the artistic longing for an infinite supply of images *in potentiis* which Leonardo articulated that prompted von Aachen to create, from nature's chance image, an image out of which other images could be made.[26]

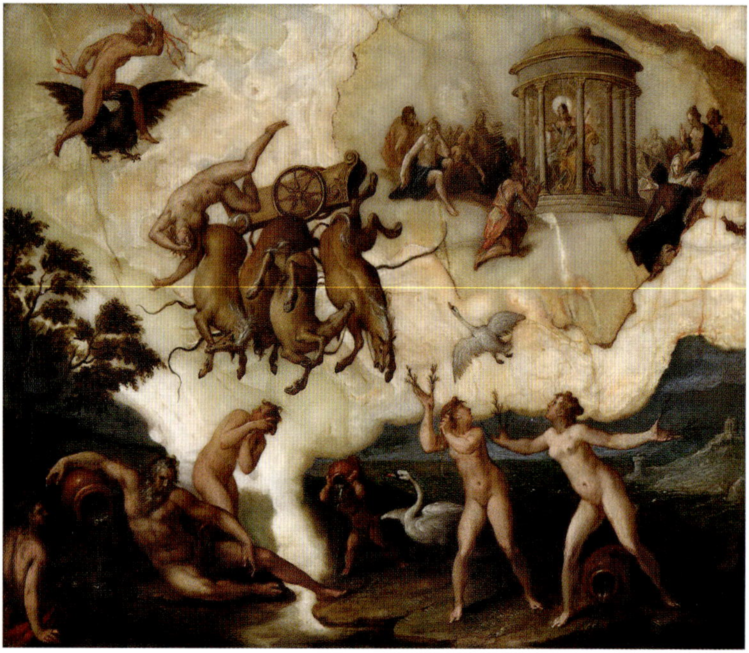

An image which harbours other images is a defining feature of Arcimboldo's *Flora*, which like his invertible paintings he completed in Milan, and as with *Vertumnus* he sent to Rudolf's court in Prague. In *Flora* a woman turns to peer out at the viewer. Her torso, garment, hair and face are composed of an abundance and diversity of flowers, perfectly intact and in full bloom. The relationship between the individual components of the painting and the whole was taken up by at least two authors in Arcimboldo's Milanese milieu. Comanini composed a madrigal that is read aloud by Signor Guazzo in *Il Figino*.

If a flower, how can my features
Laugh like Flora? And if
I am Flora,

74 Hans von Aachen, *Fall of Phaeton*, *c*. 1600, painting on alabaster.

How can I be Flora and only Flowers?
But I am not flowers, and I am not Flora.
I am both Flora and flowers.
A thousand flowers, a single Flora
Since Flowers make Flora, and Flora the flowers
How? An artful painter
Changed flowers into Flora.
Flora into Flowers.[27]

For Comanini, the figure's double nature – as the poem says she is both flowers and Flora – manifests itself as a quantitative, existential and ontological crisis. Both singular and millenary, the figure asks how something or someone embodying such a contradiction could exist, and without pause Flora responds that her impossible nature is the work of 'an artful painter'.

It is not only the twofoldness of *Flora*, or the time and place of the painting's design and manufacture, that aligns her with Arcimboldo's invertible paintings. Lomazzo reminds us that, in the case of the invertible heads, it is the viewer's proximity and orientation to the picture that must change to grasp its complexity and ingenuity. In *Idea of the Temple of Painting*, after reporting that *Flora* 'was especially prized' by Rudolf II, he writes, 'From far away this painting [*Flora*] represents nothing but a very beautiful woman. But up close, while the appearance of the woman persists, it displays only flowers and leaves, assembled and composed together.'[28] Though *Flora* and the invertible paintings demand that the viewer consciously alter their proximity and orientation to grasp the paintings' conceit, the intentional structures of the works differ. The invertible paintings propose that Arcimboldo captured and recorded an image that chance authored, and not himself, whereas the sheer impossibility of a woman made up entirely of flowers signals its origin in the artist's imagination. Indeed, just before reciting Comanini's madrigal, Signor Guazzo states that Flora could have had 'no existence in any other intellect'.[29]

Even though the invertible paintings propose that they are mere documents of an accident, we know that they were meticulously crafted by the artist. A reflectogram of *The Vegetable Gardener* taken in 2000 provides insight into the order of Arcimboldo's operations. At the outset, Arcimboldo laid down a preparatory drawing directly on to the work's wooden support. While similar, this under-drawing and the finished work do not directly correspond. In addition to revealing that Arcimboldo shifted the placement and size of some of the vegetables, the reflectogram also makes clear that Arcimboldo initially placed leaves near the base of the bowl, which do not appear in the definitive composition. We can also see from the reflectogram that the bowl and the background were only completed once the artist had finished manipulating the arrangement of vegetables, so that he could achieve his double composition without having to contend with a vessel/hat simultaneously.[30] Beyond giving us a sense of the order in which Arcimboldo laid down his invertible paintings, perhaps most importantly, the reflectogram tells us that the artist did not operate with any improvisational freedom. He worked and revised his composition, so that the individual details that made up the still life had a double duty. This is because once those individual components were turned upside down, they had to become an eye, a nose, a mouth, and they also had to gel into a face. Furthermore, when the painting was oriented to appear as a still life, the individual components could not look like an upside-down eye, nose and mouth. And this must have been extremely difficult because for a face to emerge once the still life was turned on its head, Arcimboldo had to accentuate some significant features of human physiognomy, such as the red mushroom caps, slightly parted to signal lips, the empty acorn husks, which function as the figure's eye, and the dandelion greens, remarkably aligned to create a jutting chin and fulsome beard. This is a representation that was painstakingly crafted to appear accidental. Arcimboldo worked meticulously so that the work could serve an exegetical function. To be sure, Arcimboldo's invertible paintings possess, in Michael Weeman's words, 'a paradoxical dimension meant to shake the reader and provoke a break with his usual conception of existence, thereby lead[ing] to a reorientation through dis-orientation'.[31] To put it slightly differently, Arcimboldo's invertible heads force the viewer to ask not only 'What am I seeing?' but 'Did the artist mean for me to see this?' Such questions create a sense of doubt around the mimetic claims of the work, while at the same time generating a sense of distrust in the artist.

Furthermore, these questions and others that the invertible heads ignite force viewers to wonder about the extent to which their experience of the painting and their distrust of the artist are part of the work's content. To be sure, Arcimboldo's invertible paintings create the opportunity for something out of the ordinary. These are not typical early modern paintings, nor does one view them as one might view other highly readable early modern paintings. They not only arouse, in the mind of the viewer, a world in reverse but provide the chance to ponder the possibility of two images which are one. The paintings thus facilitate an alternative way of seeing and simultaneously demand meta-pictorial reflection on that unfamiliar way of seeing.

But that is not all. While the works open multiple pictorial possibilities within a single form, they also seek to school the eye to see something particular. Arcimboldo's invertible paintings do this by channelling the viewer's attention to specific telling details. Take, for example, the three bunches of green grapes that, when the painting is seen oriented as a still life, defy gravity in *Basket with Fruit*. Or consider the golden pear in the same work. Tipped forward, its placement in the basket is precarious at best. And what is the piece of white fabric doing? Is it in the basket? Is it behind the basket? The strangeness of these pictorial elements cues the attentive viewer that something peculiar is afoot in this work, and once the viewer understands their analogical form representationally, the viewer perceives these details as facial features. As a result, Arcimboldo's invertible paintings try to induce what philosophers call 'seeing as'.[32] With these pictorial clues we can see the invertible paintings as either a still life or a humanoid face, leaving the painting and the viewer in a suspended state. The paintings therefore foreclose the human predisposition to perceive form where none exists because they do this for the viewer.

A double suspension like that described above was considered a defining feature of a 'capriccio' in art theory and literature before and during the period Arcimboldo was painting in Milan. A capriccio, first and foremost, was considered a product of the artist's imagination or a fantasia. Unlike something which an artist witnessed and documented, it was instead an image that the artist conjured in his or her mind and then drew, painted or sculpted. In addition to a display of artistic invention, capriccio also denoted a work's resistance to intelligibility.[33] It is precisely this combination of fantasia and obscurity that Arcimboldo's friend and interlocuter Lomazzo lauded in his *Idea of the Temple of Painting*: 'Transferring things imagined into representation produces such effects that the world admires them not only with utmost pleasure but in complete amazement, as if they were miracles: we see one thing shown as another, when it really is the same.'[34] Capriccio also connotes an ostentatious display of artistic skill. And what is more skilful and what is cleverer than to devise and paint a picture that is two images at once but appears to be something you might pass by unnoticed, like a basket of fruit or a bowl of vegetables? And how ingenious is it for an artist to manufacture a work to seem as if its main conceit was a mere accident, and an accident typically attributed to nature herself? Who is imitating whom here?

In his efforts to manufacture contingency Arcimboldo created works in which the mundane and the fantastical inhabited the same representational field. A consequence of this bounty of paradoxes was the erosion of the boundaries that separated categories of images, which, in turn, contributed to the impossibility of providing a narrow determination of the works' meaning. Instead, the invertible paintings invite us to contemplate the artistic process itself. Moreover, the invertible paintings make us question the signifying potential of nature, and simultaneously generate doubt in our own sensory experience of nature. In this way these works that Arcimboldo devised towards the end of his life stand in opposition to his studies of plants and animals, which attempt to evidence and perhaps even transfer to the viewer the artist's authoritative experience of nature.

Uncertainty in our experience of nature also comes into play in the imperial allegories. One crucial aspect of the imperial allegories that I have stressed throughout this book is that they argue that our experience of nature fails to perceive who controls nature, and they claim to show us who does – the emperor. As such, Arcimboldo's composite pictures powerfully demonstrate the need to portray imperial political power as limitless and therefore imperceptible, which in turn risks revealing that kind of political power as impossible.

Conclusion

This book is entitled *Impossible Nature* because Arcimboldo's most renowned works embody this paradox. But I wonder if I could not have titled the book *Impossible Politics.* So much of Arcimboldo's work – his collaborative ecclesiastical commissions in Lombardy, through his nature studies executed at the imperial courts in Vienna and Prague, his allegories of the Seasons and the Elements, his choreographed imperial tournament procession of 1571, his portrait of Holy Roman Emperor Rudolf II as Vertumnus and the invertible paintings he executed at the end of his life – was painstakingly designed and produced against the backdrop of a world that was about to undergo a dramatic change. In 1618, 31 years after Arcimboldo retired to Milan, Rudolf II's cousin, Holy Roman Emperor Ferdinand II (1578–1637), revoked the religious freedom of Protestants in the Kingdom of Bohemia. Bohemian Protestant nobles responded by throwing three of Ferdinand II's Catholic ministers out of one of Hradčany Castle's windows, igniting the Thirty Years' War and ending a period of imperial attempts to reconcile the theological differences between Catholics and Protestants.

I hope my readers have read *Impossible Nature* with attention to how Arcimboldo's extraordinary descriptions of nature, the cosmos and the Holy Roman Emperor make evident the crisis of sovereign legitimacy in the Holy Roman Empire after the Reformation. I also hope that readers have come to understand the uneasy relationship between art and politics in the Holy Roman Empire at the end of the sixteenth century. Initially, the extended metaphorics of sovereignty Arcimboldo developed to account for Maximilian II's and Rudolf II's unsteady political power appears to be mutually beneficial to the artist and his patrons. To be sure, the novel portrayal of imperial power in Arcimboldo's allegories and court spectacles attests to a yearning for recognition of the artist and the House of Habsburg. Arcimboldo presented himself as an object of praise through his superior skill in portraying Maximilian and Rudolf as objects of praise. The paintings of the Seasons and the Elements, Vertumnus and the tournament procession of 1571 claim that neither Maximilian nor Rudolf beset themselves with worry over self-preservation, for each of them, like nature, is eternal. This is a very potent political argument: if one does not have to worry about oneself, one can govern honestly. This very argument is the reason why the imperial allegories examined in these pages exceed their role as referential indications of actual persons.

Yet does such a picture, which veers so far away from reality, not run the risk of turning the emperor into merely an object of symbolic value? It is in posing this question that we can begin to detect that the politics motivating the works – the instability of the emperor's legitimacy – reappears in the works' own effects. Whether Arcimboldo knew this to be the case when he devised the paintings and spectacles is beside the point. At some moment in time, perhaps during his early forays into the study and description of nature, Arcimboldo realized that nature might be able to bear the oceanic weight of the sovereign body and the cosmos. His fantastical arrangements of intensely mimetic representations of flora, fauna and the man-made world gave the impression that the world and the Habsburgs were indivisible. Arcimboldo attempted to naturalize sovereignty by portraying in unnatural terms the sovereign as nature.

However, even though Arcimboldo clearly helped to create a new imperial posture, his works also undermined it. This damage is in part a consequence of the serious mental effort that went into creating the imperial allegories. Each of the four Seasons and the four Elements, as well as his portrait of Rudolf as Vertumnus, could stand as an example of the cognitive dexterity required to compose the composite heads. At the most basic level the artist had to see two things at once – a fruit, vegetable, flower or animal and a facial feature or body part. Thus, each component that represents a part of the figure does not signify through a positive identification with the facial element the object is standing in for, but rather it is identified with what it is standing in for through its difference from it. Another major tension in the image rests in the gap between the intensely mimetic components of the images and their unnatural composition of components. Since Arcimboldo does not provide the disparate components of the composite heads with a clearly articulated connective tissue, it permits, or even encourages, the viewer mentally to pull the components apart. The composite heads activate the mind of the viewer to reverse the process the artist went through to create the image. Thus, just as in his invertible paintings, the artist shows us what it means to behold. The act of viewing involves detecting visual analogies, rotating components and taking apart the work piece by piece, all within the space of the mind. Yet, the composite heads not only compel the viewer to decompose the composition but destroy an image predicated on nature's eternal indestructability. As such, the imperial allegories train us to cross them out, and taken to its logical end, this latent iconoclasm becomes the imperial message. They reveal the prospect of the demise of the empire, by way of a loss of form, and in the end we see that art and empire can be mutually constitutive and mutually destructive, an impossible situation indeed.

REFERENCES

Introduction

1 The work is described in Gregorio Comanini's treatise on art, *Il Figino*. Gregorio Comanini, *Il Figino, or On the Purpose of Painting*, trans. Ann Doyle-Anderson and Giancarlo Maiorino (Toronto, 2001), p. 27.
2 In the sixteenth century wit was by and large considered to be the ability to see unexpected and veiled correspondences between two entities. See Thomas DaCosta Kaufmann, 'Arcimboldo's Imperial Allegories', *Zeitschrift für Kunstgeschichte*, XXXIX (1976), p. 94.
3 *Four Seasons in One Head* is akin to composite paintings Arcimboldo made for Maximilian II and Rudolf II, though we are not certain if he made this painting for either of them. Dated 1590, the arboreal figure was devised and painted in Milan near to the end of Arcimboldo's career and life. The date and place of execution are shored up by a description of a work like it in *Il Figino*. Comanini, *Il Figino*, p. 27.
4 Howard Louthan, *The Quest for Compromise* (Cambridge, 1997), p. 3.
5 See the Select Bibliography.

1 Lost Origins

1 Thomas DaCosta Kaufmann, *Arcimboldo: Visual Jokes, Natural History, and Still-Life Painting* (Chicago, IL, 2009), p. 20. For transcriptions and summaries of documents relating to Arcimboldo's early life in Milan, see Silvio Leydi, 'Giuseppe Arcimboldo in Milan: Documents and Hypotheses – Summary of Documents Relating to the Milanese Period', in *Arcimboldo 1526–1593*, exh. cat., Kunsthistorisches Museum, Vienna (2007), pp. 37–52 and 297–302.
2 Leydi, 'Giuseppe Arcimboldo in Milan', p. 298.

3 Robert S. Miller, 'Arcimboldo e il contesto Milanese: la scuola di San Luca nel 1548–1549 e gli esordi del pittore fino al 1562', in *Arcimboldo: Artista Milanese tra Leonardo e Caravaggio*, exh. cat., Palazzo Reale, Milan (2011), p. 85; Kaufmann, *Arcimboldo*, p. 237, n. 9.
4 Gregorio Comanini, *The Figino, or On the Purpose of Painting*, trans. Ann Doyle-Anderson and Giancarlo Maiorino (Toronto, 2001), p. 27.
5 Leydi, 'Giuseppe Arcimboldo in Milan', p. 39.
6 Giacomo Berra, 'Un autoritratto cartaceo di Giuseppe Arcimboldi', *Arte Lombarda*, CXVI/1 (1996), pp. 54–5.
7 For an overview of Milanese history during Arcimboldo's lifetime, see Stefano D'Amico, *Spanish Milan: A City within the Empire* (New York, 2012).
8 Thomas DaCosta Kaufmann, 'Le opere di Arcimboldo a Monza e la carriera iniziale dell'artista/Arcimboldo's Work in Monza and the Artist's Early Career', *Studi Monzesi*, III (1988), pp. 5–17; Leydi, 'Giuseppe Arcimboldo in Milan', pp. 37–52; Miller, 'Arcimboldo e il contesto Milanese', pp. 85–101.
9 Kaufmann, *Arcimboldo*, p. 73.
10 Francis Haskell, *History and Its Images: Art and the Interpretation of the Past* (New Haven, CT, 1993), p. 19.
11 Leydi, 'Giuseppe Arcimboldo in Milan', p. 37.
12 As quoted in D'amico, *Spanish Milan*, p. 7.
13 Ibid., p. 123.
14 Ibid., p. 94.
15 As quoted ibid., p. 23.
16 Based on documentary evidence, Miller has claimed that the hands of Meda and Arcimboldo cannot be parsed in the frescoes. See Robert S. Miller, 'Gli affreschi cinquecenteschi: Giuseppe Arcimboldo, Giuseppe Meda e Giovanni Battista della Rovere detto il Fammenghino', in *Il Duomo di Monza: la storia e l'arte* (Milan, 1989), vol. II, pp. 216–30. Based on stylistic analysis, Kaufmann has suggested Arcimboldo was primarily responsible for the figures in the Tree of Jesse fresco in Monza. See Kaufmann, *Arcimboldo*, pp. 223–5.
17 Miller, 'Arcimboldo e il contesto Milanese', p. 95.
18 Leydi, 'Giuseppe Arcimboldo in Milan', p. 40.
19 Kaufmann, *Arcimboldo*, p. 237, n. 10.
20 Leydi 'Giuseppe Arcimboldo in Milan', p. 40; Miller, 'Arcimboldo e il contesto Milanese', pp. 90–91.
21 Kaufmann, *Arcimboldo*, p. 24.

22 Miller, 'Arcimboldo e il contesto Milanese', p. 90.
23 Nello Forti Grazzini, *L'arazzo ferrase* (Milan, 1982), pp. 81–4; Nello Forti Grazzini, *Arazzi del cinquecento a Como* (Como, 1986), pp. 43–7.
24 Kaufmann has drawn attention to the portrayal and arrangement of fruit and sees in it a prefiguration of Arcimboldo's handling of fruit in the Seasons. See Kaufmann, *Arcimboldo*, p. 24. However, Leydi and Miller have suggested that the festooning may have been the work of the workshop in Ferrara that produced the tapestry. Leydi, 'Giuseppe Arcimboldo in Milan', pp. 41–3; Miller, 'Arcimboldo e il contesto Milanese', p. 95.
25 Together with Forti Grazzini, Kaufmann has attributed this work to Arcimboldo on stylistic grounds. Kaufmann, *Arcimboldo*, p. 237, no. 9.
26 Leydi, 'Giuseppe Arcimboldo in Milan', pp. 41–3.
27 Ibid., p. 41.
28 Kaufmann has pointed out that Ferrari's treatment of drapery and 'blocky forms' was taken up by Arcimboldo in later works. Kaufmann, *Arcimboldo*, pp. 25–6, 223–5.
29 Ibid., pp. 21–2; Miller, 'Arcimboldo e il contesto Milanese', p. 93; G. Bora, 'Milano nell'età di Lomazzo e di San Carlo: riaffermazione e difficoltà di sopravvivenza di una cultura', in *Rabisch: il grottesco nell'arte del cinquecento – l'Accademia della Val di Blenio, Lomazzo e l'ambiente Milanese*, exh. cat. (Lugano, 1998), pp. 40–42.
30 Francesca Alberti, 'Menacing Laughter in Sixteenth-Century *pittore ridicule*', RES, LXXIII–LXXIV (2020), pp. 41–59.
31 See Sylvia Ferino-Pagden, 'Giuseppe Arcimboldo: Court Artist, Philosopher, "rhétoriqueur", Magician or an Entertainer?', in *Arcimboldo 1526–1593*, exh. cat., Kunsthistorisches Museum, Vienna (2007), pp. 15–24; Andrea Bayer, '". . . il gran pittore Giuseppe Arcimboldi": On the Construction of Arcimboldo's Fame', in *Arcimboldo 1526–1593*, exh. cat., Kunsthistorisches Museum, Vienna (2007), pp. 25–31.
32 On naturalism in the Lombardy, see Andrea Bayer, 'Defining Naturalism in Lombard Painting', in *Painters of Reality: The Legacy of Leonardo and Caravaggio in Lombardy*, exh. cat., Metropolitan Museum of Art, New York (2004), pp. 3–21.
33 See, for example, Giacomo Berra, 'Arcimboldi: le teste "caricate" leonardesche e le "grillerie" dell'Accademia della Val di Blenio', in *Rabisch: il grottesco nell'arte del cinquecento – l'Accademia della Val di Blenio, Lomazzo e l'ambiente Milanese*, exh. cat. (Lugano, 1998), pp. 57–68; Kaufmann, *Arcimboldo*, p. 22, n. 13, and pp. 219–22.

34 T. Wilson, 'Un "intracamento" tra Leonardo ed Arcimboldo', *Ceramica Antica*, XV/2 (2005), pp. 10–16; Raymond B. Waddington, 'Before Arcimboldo: Composite Portraits on Italian Medals', *The Medal*, XIV (1989), pp. 12–23.
35 Kaufmann, *Arcimboldo*, pp. 26–7.
36 On Leonardo's caricatures circulating in Milan, see Giacomo Berra, 'Arcimboldi: le teste "caricate"', pp. 57–68.
37 Kaufmann, *Arcimboldo*, p. 27.
38 Linda Wolk-Simon, 'Naturalism in Lombard Drawing from Leonardo to Cerano', in *Painters of Reality: The Legacy of Leonardo and Caravaggio in Lombardy*, exh. cat., Metropolitan Museum of Art, New York (New York, 2004), p. 49.
39 Kenneth Clark, 'Francesco Melzi as Preserver of Leonardo da Vinci's Drawings', in *Studies in Renaissance and Baroque Art Presented to Anthony Blunt on his 60th Birthday* (London, 1967), p. 24.
40 Kaufmann, *Aricimboldo*, p. 29.
41 Francesco Porzio, *Arcimboldo: Artista Milanese tra Leonardo e Caravaggio*, exh. cat., Palazzo Reale, Milan (2011), pp. 222–8.

2 Nature Studies

1 The literature on sixteenth-century natural history illustration is extensive. For the most recent overview of the topic, with a recent bibliography, see Florike Egmond, *Eye for Detail: Images of Plants and Animals in Art and Science, 1500–1650* (London, 2017).
2 On early modern interest in the monstrous, see Lorraine Daston and Katharine Park, *Wonders and the Order of Nature, 1150–1750* (New York, 1998).
3 Cod. Min. 42 is one of three compendia in Rudolf's imperial Kunstkammer that contained animal studies by or based on works by Arcimboldo in the Austrian National Library. A watercolour of a mountain coati that scholars take to be a copy of one by Arcimboldo was pasted into the compendium that now goes by Cod. Min. 129, and a watercolour of an aplomado falcon also derived from a watercolour in Arcimboldo's hand now resides in compendium Cod. Min. 130. Often referred to as Rudolf's *Museum*, Cod. Min. 129 and Cod. Min. 130 picture a number of objects from Rudolf's collection, such as a mounted rhinoceros horn, as well as reproducing plant and animal studies from Rudolf's collection. Several artists were involved in producing the images that make up Cod. Min. 129 and Cod. Min.

130, among them Daniel Fröschl, Rudolf's imperial miniature painter and later imperial antiquarian. On Cod. Min. 42, see Fritz Koreny, *Albrecht Dürer and the Animal and Plant Studies of the Renaissance* (Boston, MA, 1985), pp. 21, 28–9, 130; Manfred Staudinger, 'Naturstudien Kaiser Rudolfs II (1576–1612): Zur Kunstkammer auf der Praguer Burg', in *Thesaurus Austriacus: Europas Glanz im Spiegel der Buchkunst, Handschriften und Kunstalben von 800 bis 1600* (Vienna, 1996), pp. 229–86; Lee Hendrix, 'Natural History Illustration at the Court of Rudolf II', in *Rudolf II and Prague: The Court and City*, ed. Eliška Fucíková (London, 1997), pp. 157–71; Thomas DaCosta Kaufmann, *Arcimboldo: Visual Jokes, Natural History, and Still-Life Painting* (Chicago, IL, 2009), pp. 115–48, 226–32; Sylvia Ferino-Pagden, 'Arcimboldo as "Conterfetter of Nature"', in *Arcimboldo, 1526–1593*, exh. cat., Kunsthistorisches Museum, Vienna (2007), pp. 303–9, 159–67.

4 In 1992 Lucilla Conigliello attributed several natural history illustrations to Arcimboldo based on the inscriptions scrawled on the watercolours of deformed goat hooves. See Lucilla Conigliello, 'L'altra faccia di Arcimboldo', *Paragone*, XLII (1992), pp. 44–9; see also Kaufmann, *Arcimboldo*, pp. 125–7.

5 Claudia Swan, 'Ad vivum, naer het leven, from the life: Considerations on a Mode of Representation', *Word & Image*, XI (1995), pp. 353–72; Joanna Woodall et al., *Ad vivum? Visual Materials and the Vocabulary of Life-Likeness in Europe before 1800* (Leiden, 2019); Marisa Bass, *Insect Artifice: Nature and Art in the Dutch Revolt* (Princeton, NJ, 2019), pp. 228–40.

6 On Arcimboldo's natural history illustrations in Dresden, see Thomas DaCosta Kaufmann, 'For the Birds: Collecting, Art, and Natural History in Saxony', in *For the Sake of Learning: Essays in Honor of Anthony Grafton*, vol. I, ed. Ann Blair and Anja-Silvia Goeing (Leiden, 2016), pp. 481–504; Christien Melzer, *Von der Kunstkammer zum Kupferstich Kabinett: Zur Frühgeschichte des Graphiksammelns in Dresden (1560–1738)*, https://skd-online-collection (Hildesheim, 2010), pp. 102ff.

7 Kaufmann, *Arcimboldo*, pp. 115–66.

8 Both letters are reproduced in Ferino-Pagden, 'Arcimboldo as "Conterfetter of Nature"', pp. 303–4.

9 Ibid.

10 See Kaufmann, *Arcimboldo*, pp. 125–7; Staudinger, 'Naturstudien Kaiser Rudolfs II', pp. 209–25.

11 Kaufmann, *Arcimboldo*, p. 121. On Maximilian's gardens, menagerie and residence at Klatterberg, see Dirk Jacob Jansen, *Jacopo Strada and*

Cultural Patronage at the Imperial Court: The Antique as Innovation (Leiden, 2019), pp. 434–8.

12 Peter Parshall, 'Imago Contrafacta: Image and Facts in the Northern Renaissance', *Art History*, XVI/4 (1993), pp. 560–61.

13 David Freedberg, *The Eye of the Lynx: Galileo, His Friends, and the Beginnings of Modern Natural History* (Chicago, IL, 2002), p. 202.

14 Harry Berger Jr, 'The Fictions of the Pose: Facing the Gaze of Early Modern Portraiture', *Representations*, XLVI (1994), pp. 87–120.

15 Ibid., p. 104.

16 Paula Findlen, 'Natural History', in *Early Modern Science*, ed. Lorraine Daston and Katharine Park (Cambridge, 2008), pp. 435–68; on artisanal knowledge and natural history, see Pamela Smith, *The Body of the Artisan: Art and Experience in the Scientific Revolution* (Chicago, IL, 2006).

17 Karen Leonhard, *The Fertile Ground of Painting: Seventeenth-Century Still Lifes & Nature Pieces* (London, 2020), p. 11.

18 On the changing status of natural history and natural illustration, see Brian W. Ogilvie, *The Science of Describing: Natural History in Renaissance Europe* (Chicago, IL, 2006).

19 For instance, the imperial collection contained moose antlers and Arcimboldo executed studies of moose antlers which were in turn pasted into compendia. See R. Bauer and H. Haupt, 'Das Kunstkammerinventar Kaiser Rudolfs II', *Jahrbuch der Kunsthistorischen Sammlung in Wien*, LXXII (1976), p. 9, no. 11; Kaufmann, *Arcimboldo*, p. 154.

20 T. Vignau-Wilberg, 'Le "Museum" de l'empereur Rodolphe II et le Cabinet des arts et curiosités', in *Le bestiaire de Rodolphe II*, ed. M. Staudinger et al. (Paris, 1990), pp. 40–41; Ferino-Pagden, 'Arcimboldo as "Conterfetter of Nature"', p. 162.

21 Bauer and Haupt, 'Das Kunstkammerinventar Kaiser Rudolfs II, 1607–1611', p. 8, n. 100.

22 Kaufmann, *Arcimboldo*, p. 152.

23 M. Staudinger, 'Arcimboldo and Ulisse Aldrovandi', in *Arcimboldo 1526–1593*, exh. cat., Kunsthistorisches Museum, Vienna (2007), pp. 114–17.

24 Hendrix, 'Natural History Illustration at the Court of Rudolf II', p. 161.

25 Koreny, *Albrecht Dürer and the Animal and Plant Studies of the Renaissance*, p. 21.

26 Ferino-Pagden, 'Arcimboldo as "Conterfetter of Nature"', p. 159. Staudinger, *Le bestiaire de Rodolphe II*, pp. 132–3.

27 On the copying of Gessner, see Lee Hendrix, 'Joris Hoefnagel and the *Four Elements*: A Study in Sixteenth-Century Nature Painting',

PhD diss., Princeton University, 1984, p. 66; Nadia Baadj, *Jan van Kessel I (1626–79): Crafting a Natural History of Art in Early Modern Antwerp* (London, 2016), p. 129; Bass, *Insect Artifice*, pp. 191–8.

28 See Sachiko Kusukawa, *Picturing the Book of Nature: Image, Text, and Argument in Sixteenth-Century Human Anatomy and Botany* (Chicago, IL, 2012); Angela Fischel, *Natur im Bild: Zeichnung und Naturerkenntnis bei Conrad Gessner und Ulisse Aldrovandi* (Berlin, 2009); Angela Fischel, 'Collections, Images and Form in Sixteenth-Century Natural History: The Case of Conrad Gessner', *Intellectual History Review*, XX/1 (2010), pp. 147–64.

29 The chick and the deformed goat hooves are the exceptions.

30 As quoted in Ferino-Pagden, 'Arcimboldo as "Conterfetter of Nature"', p. 108.

31 On Aldrovandi's collection, see Paula Findlen, *Possessing Nature: Museums, Collecting, and Scientific Culture in Early Modern Italy* (Berkeley, CA, 1994), pp. 17–47.

32 Staudinger, 'Arcimboldo and Ulisse Aldrovandi', pp. 113–17; Kaufmann, *Arcimboldo*, pp. 121–5.

33 Hendrix, 'Natural History Illustration at the Court of Rudolf II', p. 163.

34 On early modern princes' interest in the natural world and its political significance, see Smith, *The Body of the Artisan*, pp. 32–7.

35 Florike Egmond, *The World of Carolus Clusius: Natural History in the Making, 1550–1610* (London, 2010), pp. 21–2.

36 On Mattioli at Habsburg courts, see Miroslava Hejnová, *Pietro Andrea Mattioli 1501–1578* (Prague, 2001); Kaufmann, *Arcimboldo*, p. 121.

37 Staudinger, 'Naturstudien Kaiser Rudolfs II', pp. 209–25.

38 As quoted in Dirk Jansen, *Jacopo Strada and Cultural Patronage at the Imperial Court: The Antique as Innovation* (Leiden, 2019), p. 455.

39 Hilda Lietzmann, *Das Neugebäude in Wien: Sultan Süyleman's Zeit – Kaiser Maximilian II Lustschloß* (Munich, 1987), pp. 206ff., doc. n. 2.

40 Pieter Diemer, Elke Bujok and Dorothea Diemer, *Johann Baptist Fickler: Das Inventar der Münchner herzoglichen Kunstkammer von 1598* (Munich, 2004), p. 129, no. 1455.

41 Clusius continued at the court into Rudolf's reign. He departed in 1588 and later became the director of the famed garden at the University of Leiden. Howard Louthan, *The Quest for Compromise: Peacemakers in Counter-Reformation Vienna* (Cambridge, 1997), p. 189.

42 Andrea Bubenik, 'The Art of Albrecht Dürer in the Context of the Court of Rudolf II', *Studia Rudolphina*, V (2005), p. 19.

43 Annemarie Jordan Gschwend, ed., *Hans Khevenhuller at the Court of Philip II of Spain: Diplomacy and Consumerism in a Global Empire* (London, 2017); Sylva Dobalova, 'The Amsterdam Dealer Hans le Thoor at the Court of Rudolf II', *Journal of the History of Collections*, XXXV/3 (2023), pp. 413–24.
44 On storage in Rudolf II's Kunstkammer, see Jessica Keating, 'Hidden in Plain Sight: On Copiousness in the *Kunstkammer* of Emperor Rudolf II', *Journal of the History of Collections*, XXXIII/3 (2021), pp. 447–58.
45 Bauer and Haupt, 'Das Kunstkammerinventar Kaiser Rudolfs II, 1607–1611', p. 135, nos 2688–97, 2702, 2705, p. 138, nos 2780, 2782.
46 Koreny, *Albrecht Dürer and the Plant and Animal Studies of the Renaissance*, p. 28.
47 Kaufmann, *Arcimboldo*, p. 153.
48 Ferino-Pagden, 'Arcimboldo as "Conterfetter of Nature"', p. 108.
49 Ibid.
50 Staudinger, 'Naturstudien Kaiser Rudolfs II', pp. 254–7, 258–60.
51 Anke te Heesen, 'News, Paper, Scissors: Clippings in the Sciences and Arts around 1920', in *Things that Talk: Object Lessons from Art and Science*, ed. Lorraine Daston (New York, 2004), p. 299.
52 On this practice in natural history collections, see Fischel, 'Collections, Images and Form in Sixteenth-Century Natural History', p. 150.
53 On the practice of cutting and pasting biblical images and text and ways in which uniformity among fragments was achieved, see Michael Gaudio, *The Bible and Printed Image in Early Modern England: Little Gidding and the Pursuit of Scriptural Harmony* (London, 2017), p. 30.

3 Nature and Empire

1 Kaufmann points out that Arcimboldo was also paid 100 thaler *aus Gnaden* in May 1570, and proposes that this second payment might also have come as 'recognition' of the Seasons and Elements. He also notes that the payment might have been given in 'recognition' of Arcimboldo's participation in a tournament held in Prague in May 1570 as well. Thomas DaCosta Kaufmann, *Arcimboldo: Visual Jokes, Natural History, and Still-Life Painting* (Chicago, IL, 2009), p. 56.
2 The earliest manuscript of Fonteo's poem is dated 1568. Kaufmann mentions that it is unclear if Fonteo's poem was a programme for the paintings, an ekphrasis of the paintings or an explanation.

Thomas DaCosta Kaufmann, 'Metamorphoses of Nature', in *The Mastery of Nature: Aspects of Art, Science, and Humanism in the Renaissance* (Princeton, NJ, 1993), p. 105. The manuscript of Fonteo's poem on Arcimboldo's paintings is located in the Austrian National Library under ONB Cod. 10152. ONB Cod. 102006 contains a revised version of the poem as well as additional marginal comments. A transcription of ONB Cod. 10152 was published in Thomas DaCosta Kaufmann, *The Mastery of Nature*, appendix 2.

3 Thomas DaCosta Kaufmann, 'Metamorphoses of Nature', pp. 100–128, 268–73.

4 It has been suggested that taken together the Seasons represent successive stages of growth and decline: Youth/Spring, Young Adult/Summer, Mature Adult/Autumn, Aged Adult/Winter. Ibid., pp. 110–17.

5 Kaufmann's work on the imperial significance of Arcimboldo's Seasons and Elements is extensive. For his most recent discussion of the works, see Kaufmann, *Arcimboldo*, pp. 43–71. See also the Select Bibliography.

6 Howard Louthan, *The Quest for Compromise: Peacemakers in Counter-Reformation Vienna* (Cambridge, 1997).

7 Kaufmann, *Arcimboldo*, p. 55.

8 In his discussion of *Winter*, Berra emphasizes that the anthropomorphism of the tree trunk which forms Winter's neck and head is largely dependent on Leonardo's physiognomic studies. Giacomo Berra, 'Un autoritratto cartaceo di Giuseppe Arcimboldi', *Arte Lombarda*, CXVI/1 (1996), p. 62.

9 Winter's cloak also contains a striking iron, which formed part of the chain of the Habsburg order of the Golden Fleece. Kaufmann, 'Metamorphoses of Nature', pp. 123–4.

10 Cod. 10206, fol. 53r, has the marginal note: 'Caput humanum inventum a fabricatoribus capitolij portendit, romanos potituros hominum imperio.' As quoted in Kaufmann, 'Metamorphoses of Nature', p. 264, n. 66.

11 Alexander Thein, 'Capitoline Jupiter and the Historiography of Roman World Rule', *Histos*, VIII (2014), pp. 284–319.

12 Livy I. 55.7–9; D. Hal. A.R.5.50.5.

13 Ov. Fast 1.79–89.

14 See *Katalog der Gemäldegalerie* (Vienna, 1965), pp. 4–5.

15 On this possibility, see Thomas DaCosta Kaufmann, *L'Ecole de Pragues* (Paris, 1985), p. 211, cat. nos 2–3.

16 The identification of all the plants that make up Spring is entirely dependent on Sam Segal's work. See Sylvia Ferino-Pagden, *Arcimboldo 1526–1593*, exh. cat., Kunsthistorisches Museum, Vienna (2007), pp. 125–6, cat. no. IV.2.

17 Ibid.

18 Ibid., pp. 151–6, cat. no. IV.20.

19 All Arcimboldo's versions of the Seasons in the Louvre date to 1573. All have been supplemented with a garland border that post-dates Arcimboldo's execution. All are painted on canvas rather than panel. On the versions of the Seasons that Maximilian II gave to August of Saxony, see Thomas DaCosta Kaufmann, 'Arcimboldo and the Elector of Saxony', in *Scambio culturale con il nemico religioso: Italia e Sassonia attorno al 1600*, ed. Sybille Ebert-Schifferer (Rome, 2007), pp. 27–36.

20 I am deeply indebted to Jennifer Nelson for pointing out the ways in which the splayed roots in Arcimboldo's composite paintings signal the displacement of nature's bounty.

21 Karin Leonhard, 'Pictura's Fertile Field: Otto Marseus van Schrieck and the Genre of *sottobosco* Painting', *Simiolus*, XXXIV/2 (2009–10), p. 114. See also Henry Harris, *Things Come to Life: Spontaneous Generation Revisited* (Oxford, 2002).

22 In Fonteo's poem, couples conduct dialogues with each other. Kaufmann, 'Metamorphoses of Nature', p. 119.

23 Karin Leonhard, *The Fertile Ground of Painting: Seventeenth-Century Still Lifes & Nature Pieces* (Brussels, 2021).

24 On imagery of the Golden Fleece in Arcimboldo's paintings of the Elements, see Kaufmann, 'Metamorphoses of Nature', pp. 122–6.

25 Take, for instance, Adrian de Vries' bust of Rudolf II of 1609, currently in the Victoria and Albert Museum. It features a similar lion skin as well as representations of the labours of Hercules. Acc. nos 6920–1860.

26 Annemarie Jordan Gschwend, *The Story of Süleyman: Celebrity Elephants and Other Exotica in Renaissance Portugal* (Cambridge, 2010).

27 Gregorio Comanini, *The Figino, or On the Purpose of Painting*, trans. Ann Doyle-Anderson and Giancarlo Maiorino (Toronto, 2001), pp. 25–6. On the Plinian physiognomy of Arcimboldo's *Earth*, see R. J. Evans, *Rudolf II and His World: A Study in Intellectual History, 1576–1612* (Oxford, 1984), p. 174.

28 The identifications of all the fish and sea creatures that make up *Water* is entirely dependent on Sam Segal's work. See Ferino-Pagden,

Arcimboldo 1526–1593, exh. cat., Kunsthistorisches Museum, Vienna (2007), pp. 151–6.

29 Giorgio Vasari, *The Lives of the Artists*, trans. Julia Conway Bondella and Peter Bondella (Oxford, 1991), p. 288.

30 Ibid.

31 Kaufmann, *Arcimboldo*, pp. 55–6.

4 Harmonious Bodies

1 As quoted in Erwin Panofsky, *The Life and Art of Albrecht Dürer* (Princeton, NJ, 2005), p. 178.

2 For more on this tapestry and others like it, see Thomas P. Campbell, *Henry VIII and the Art of Majesty* (New Haven, CT, 2007), p. 147.

3 On the coronation motet, see Jonas Pfohl, *Motetten am Hof Maximilians II (1527–1576): Komponieren im Zeitalter der Konfessionalisierung* (Vienna, 2022), pp. 57–9.

4 As quoted in Howard Louthan, *The Quest for Compromise: Peacemakers in Counter-Reformation Vienna* (Cambridge, 1997), p. 81.

5 Nor did he mention that he spent many florins of his own money to make modifications to the space of the library to keep nature at bay. Ibid., p. 69.

6 The fountain was not completed until 1578, during Rudolf's reign. A lengthy seventeenth-century description of the object provides information on iconography and design. See Dirk Jansen, *Jacopo Strada and Cultural Patronage at the Imperial Court: The Antique as Innovation* (Leiden, 2018), vol. I, pp. 96–9.

7 My account of the 1571 tournament procession is deeply indebted to Thomas Kaufmann's account in his magisterial *Variations on an Imperial Theme in the Age of Maximilian II and Rudolf II* (New York, 1978), especially pp. 33–9. Other sources on the 1571 event include K. Vocelka, *Habsburgische Hochzeiten 1550–1600* (Vienna, 1976), pp. 63–85, 168–83; R. Lindell, 'The Wedding of Archduke Charles and Maria of Bavaria in 1571', *Early Music*, XVIII/2 (1990), pp. 253–69; Thomas DaCosta Kaufmann, 'The Festival Designs of Jacopo Strada Reconsidered', *Artibus et Historae*, LXII (2010), nn. 15, 16 and 17.

8 J. R. Mulryne and Elizabeth Goldring, eds, *Court Festivals of the European Renaissance: Art, Politics, and Performance* (Burlington, VT, 2002).

9 Veronika Sandbichler, 'Element of Power in Court Festivals of Habsburg Emperors in the Sixteenth Century', in *Ceremonial Entries in Early Modern Europe: The Iconography of Power*, ed. J. R. Mulryne

(London, 2015), pp. 167–87; Borbála Gulyás, 'Triumphal Arches in Court Festivals under the New Holy Roman Emperor, Habsburg Ferdinand I', in *Occasions of State: Early Modern European Festivals and the Negotiations of Power*, ed. J. R. Mulryne (London, 2018), pp. 54–82.

10 Mikael Bøgh Rasmussen, 'Vienna, a Habsburg Capital Redecorated in Classical Style: The Entry of Maximilian II as King of the Romans in 1563', in *Architectures of Festival in Early Modern Europe: Fashioning and Refashioning Urban and Courtly Space*, ed. J. R. Mulryne (London, 2017), pp. 55–8.

11 On the chivalric elements of the event, see Andrea Bayer, 'The Princely Stage: Arcimboldo's Costumes and Drawings for Court Festivities and Tournaments', in *Arcimboldo 1526–1593*, exh. cat., Kunsthistorisches Museum, Vienna (2007), pp. 243–61.

12 For an overview of such events at the Habsburg court, see W. Seipel, ed., *Wir sind Helden: Habsburgische Feste in der Renaissance* (Innsbruck, 2005).

13 As quoted in Bayer, 'The Princely Stage', p. 243.

14 For the fullest description, see Kaufmann, *Variations on an Imperial Theme*, pp. 33–9.

15 On how designs for processions and masks were often copied, see Thomas DaCosta Kaufmann, 'The Festival Designs of Jacopo Strada Reconsidered', p. 174.

16 On the drawings in particular, see Kaufmann, *Variations on an Imperial Theme*, pp. 51–6; Bayer, 'The Princely Stage', pp. 244–61.

17 Sylvia Ferino-Pagden, *Arcimboldo 1526–1593*, exh. cat., Kunsthistorisches Museum, Vienna (2007), p. 248, cat. no. VII.8.

18 As quoted in Bayer, 'The Princely Stage', pp. 246–7.

19 Thomas Kaufmann unearthed both documents in the Austrian National Library, and he has meticulously described and analysed the 1571 tournament in his foundational book *Variations on an Imperial Theme in the Age of Maximilian II and Rudolf II*. For that reason, I will focus on the aspects of the 1571 tournament procession that afford us a glimpse into the development of Arcimboldo's imperial allegorical imagery and how Arcimboldo portrayed the Habsburgs as utterly 'natural' rulers. Kaufmann, *Variations on an Imperial Theme*, pp. 33–9.

20 The costume for the King of America may have been designed by Jacopo Strada, ONB, Sammlung von Handschriften und alten Drucken, Cod. Min. 21, vol. III, fol. 33r. Kaufmann, 'The Festival Designs of Jacopo Strada Reconsidered', pp. 174, 176.

21 For the Platonic system, see Plato, *Timeaus*, 31b–32c. For one of its early medieval elaborations, see Isidore of Seville, *De natura rerum*, 9.1–2. The number 4 informed almost everything in Agrippa of Nettesheim's cosmology. Agrippa, *De occulta philosophia libri tres* (Cologne, 1533).
22 Kaufmann, *Variations on an Imperial Theme*, p. 39.
23 On early modern cosmological elaborations, see S. K. Heninger Jr, *The Cosmographical Glass: Renaissance Diagrams of the Universe* (San Marino, 1977), pp. xv–xvii.
24 Conrad Rudolph, *The Mystic Ark: Hugh of Saint Victor, Art, and Thought in the Twelfth Century* (Cambridge, 2014), p. 128; Conrad Rudolph, 'Macro/Microcosm at Vézelay: The Narthex Portal and Non-Elite Participation in Elite Spirituality', *Speculum*, XCVI/3 (2021), pp. 627–9.
25 Heninger, *The Cosmographical Glass*, pp. 81–2.
26 On the political significance of a procession's movement through space and time, see Jessica Keating, *Animating Empire: Automata, the Holy Roman Empire, and the Early Modern World* (University Park, PA, 2018), pp. 77–83.
27 Louthan, *The Quest for Compromise*, passim.
28 Andrew L. Thomas, *A House Divided: Wittelsbach Confessional Court Cultures in the Holy Roman Empire* (Leiden, 2010), pp. 65–99.

5 Impossible Desires

1 These drawings strongly suggest that Arcimboldo was present for Rudolph's coronation as King of Bohemia as well as his imperial coronation. Thomas DaCosta Kaufmann, *Variations on an Imperial Theme* (New York, 1978), p. 43. On the drawings, see Sylvia Ferino-Pagden, *Arcimboldo 1526–1593*, exh. cat., Kunsthistorisches Museum, Vienna (2007), p. 94, cat. no. III.11.
2 The inscription reads: 'La corona dove si corono Re de Romano Rodolpho el primo di Novembre 1575 in Ratisbona corona cheva in aquiscrana che fece far Carlo Magno et era di tanta larghezza et gli avanzava doi dita per parte era tutta d'oro e della medema fatura. Io Giuseppe Arcimboldo fui pre[sen]te.' As transcribed in Ferino-Pagden, *Arcimboldo 1526–1593*, p. 94, cat. no. III.11.
3 The entire inscription reads: 'La Corona dove si corono Rudolpho Re Bohemia de medemo garbo come si vede nel pre[sen]te disegno 1575 il giorno de Sto. Matia Settemb. Io Giuseppe Arcimboldo fui

pre[sen]te.' As transcribed in Ferino-Pagden, *Arcimboldo 1526–1593*, p. 94, cat. no. III.II.

4 *Meisterwerke der Weltlichen Schatzkammer*, ed. Sabine Haag, exh. cat., Kunsthistorisches Museum, Vienna (2014), pp. 156–8.

5 Most scholars agree with Larsson that they were preparatory sketches for an official portrait. Lars Olof Larsson, 'Portraits of Emperor Rudolf II', in *Rudolf II and Prague*, ed. Eliška Fucíková (London, 1997), p. 122. Fucíková suggested that they might have been made for portrait medals that would have commemorated both coronations. Eliška Fucíková, ed., *Rudolf II and Prague: The Court and City* (London, 1997), p. 15.

6 Christopher Wood, *Forgery, Replica, Fiction: Temporalities of German Renaissance Art* (Chicago, IL, 2008), pp. 149–55.

7 As quoted in Wood, *Forgery, Replica, Fiction*, p. 151.

8 Ovid, *Metamorphoses*, XIV: 623–771.

9 Kaufmann has taken these manifestations of Vertumnus to suggest that we should consider Vertumnus not only god of the seasons but god of the elements – water (fisherman), air (fowler) and earth (hunter). Thomas DaCosta Kaufmann, 'Metamorphoses of Nature', in *The Mastery of Nature: Aspects of Art, Science, and Humanism in the Renaissance* (Princeton, NJ, 1993), p. 133.

10 Jean-Pierre Vernant, 'Dim Body, Dazzling Body', in *Fragments for a History of the Human Body*, ed. Michel Feher (New York, 1989), p. 38.

11 Ibid.

12 Thomas DaCosta Kaufmann, 'Arcimboldo and Propertius: A Classical Source for Rudolf II as Vertumnus', *Zeitschrift für Kunstgeschichte*, XLVIII/1 (1985), pp. 117–23.

13 Thomas DaCosta Kaufmann, *Arcimboldo: Visual Jokes, Natural History, and Still-Life Painting* (Chicago, IL, 2009), p. 93.

14 Jessica Keating, 'Hidden in Plain Sight: On Copiousness in the *Kunstkammer* of Emperor Rudolf II', *Journal of the History of Collections*, XXXIII/3 (2021), pp. 455–6.

15 Thomas DaCosta Kaufmann, 'Arcimboldo and Propertius: A Classical Source for Rudolf II as Vertumnus', pp. 117–23.

16 Propertius, *The Elegies*, IV.2, 1–49.

17 Ibid., IV.2, 3–4.

18 Thomas S. Suits, 'The Vertumnus Elegy of Propertius', *Transactions and Proceeding of the American Philological Association*, C (1969), pp. 475–86.

19 Gregorio Comanini, *Il Figino, or On the Purpose of Painting*, trans. Ann Doyle-Anderson and Giancarlo Maiorino (Toronto, 2001), p. 16.

20 Ibid., p. 18.
21 Ibid.
22 Ibid., p. 19.
23 Ibid., pp. 23–34.
24 Ibid., p. 25.
25 Ibid.

6 To Make a Face

1 There is another invertible painting in Stockholm that has been 'hesitantly' attributed to Arcimboldo. It is referred to as *The Cook*, dated circa 1570. Given its date and the questions around its attribution, I have chosen not to address it here.
2 See Paula Findlen, 'Jokes of Nature and Joke of Knowledge: Playfulness in Scientific Discourse in Early Modern Europe', *Renaissance Quarterly*, XLIII (1990), pp. 318–20.
3 Accounts of invertible paintings like those addressed in this chapter appear in Philip Hainhoffer's account of the Dresden Kunstkammer. See Oscar Doering, *Des Augsburger Patriciers Phillip Hainhoffer Reisen nach Innsbruck und Dresden* (Vienna, 1894), p. 174; Thomas DaCosta Kaufmann, 'Arcimboldo and the Elector of Saxony', in *Scambio culturale con il nemico religioso: Italia e Sassonia attorno al 1600*, ed. Sybille Ebert-Schifferer (Rome, 2007), p. 29; Thomas DaCosta Kaufmann, 'For the Birds: Collecting, Art, and Natural History in Saxony', in *For the Sake of Learning: Essays in Honor of Anthony Grafton*, ed. Ann Blair and Anja-Silvia Goeing (Leiden, 2016), p. 491.
4 Thomas DaCosta Kaufmann, *Arcimboldo: Visual Jokes, Natural History, and Still-Life Painting* (Chicago, IL, 2009), pp. 199–200.
5 William R. Newman, 'The Homunculus and the Mandrake: Art Aiding Nature versus Art Faking Nature', in *Genesis Redux: Essays in the History of Philosophy and Artificial Life*, ed. Jessica Riskin (Chicago, IL, 2007), pp. 119–30.
6 Stephen Campbell, 'Naturalism and Venetian "Poesia": Grafting Metaphor and Embodiment in Giorgione, Titian, and the Campagnolas', in *Subjects as Aporia in Early Modern Art*, ed. Alexander Nagel and Lorenzo Pericolo (Burlington, VT, 2010), pp. 115–16.
7 Census reveals this information. Silvio Leydi, 'Giuseppe Arcimboldo in Milan: Documents and Hypotheses – Summary of Documents Relating to the Milanese Period', in *Arcimboldo 1526–1593*, exh. cat., Kunsthistorisches Museum, Vienna (2007), pp. 301–2.

8 Ibid., p. 302. On the significance of this type of imperial patent, see Dirk Jacob Jansen, 'The Instruments of Patronage: Jacopo Strada and the Court of Maximilian II – A Case Study', in *Maximilian II: Kultur und Politik im 16 Jahrhundert* (Vienna, 1992), pp. 194–5.

9 On the circle of intellectuals who welcomed Arcimboldo back to Milan, see Kaufmann, *Arcimboldo*, pp. 83–8.

10 [Gio. Filippo Gherardini], *All'Iventtissimo Cesare Rodolfo Secondo componimenti sopra le due quadri Flora et Vertumno fatti à sua sacra cesara maestà da Giuseppe Arcimboldo* (Milan, 1591). See also Giacomo Berra, 'Allegoria e mitologia nella pittura dell'Arcimboldi: la *Flora* e il *Vertunno* nei versi di un libretto sconosciuto di rime', *Acme*, XLI (1988), pp. 11–39.

11 Givan Paolo Lomazzo, *Idea of the Temple of Painting*, trans. Jean Julia Chai (University Park, PA, 2013), pp. 165–6.

12 The others include another self-portrait drawing, which is now housed in the Národní Galerie in Prague, and a lost painted self-portrait.

13 Gregorio Comanini, *Il Figino, or On the Purpose of Painting*, trans. Ann Doyle-Anderson and Giancarlo Maiorino (Toronto, 2001), p. 26.

14 On naturalism in Lombard painting, see Andrea Bayer and Mina Gregori, eds, *Painters of Reality: The Legacy of Leonardo and Caravaggio in Lombardy*, exh. cat., Metropolitan Museum of Art, New York (2004). For a more recent assessment of naturalism in Italian Renaissance painting, see Stephen Campbell, *The Endless Periphery: Toward a Geopolitics of Art in Lorenzo Lotto's Italy* (Chicago, IL, 2019), pp. 51–97.

15 On Metsy's rendering of Folly and on folly writ large, see Larry Silver, *Fools and Folly in Flemish Art* (Antwerp, 2022), especially pp. 7–17.

16 Lorraine Daston, 'Cloud Physiognomy: Describing the Indescribable', *Representations*, CXXXV (2016), pp. 45–71.

17 For the classic account, see Horst W. Janson, 'The "Image Made by Chance" in Renaissance Thought', in *De artibus opuscula XL: Essays in Honor of Erwin Panofsky*, ed. Millard Meiss (New York, 1961), pp. 254–66. See also Ernst Gombrich, *Art and Illusion: A Study in the Psychology of Pictorial Representation* (Princeton, NJ, 1960), pp. 181–202. For a reassessment, see Amy Knight Powell, 'Images (Not) Made by Chance', *Art History*, XL/2 (2017), pp. 380–403.

18 Leonardo da Vinci, *Treatise on Painting*, trans. Philip A. McMahon (Princeton, NJ, 1956), vol. I, p. 50.

19 Leon Battista Alberti, *On Painting and Sculpture: The Latin Texts of De pictura and De statua*, trans. Cecil Grayson (London, 1972), p. 117.
20 On potential images, see Dario Gamboni, *Potential Images: Ambiguity and Indeterminacy in Modern Art* (London, 2002), pp. 15–19.
21 My thinking on the intentional structure of Arcimboldo's invertible paintings is indebted to Joseph Koerner, 'Bosch's Contingency', in *Kontingenz*, ed. Gerhart von Graevenitz and Odo Marquard (Berlin, 1998), pp. 245–51.
22 'It is no accident that the cabinets of curiosities favored mannerist art, above all anamorphic and trompe l'oeil paintings and displayed these works promiscuously next to bits of landscape marble, branching trees of coral, seashells, and other "works" of nature. What curious art and curious nature shared was exquisite workmanship, echoing the root sense of "curiosity" (from the Latin *cura*) as painstaking, even excessive care or artistry.' Lorraine Daston, 'Curiosity in Early Modern Science', *Word and Image*, XI/4 (1995), p. 398.
23 R. Bauer and H. Haupt, 'Das Kunstkammerinventar Kaiser Rudolfs II', *Jahrbuch der Kunsthistorischen Sammlung in Wien*, LXXII (1976), inv. nos, 258, 271, 254, 242, 243, 1400, 1401, 1497.
24 Findlen, 'Jokes of Nature', p. 295.
25 Ambroise Paré, *On Monsters and Marvels*, trans. Janis Pallister (Chicago, IL, 1982), p. 107.
26 Von Aachen was not the first artist to make works that imitated nature's productivity. See Joseph Leo Koerner, 'Bosch's Equipment', in *Things that Talk: Object Lessons from Art and Science*, ed. Lorraine Daston (New York, 2004), pp. 27–65, especially p. 57.
27 Comanini, *Il Figino*, p. 18.
28 Lomazzo, *Idea*, p. 165.
29 Comanini, *Il Figino*, p. 17.
30 Mario A. Lazzari and Mario Marubbi, 'Technical Analysis of *The Vegetable Gardener*', in *Arcimboldo 1526–1593*, exh. cat., Kunsthistorisches Museum, Vienna (2007), p. 296.
31 Michel Weemans, 'Herri met de Bles's Sleeping Peddler: An Exegetical and Anthropomorphic Landscape', *Art Bulletin*, LXXXVIII/3 (2006), p. 459.
32 Richard Wollheim, *Painting as an Art* (Princeton, NJ, 1987), pp. 45–63.
33 The literature on capriccio is vast. For an excellent overview, see Patricia Emison, 'The Ignudo as Proto-Capriccio', *Word and Image*, XIV/3 (1998), pp. 281–95; on Arcimboldo and capriccio, see Thomas

DaCosta Kaufmann, 'Caprices of Art and Nature: Arcimboldo and the Monstrous', in *Kunstform Capriccio: Von der Groteske zur Spieltheorie der Moderne*, ed. Ekkehard Mai and Joachim Rees (Cologne, 1997), pp. 33–51.

34 Lomazzo, *Idea*, p. 69.

SELECT BIBLIOGRAPHY

The following offers a list of key sources, exhibition catalogues, monographs and edited volumes for further reading on Arcimboldo.

Sources

Bauer, Rotraud, and Herbert Haupt, eds, 'Das Kunstkammerinventar Kaiser Rudolfs II., 1607–1611', *Jahrbuch der Kunsthistorischen Sammlungen in Wien*, LXXII (1976)

Comanini, Giovanni Paolo, 'Il Figino; overo del fine della pittura', in *Trattati d'arte del cinquecento*, vol. III, ed. Paola Barocchi (Bari, 1962)

—, *The Figino; or On the Purpose of Painting: Art Theory in the Late Renaissance*, trans. and ed. Ann Doyle-Anderson and Giancarlo Maiorino (Toronto, 2001)

Gherardini, Giovanni, *All'Invittissimo Cesare Rodolfo Secondo componimenti sopra le due quadri Flora et Vertumno fatti à sua sacra cesara maestà da Giuseppe Arcimboldo* (Milan, 1591)

Kreyczi, Franz, 'Urkunden und Regesten aus dem K. und K. Reichs-Finanz-Archiv', *Jahrbuch der Kunsthistorischen Sammlungen des Allerhöchsten Kaiserhauses*, V (1887), part 2, pp. i–xlviii

Leydi, Silvio, 'Giuseppe Arcimboldo in Milan: Documents and Hypotheses – Summary of Documents Relating to the Milan Period', in *Arcimboldo 1526–1593*, ed. Sylvia Ferino-Pagden (Paris, 2007), pp. 37–52 and 297–302

Lomazzo, Giovan Paolo, *Idea del Tempio della Pittura* (Milan, 1590)

—, *Idea of the Temple of Painting*, trans. and ed. Jean Julia Chai (University Park, PA, 2013)

—, *Trattato dell'arte pittura, scoltura et archittetura* (Milan, 1584)

Morigia, Paolo, *Historia dell'antichità di Milano* (Venice, 1592)
—, *La nobiltà di Milano* (Milan, 1595)
Staudinger, Manfred, 'Archival Documents Concerning the Appointment of Arcimboldo at the Imperial Court', in *Arcimboldo 1526–1593*, ed. Sylvia Ferino-Pagden (Paris, 2007), pp. 304–7
Uhlirz, Karl, ed., 'Urkunden und Regesten aus dem Archiv der k. k. Reichshaupt und Residenzstadt Wien', *Jahrbuch der Kunsthistorischen Sammlungen des Allerhöchsten Kaiserhauses*, XVIII (1897), pp. i–cc
Zimerman, Heinrich, ed., 'Das Inventar der Prager Schatz- und Kunstkammer von 6. Dezember 1621 nach Akten des K. und K. Reichsfinanzarchiv in Wien', *Jahrbuch der Kunsthistorischen Sammlungen des Allerhöchsten Kaiserhauses*, XXV (1905), part 2, pp. xx–li
—, 'Inventare, Acten und Regesten aus der Schatzkammer des Allerhöchsten Kaiserhauses', *Jahrbuch der Kunsthistorischen Sammlungen des Allerhöchsten Kaiserhauses*, X (1889), pp. cci–cccxxiv

Secondary Sources

Alfons, Sven, 'Giuseppe Arcimboldo (Symbolister 3)', *Tidskrift för Konstvetenskap*, LI (1957)
Barthes, Roland, *Arcimboldo*, trans. John Shepley (Milan, 1980)
Berra, Giacomo, 'Allegoria e mitologia nella pittura dell'Arcimboldi: la *Flora* e il *Vertunno* nei versi di un libretto sconosciuto di rime', *Acme (annali della facoltà di lettere e filosofia dell'Università degli Studi di Milano)*, XLI/2 (1988), pp. 11–39
—, 'Arcimboldi e Caravaggio: "Dilegenza'e patienza" nella natura morta arcaica', *Paragone*, VIII–X (1996), pp. 108–61.
Casati, Carolo, 'Giuseppe Arcimboldi, pittore milanese', *Archivo Storico Lombardo*, ser. 2, II (1885), pp. 86–94
Fend, Doris, and Monika Strolz, 'Arcimboldos *Teste Composte*: Beiträge zur Restaurierung', *Jahrbuch des Kunsthistorischen Museum Wien*, I (1999), pp. 282–90
Haupt, Herbert, ed., *Le bestiaire de Rodolphe II, Cod. Min. 129 et. 130 de la Bibliothèque nationale d'Autriche* (Paris, 1990)
Hendrix, Lee, 'Natural History Illustration at the Court of Rudolf II', in *Rudolf II and Prague: The Court and the City*, ed. Eliška Fucíková (London, 1997), pp. 107–71
Kaufmann, Thomas DaCosta, *Arcimboldo: Visual Jokes, Natural History, and Still Life Painting* (Chicago, IL, 2009)

—, 'Arcimboldo and the Elector of Saxony', in *Scambio culturale con il nemico religioso: Italia e Sasonia attorno 1600*, ed. Sybille Ebert Schifferer (Rome, 2007), pp. 27–36
—, 'Arcimboldo and Propertius: A Classical Source for Rudolf II as Vertumnus', *Zeitschrift für Kunstgeschichte*, XLVIII (1985), pp. 117–23
—, 'Arcimboldo au Louvre', *La revue du Louvre et des musées de France*, V–VI (1977), pp. 337–42
—, 'Arcimboldo's Imperial Allegories', *Zeitschrift für Kunstgeschichte*, XXXIX (1976), pp. 275–96
—, 'Arcimboldo's Serious Joke: Mysterious but Long Meaning', in *The Verbal and the Visual: Essays in Honor of William Heckscher*, ed. Karl-Ludwig Selig and Elizabeth Sears (New York, 1990), pp. 57–86
—, 'The Artificial and the Natural: Arcimboldo and the Origins of Still Life', in *The Artificial and the Natural: An Evolving Polarity*, ed. Bernadette Bensaude-Vincent and William Newman (Cambridge, MA, 2007), pp. 149–84
—, 'Caprices of Art and Nature: Arcimboldo and the Monstrous', in *Kunstform Capriccio: Von der Groteske zur Spieltheorie der Moderne*, ed. Ekkehard Mai and Joachim Rees (Cologne, 1997), pp. 33–51
—, *Court, Cloister, and City: The Art and Culture of Central Europe 1450–1800* (Chicago, IL, 1995)
—, 'The Dating of Arcimboldo's First Composite Heads', *Studia Rudolphina*, V (2005), pp. 28–32
—, 'Giuseppe Arcimboldo, the Habsburgs' Leonardo', in *Rudolf II, Prague and the World*, ed. Buket Bukovinskà (Prague, 1999), pp. 169–76
—, 'The Kunstkammer as a Form of Representation: Remarks on the Collections of Rudolf II', *Art Journal*, XXXVIII (1978), pp. 526–37
—, *The Mastery of Nature: Aspects of Art, Science, and Humanism in the Renaissance* (Princeton, NJ, 1993)
—, 'Le opere di Arcimboldo a Monza e la carriera iniziale dell'artista/ Arcimboldo's Work in Monza and the Artist's Early Career', *Studi Monzesi*, III (1988), pp. 5–17
—, *Variations on the Imperial Theme in the Age of Maximilian II and Rudolf II* (New York, 1978)
Kriegeskorte, Werner, *Giuseppe Arcimboldo 1527–1593: Ein manieristischer Zauberer* (Cologne, 1988)
Maiorino, Giancarlo, *The Portrait of Eccentricity: Arcimboldo and the Mannerist Grotesque* (University Park, PA, 1991)
Mandiargues, André Pieyre de, *Arcimboldo the Marvelous* (New York, 1978)

Miller, Robert S., 'Gli affreschi cinquecenteschi: Giuseppe Arcimboldo, Giuseppe Meda e Giovanni Battista della Rovere detto il Fiammenghino', in *Il Duomo di Monza: la storia e l'arte*, vol. II (Milan, 1989), pp. 216–30
Porzio, Francesco, 'Fonti carnevalesche del naturalismo nel cinquecento Milanese: alcune ipotesi su Giuseppe Arcimboldi', *Arte Lombarda*, 105 (1993), pp. 37–42
Waddington, Raymond B., 'Before Arcimboldo: Composite Portraits on Italian Medals', *The Medal*, XIV (1989), pp. 13–23

Exhibition Catalogues

Bayer, Andrea, *Painters of Reality: The Legacy of Leonardo and Caravaggio in Lombardy*, exh. cat., Metropolitan Museum of Art, New York (2004)
Bora, Giulio, *Rabisch: il grotessco nell'arte del cinquecento – l'Accademia della Val di Blenio, Lomazzo e l'ambiente Milanese*, exh. cat., Museo Canonale d'Arte, Lugano (1998)
Irblich, Eva, *Thesaurus Austriacus: Europas Glanz im Spiegel der Buchkunst: Handschriften und Kunstalben von 800 bis 1600*, exh. cat., Das Nationalbibliothek, Vienna (1996)
Pagden, Sylvia, *Arcimboldo 1526–1593*, exh. cat., Kunsthistorische Museum, Vienna (2007)
—, *Arcimboldo: Artista Milanese tra Leonardo e Caravaggio*, exh. cat., Palazzo Reale, Milan (2011)
Rasponit, Simonetta, ed., *The Arcimboldo Effect: Transformations of the Face from the Sixteenth to the Twentieth Century*, exh. cat., Palazzo Grassi, Venice (1987)
Seipel, Wilfrid, ed., *Die Entdeckung der Natur: Naturalien in den Kunstkammern des 16. und 17. Jahrhunderts*, exh. cat., Kunsthistorisches Museum, Vienna (2006)

ACKNOWLEDGEMENTS

I am in the fortunate position of having too many family, friends, mentors and colleagues to acknowledge individually, but I would like to convey my deep gratitude to Thomas DaCosta Kaufmann for his faith in me, and to Michael Leaman and François Quiviger for inviting me to write for the Renaissance Lives series. Thanks also go to Claudia Swan, Kathleen Ryor, David Lefkowitz, Clara Hardy, Cathy Yandell, Timothy Raylor, Bill North, Victoria Morse, Jennifer Nelson and Lia Markey for reading various drafts of this book, and to Daniela Bleichmar, Caroline Kumsta, Sondra Barringer, Lauren Cagle and Celeste Pilegard for their tireless support. Finally I wish to thank Larry Cooper, who inspired me to write this book and who made the impossible possible.

PHOTO ACKNOWLEDGEMENTS

The author and publishers wish to express their thanks to the sources listed below for illustrative material and/or permission to reproduce it. Some locations of artworks are also given below, in the interest of brevity:

Alte Pinakothek, Munich (CC BY-SA 4.0): 44, 45, 46, 47 (photo bpk Bildagentur/Art Resource, NY); © Ashmolean Museum, University of Oxford/Bridgeman Images: 34; Biblioteca Universitaria di Bologna (vol. VI/2, fol. 87): 58; The British Museum, London: 37, 38, 40, 62, 71; Château royal de Blois: 53; David Rumsey Map Collection, David Rumsey Map Center, Stanford Libraries: 20; Duomo di Como, photo Renáta Sedmáková/AdobeStock: 23; Gabinetto dei Disegni e delle Stampe degli Uffizi, Florence (inv. no. 3156), photo Cristian Ceccanti, courtesy Ministero Beni e Attività Culturali, all rights reserved: 66; Galleria dell'Accademia, Gabinetto dei Disegni e delle Stampe, Venice: 39; Gallerie degli Uffizi, Florence: 43; Germanisches Nationalmuseum, Nuremberg: 69; Kaiserliche Schatzkammer, Vienna, photo Markus Luttenberger/Wikimedia Commons (CC BY-SA 3.0): 68; Koninklijk Museum voor Schone Kunsten Antwerpen (KMSKA): 72; Kunsthistorisches Museum, Vienna: 2, 4, 8, 9, 56, 64, 70; Kupferstich-Kabinett – Staatliche Kunstsammlungen Dresden (Inv.-Nr. Ca 213/002), photo bpk Bildagentur/Art Resource, NY: 63; Landesmuseum, Hannover: 57; The Metropolitan Museum of Art, New York: 21, 29, 30, 33; Musée du Louvre, Paris: 5, 26 (photo © Erich Lessing/Bridgeman Images); Musei di Strada Nuova, Gabinetto Disegni e Stampe di Palazzo Rosso, Genoa: 19; Museo civico 'Ala Ponzone', Cremona: 10; © Museo e Tesoro del Duomo di Monza, photos Piero Pozzi: 22, 24; photos © Museum of Fine Arts, Boston: 11, 12; Národní muzeum – Historické muzeum, Prague (CC BY 4.0): 67; The National Gallery, London: 41, 42; National Gallery of Art, Washington, DC: 1, 35, 36; National Galleries of Scotland, Edinburgh: 31; Nationalmuseum,

Stockholm, photo Cecilia Heisser: 13; Österreichische Nationalbibliothek, Vienna (Cod. Min. 42): 50 (fol. 46r), 51 (fol. 23r), 52 (fol. 6r), 54 and 55 (fol. 19r), 61 (fol. 8r); The Phoebus Foundation, Antwerp: 73; private collection: 6, 7 (photo Artothek/Bridgeman Images), 15, 16; Real Academia de Bellas Artes de San Fernando, Madrid: 3; Rijksmuseum, Amsterdam: 48, 49, 65; photo Ghigo Roli/Bridgeman Images: 27; Santa Maria delle Grazie, Milan: 25; Schloss Ambras, Innsbruck: 74; photo © Yoav Sinai/Dreamstime.com: 17; Skoklosters slott, photo Erik Lernestål/SHM: 14; Veneranda Biblioteca Ambrosiana, Milan: 32; Veneranda Fabbrica del Duomo di Milano/image by Google: 18; Wellcome Collection, London: 59, 60; photo Martin Jung/imageBROKER.com/Alamy: 28.

INDEX

Illustration numbers are indicated by *italics*.
Artworks are by Giuseppe Arcimboldo unless otherwise indicated.